HUNTING
with Air Rifles

HUNTING
with Air Rifles

THE COMPLETE GUIDE

Mathew Manning

northumbria|press

Published by McNidder & Grace Limited
4 Chapel Lane, Alnwick NE66 1XT, UK
www.mcnidderandgrace.co.uk

First Published 2010
Reprinted 2010, 2012
Copyright © Mathew Manning

British Library Cataloguing in Publication Data. A Catalogue Record
for this book is available from the British Library.

ISBN: 978 0 85716 001 0

Designed by Northumbria Graphics, Northumbria University
Printed in Slovenia on behalf of Latitude Press Limited

All photographs by Mathew Manning and Kev Hawker. Gun shop picture
(p.11) courtesy of Don Brunt. Illustrations by Jon Brammer.

To Sally, George and Violet.
Thank you for your patience.

Foreword

If you read the national press you might well see the airgun portrayed as "a lethal, high-powered firearm." Listen to some shooters and you might dismiss it as a toy. In reality, it is neither second cousin to the AK47 nor to the catapult: the truth lies in between.

Used properly, it is an effective hunting weapon but it has serious limitations. If you know those limitations, and how to get the best from it, an airgun can provide superb sport. More than that, its limitations demand a level of skill which many would argue is unequalled by any other shooting sport. There is little margin for error and, as well as learning to shoot accurately, you will need a wealth of fieldcraft - for the newcomer to airguns that can be a daunting prospect.

It needn't be, if you read this book.

This is the distillation of years of experience by one of the country's most respected airgunners. It is concise, clear and above all a damn good read. If you weren't hooked on the sport before, you will be after reading this.

Mathew's constant emphasis on safe and humane shooting will ensure that you get off to a good start. His down-to-earth, practical advice, all garnered from first-hand knowledge, will keep you on the right path.

The great thing about airguns is that they suffer from fewer restrictions than most other guns and pest shooting is generally accessible and free. But always remember that in law airguns are firearms and subject to the same legislation as a shotgun or full-bore rifle. There are at least 32 offences you can commit and some carry a heavy jail sentence. The legal advice may not be the most exciting part of the book but it really is essential reading.

Today airguns are coming under increasing pressure as a result of pea-brained yobs, a sensationalist press and populist politicians, and there has never been a greater need for airgunners to be first-class ambassadors for their sport. Follow Mathew's advice and you will be. You will also enjoy some tremendous sport and – this is the big bonus – bring something home for your supper.

Good shooting!

Jeffrey Olstead
Head of Publications
British Association for Shooting and Conservation

Contents

Introduction

Hunting with air rifles has provided me with an enjoyable pastime and meat for the table for more than twenty years. Through this book, I hope to be able to share some of the pleasure this fascinating hobby has given me and some of the knowledge I have managed to gain through my trials and tribulations since first setting out with a gun.

Although they are relatively low-powered, modern air rifles are incredibly accurate and capable of packing a lethal punch. Ammunition is inexpensive, so even newcomers should be able to put in sufficient practice to quickly become a competent shot. Furthermore, air rifles are very quiet in operation, making them the ideal tool for discreet pest control in situations that rule out the use of high-powered guns.

As modern society has drifted away from the grass roots of food production, the subject of hunting – either for the pot or for pest control – has become an emotive issue. However, I don't believe anyone should need to defend their choice to partake in this engaging pursuit; provided, of course, that there is always a good reason for their actions. Most people eat meat and I believe that harvesting your own is far more dignified than leaving it to someone else to farm and kill animals that have endured goodness knows what just so you can fill your belly.

To the benefit of animal welfare, the environment and countryside sports, people appear to be thinking more carefully about where their food comes from. Consequently, people are once again learning to appreciate just how gratifying and important it is to grow, forage and even hunt your own ingredients. The treatment of livestock, the impact on the natural world and the reduction of food miles are key factors of sustainable food production, and hunting with an air rifle ticks all these boxes and brings the added bonuses of pleasure, satisfaction and exercise. Furthermore, because airgun quarry species are regarded as vermin, they provide a free source of meat, so there are significant economic gains too.

A rabbit or pigeon shot with an air rifle was born in the wild, it fed and grew in the wild and probably bred in the wild. This compares very favourably with the existence of a farm animal, which could well have spent its entire life indoors being pumped full of antibiotics and processed feed before being transported miles and miles to queue up for slaughter.

Of course, not all pest species controlled with the air rifle make good eating – rats and crows instantly spring to mind. However, the threat they pose to human health or populations of other wild animals must provide a good enough reason for culling to maintain the balance.

Whatever the reason for hunting with air rifles, the pastime offers a lifetime of learning and enjoyment – not least because it is also an excellent excuse for not only enjoying but also becoming a part of the great outdoors. The experienced hunter appreciates that his or her quarry can literally change its habits with the weather, let alone the seasons, and he or she will need to be able to read the countryside and all the little clues provided by nature to be truly successful. A close relationship with nature is inevitable for hunters and that's why they are regarded by many as the guardians of the countryside.

This book contains information that I hope will be of great use to newcomers and experienced hunters alike – knowledge that has taken me well over half my lifetime to accumulate, and as much of it through failure as triumph. Air-rifle hunting is challenging and it has to be accepted that success may not always come quickly when you are pitting your wits against the finely tuned senses of wild creatures that manage to avoid the clutches of predators on a daily basis.

Nonetheless, it is the element of difficulty that makes our sport so rewarding. There is little satisfaction in achieving something without having to overcome challenges. Whether potting pigeons on the allotment, stalking rabbits on the hills or controlling crows on the farm, I hope this book will equip the reader with useful skills to help you to consistently meet those ever-changing challenges and to enjoy success in the field.

CHAPTER 1

Air rifles and how they work

Air rifle hunters are spoilt for choice; the walls of gun shops and the pages of the latest shooting magazines are adorned with dozens of different models made by manufacturers from all over the world. From a £75 second-hand bargain to a £1,000-plus state of the art super-gun, most will be fit for the purpose of hunting. Of course, there are a few dubious airguns out there; from cheap, mass-produced tat that is nowhere near up to the tasks likely to be encountered in the hunting field to over-designed gimmick guns with expensive extras that even the most experienced hunters are never likely to need. I hope the following paragraphs will help you to make more of an informed choice when you part with your hard-earned cash.

Before purchasing an air rifle – be it your first or the latest addition to a growing collection – it is important to make sure that it suits your needs. The best way to answer that question is to understand how the airgun works and to establish what you want to get from yours.

Power sources

In very simple terms, air rifles function by blowing a projectile (usually a lead pellet) down the barrel with a blast of compressed air. This feature is one of the key appeals of the airgun; its power source is easily, and usually inexpensively, recharged and does away with the

Modern air rifles are impressive pieces of kit but you don't have to splash out on a top of the range model like this to enjoy the sport.

need for costly and noisy explosive charges associated with the ammunition used in more conventional powder-burning, live-fire rifles.

Air rifles generally produce their blast of air via one of two power sources: spring-and-piston or pre-charged pneumatic. Two less common variations of this are the ingenious gas-ram system pioneered by British gunmaker Theoben and the CO2 capsule. I don't believe the CO2 capsule provides a reliably consistent power source for the serious hunter.

Let's start with spring-and-piston air rifles, often referred to as springers. These guns epitomise the simplicity of the airgun because the whole propulsion mechanism is self-contained.

Behind the barrel of a spring-and-piston gun sits a chamber that houses the mainspring and piston. This type of gun is cocked either by breaking the barrel or by the stroke of a side- or under-lever. The cocking stroke compresses the powerful mainspring behind the piston, ready to be released by the trigger.

When a spring-and-piston rifle is fired, the spring powers forward, driving the piston in front of it and creating a pocket of compressed air within the sealed chamber. The air escapes through a transfer port at the front of the cylinder, right behind the pellet, which it then pushes on through the barrel.

Springers are wonderfully simple in operation, and there is something very gratifying about hunting with a gun that is powered by energy produced by your own effort. The cocking stroke usually exposes the breech, into which the pellet is directly loaded. The breech is then closed and sealed by the return stroke of the barrel or cocking lever. This simple and effective mechanism has stood the test of time, giving many decades of reliable service to hunters all over the world.

Of course, the ever-ready power plant of a

Spring-powered air rifles are cocked by the stroke of a lever or, as in this case, the barrel. Their self-contained power source makes for hassle-free shooting.

Loading a pellet direct to the breech of a break-barrel air rifle.

springer has its shortcomings. The most significant disadvantage of a spring-and-piston air rifle is the fact that the moving parts that power it can also cause a fair amount of recoil. First the piston slams forward, then it bounces back off the cushion of air at the front of the cylinder. This movement can translate into quite a kick. Predictably, more expensive models tend to shoot much smoother than those at the budget end of the market. However, the effects of recoil can be tamed with good shooting technique and consistent accuracy can easily be achieved with regular practise. We'll look at that in more detail later.

Another consideration with springers is the effort needed to cock them. Achieving the power levels required for hunting can result in a gun that takes a fair amount of grunt to cock, and this might be a serious consideration – particularly for youngsters, women and older shooters. Nonetheless, however much power it takes to cock a springer, the action in a decent air rifle should be smooth with no grating – the slick cocking stroke should conclude with a crisp 'snick' as the trigger sear engages, fastening the piston in place.

Also, it has to be accepted that, after thousands and thousands of shots and probably several years of service, the spring, and most likely a few other components, will need to be replaced. Fortunately, this is a reasonably straightforward job and kits are available with easy-to-follow instructions if you're reasonably practical. If not, your local gun shop should be able to carry out the necessary repairs without breaking the bank.

A cautionary word: never fire a spring-and-piston air rifle before the barrel or cocking lever is returned to its fixed position. Although many guns are designed not to do this, there is a serious risk that the spring will be released and the piston flung forward. Without a pellet in front of the port to create a cushion of air, the piston will smash into the front of the chamber, doing untold damage to the innards of your pride and joy. The force of the workings of the gun trying to snap back into place can bend barrels, crack woodwork and dissect fingers. Don't try it.

Thoeben's gas-ram system, developed in the 1980s, is an interesting variation on the spring-and-piston power-plant. This system is still self-contained in the sense that no charging equipment is required, but instead of a steel spring, the piston is driven by a gas strut – a sealed chamber of compressed air or nitrogen. Most people will have seen a gas strut in operation, taking the weight of the tailgate when they open the boot of their car.

When a gas-ram air rifle is cocked (which is done in the same manner as with a spring-and-piston gun) the air is further compressed. When the gun is fired, the strut pushes forward behind the piston and drives air towards the pellet.

Gas-rams offer several advantages over springers. The strut doesn't wear anywhere nearly as quickly as a spring; in fact they last for decades. Also, they don't lose power when left cocked for long periods of time, so shot-to-shot consistency is very good. The mechanism also functions more quickly than a spring-and-piston system, so the pellet takes less time to leave the barrel.

The downside is that gas-rams can be harder to cock and some people just don't get on with their snappy recoil. The fast firing cycle can manifest as quite a harsh jolt that some shooters really can't get to grips with. However, like the kick of a conventional springer, this should easily be overcome with good shooting technique.

The other popular (and probably the most popular) type of air rifle is the pre-charged pneumatic, often known as PCPs.

Pre-charged air rifles have an air reservoir, usually in the shape of a long cylinder or diver-style buddy bottle, which holds enough air to power dozens, and sometimes hundreds, of shots. Each time the gun is fired, a regulator or valve releases a consistent pulse of air which propels the pellet along the barrel.

A great advantage of the PCP is the fact that the absence of any significant moving parts means the firing cycle is virtually recoilless. This

Above: In single shot mode, the probe of this pre-charged air rifle can easily be seen as it feeds a pellet into the breech.

Left: As well as having virtually no recoil, pre-charged airguns often provide the option of a multi-shot magazine for fast follow-up shots.

'dead' action means that accurate shooting is much easier to achieve than with a springer. For this reason, pre-charged pneumatics quickly found favour with target shooters when they first became readily available in the 1980s. Of course, this high degree of accuracy is also very useful in hunting situations, when straight shots literally do make the difference between life and death, and PCPs are now the first choice of many sporting shooters.

Also, because the firing power is already generated and contained within the workings of the gun, PCPs require far less effort to cock than springers, so you don't need much brawn to use them. Most pre-charged air rifles are cocked by a bolt-action or by the throw of a short lever. Many models also incorporate multi-shot magazines, from which the simple cocking

stroke also probes another pellet into the breech, ready for action. This fast, efficient loading system can be very useful to the hunter, especially when a swift follow-up shot is required.

The number of shots you get from a PCP depends on several factors. These include the efficiency of the valving system or regulator, and the size and capacity of the air reservoir. By and large, a light, compact gun is likely to produce fewer shots per fill than a large, heavy one.

When you reach the end of the useful charge you're going to need to refill, and that's the biggest disadvantage with pre-charged airguns. Many guns are fitted with a dial that tells you what air pressure you have on board – otherwise you'll just have to keep count of your shots. PCPs tend to cost a little more than springers in the first place, and remember that you're going to have to add charging kit to the equation too.

The cheapest charging method is to use a stirrup pump to manually generate the full charge of compressed air. While the stirrup pump shares the springer's appeal of generating your own power, it can also be quite a chore to operate. I find that manual pumps are perfectly adequate for small-capacity guns but the exertion of pumping a large buddy bottle up to 230 bars (bars being the pressure scale adopted by most airgun makers) makes my pulse pound so much that it takes a good ten minutes' recovery before I am able to shoot straight. Still, it's good exercise.

The lazy, and very convenient, option is to go for a large-capacity diver's bottle. A decent-sized 300-bar diving bottle will refill the average airgun several dozens of times before you have to pay for a refill. The downside is that the bottle will set you back a couple of hundred pounds or so and they are heavy, cumbersome brutes to lug around. You also have to be very careful transporting them – with all that compressed air trapped inside a metal shell, it's going to make a mess if it goes 'pop'. You'll also need your bottle tested every five years to make sure it is still up to the required standard.

In spite of the drawbacks, a diver's bottle is a useful piece of kit that makes for very convenient charging. You'll be reminded of the benefit every time you refill your gun with the simple twist of a knob. Once the gun is filled, you just let trapped air hiss out of the hose via the bleed valve, uncouple the gun and you're back in action.

It is advisable to carry out filling in a reasonably clean environment – and not in a dirty old barn. Pre-charged air rifles have delicate internals and their valves don't like grit or dust. Modern design has reduced the problem, but get dirt into the innards of a PCP and you could be looking at a costly repair bill.

Most PCP's come with the necessary couplings to fit the charging hose to them, and couplings vary from manufacturer to manufacturer. Some shooters are discouraged by the apparent hassle of having to mess about with charging kit but it is really quite straightforward.

A serious warning for owners of pre-charged air rifles is that they should only ever be filled with clean air. There are a few horror stories knocking around the air-gunning grapevine which tell of exploding metalwork, mangled fingers and lost eyes resulting from foolish experimentation with more volatile gases.

The important parts

Being a major component, the barrel seems a fairly obvious place to start. The barrel isn't just a spout through which the pellet is pointed and launched, it is a carefully designed component that actually helps the pellet maintain the power imparted by the gun's action. The inside of a rifle barrel is grooved or rifled (hence the name) in a corkscrew fashion. The twist of the rifling gives the pellet a spin that helps it cut through the air with maximum stability after it leaves the muzzle. The barrels of better-quality air rifles are often choked. The choke is a tiny narrowing, or pinch-point at the front end of the barrel, which improves down-range accuracy.

Barrel length is an important consideration. It used to be assumed that a longer barrel would set the pellet on a truer course and therefore improve accuracy but, as some modern air rifles shoot very accurately in spite of having barrels of much less than 25cm in length, this theory is largely discounted.

Nonetheless, a longer barrel improves air efficiency and needs less input from the power-plant to achieve full power. What this means is that a spring-and-piston gun with a long barrel will need a less powerful and therefore smoother-shooting spring than the equivalent model with a shorter barrel. Similarly, a pre-charged gun with a long barrel will produce more full-power shots per fill than the equivalent short-barrelled version. A long barrel also provides greater leverage and consequently an easier cocking stroke on a break-barrel springer.

But, just to further complicate the choice, short barrels have advantages too. Compact guns tend to balance better because the bulk of the weight is closer to your body, and this makes them easier to shoot. A short (or carbine) gun is also very useful if you are going to be using it in confined conditions – shooting rats inside farm buildings, for instance. In this situation, a carbine model will enable you to quickly swing onto your target whereas you would probably be worrying about bashing the muzzle of a longer gun.

A silencer is regarded by most hunters as an important, and in many cases essential, addition to the barrel. With stealth and concealment being paramount when it comes to going unnoticed by one's quarry, it makes sense to keep the sound of shots to a minimum; I certainly like to have my air rifles fitted with silencers to mute the muzzle report.

Silencers are often referred to as moderators or suppressers, which makes sense as they moderate and suppress the noise of the gun rather than silence it. As the blast of pressurised air escapes from the muzzle behind the pellet, it can make quite a crack. Inside the cylinder of a silencer is a series of baffles. As the air escapes from the muzzle into the wider chamber of the silencer, much of it is deflected and muffled by the sound-absorbing baffles, and the muzzle blast is consequently reduced. It is also claimed that some silencers improve accuracy as the turbulent air behind the pellet is stripped by the baffles, leaving the little projectile in a pocket of 'clean' air as it leaves the barrel and begins its journey to the target. Although this may be true, the effect is minimal at best and of no great significance to the hunter.

A good silencer will reduce the muzzle report of a pre-charged air rifle to a muted 'phut', which not only makes for stealthy hunting but also causes less disturbance when you're practising. The result can be quite astounding and I have lost count of the times that I have missed shots at live quarry only to be able to make a kill with the second shot because it went unheard.

Silencers have a more noticeable effect on pre-charged air rifles than on spring-and-piston models because the muzzle blast is about the only noise emitted from a PCP. Fit a silencer to a springer and it will still sound quite noisy because you can't avoid the mechanical sound of the moving spring and piston. However, the noise of the mechanism is far more noticeable to the shooter because you have your head right next to the action of the gun. Down range, where your quarry will be sitting, the sound of the gun's power-plant is less significant and a silencer will make a useful, and very noticeable, reduction to the muzzle report.

Some air rifles come with factory fitted silencers – often as a shroud or bull-barrel which stretches the entire length of the barrel – but many come without, leaving it to the shooter to select the most appropriate model. Most air rifles can be coupled with one of a variety of compatible silencers, and your gun dealer should be able to advise on what's best. The first thing to check is whether the silencer you are buying is calibre-specific, because if you fit a .177 silencer to a .22 barrel you can be pretty sure that the pellet won't come out the end!

You also need to make sure that your

The stock is the handle that marries the gun to the shooter. This thumbhole version is sculpted for an improved fit and features crisply cut chequering to improve grip.

favoured silencer is compatible with your gun because air rifles are designed to accept either a threaded, screw-fit silencer or the type with a sleeve that slides over the barrel and is secured with a small grub screw. When fitting the grub screw variety, the screw does not need to be graunched into place until it's mangled into the barrel; it only needs a gentle nip to keep things secure. Whatever kind you have, it must be absolutely aligned with the barrel. If it's slightly off-centre, the pellet will clip it and accuracy will be ruined.

When choosing a silencer, don't assume that the biggest is necessarily the best. High-tech baffles can result in surprisingly compact silencers that work incredibly well. Most of the major brands do the job fairly well but, as ever, you tend to get what you pay for. Some manufacturers are moving away from metal to carbon fibre for the construction of silencers, as

the latter material is lighter and produces a quieter sound profile. One problem with some carbon fibre silencers is that their shiny finish can reflect quite a lot of glare when the sun shines on them – and this will attract the attention of your quarry. Still, this nuisance can easily be remedied with a covering of camouflage tape or a spray of matt-black paint (before you fit it to the barrel, please).

The stock is the wooden or, increasingly often, plastic chassis into which the action of the gun is seated. It is a critical component as it forms the all-important contact with the shooter.

Plastic stocks, often described as synthetic or tactical stocks, are becoming increasingly popular. They are more robust and usually lighter than the wooden equivalent, which can be a great benefit to youngsters, women and people of smaller build. I initially had misgivings about the image portrayed by synthetic stocks, which usually come in black and are very military in appearance, but their practical advantages are undeniable – they bounce back from knocks and bumps far better than the wooden equivalent.

Being something of a traditionalist when it comes to gun stocks, I favour the wooden option because it blends in well with the countryside and has a certain sporting look about it. More expensive airguns tend to be fitted with walnut stocks and those towards the lower end of the market are generally finished in beech wood, which is a little heavier and not as prettily grained.

Materials aside, the stock plays an important role as the handle of the gun, and it should fit the shooter properly. As well as looking good, textured areas of chequering or stippling around the main handling areas will improve grip when your hands are wet with rain or sweat. These handling areas are at the fore-end and the pistol grip, where your trigger hand sits. Most stocks are fashioned to enable the thumb of your trigger hand to fit over and around the stock; the best ones also cradle your thumb in a very relaxed upward position, known as thumb-up. Many air rifles also come with a thumbhole stock option at an additional cost. Thumbhole stocks enable your thumb to fit through the woodwork and right around the pistol grip. These stocks look very elegant and some shooters favour the secure hold they provide – they are certainly worth trying if within your budget.

The height of the cheek-piece, where your cheek is cradled towards the butt end of the stock, needs to be considered relative to the type of sights you intend to use. It is not so critical if you are just using the open sights that sit low against the action of the gun, but if you're going to fit a telescopic sight, you'll probably need a stock with a raised cheek-piece, with a high comb to provide good eye alignment.

If you do plan to use a scope, make sure the gun you buy has rails machined into it – most do. These rails are the grooves onto which the mounts that hold your scope will be clamped.

At the extreme butt end of the stock sits the shoulder pad or plate. The fit of the shoulder pad will affect gun handling and eye alignment. On some guns they can be adjusted for height – a very useful feature.

So, you know about power-plants, barrels, stocks and gun-fit, but there is one element that will make or break a potentially great air rifle, and that's the trigger. This little component is the switch that enables the shooter to control his or her gun and send the pellet on its way when the aim is good. There are good triggers and there are bad triggers and, unfortunately, some otherwise good air rifles have terrible triggers.

Because the trigger is the control by which the shooter unleashes the shot – translating what's going on in the sight picture via your eye, brain and muscles – its operation is paramount.

You really don't want a trigger that takes a great effort to pull because you'll yank the gun off aim before the shot is released, but an unpredictably light trigger is dangerous and equally difficult to operate with any degree of consistency. A good trigger should be crisp and easy to predict and there should be no detectable roughness to its movement.

Modern air rifles usually come with decent two-stage triggers. The first stage offers some movement against light pressure until it comes to rest against the second stage. Most shooters hold the trigger in this position while making final adjustments to their aim before touching off the second stage to release the sear and unleash the shot when the aim is just right. There is no pre-tensioning with a single-stage

The trigger unit can make or break the performance of an airgun. A smooth, crisp mechanism with a comfortable blade is essential for accurate shooting.

The advice of a reputable gun dealer is invaluable. The best will allow you to try before you buy.

trigger; the sear releases under the initial movement. Although a good two-stage trigger should be your first choice, a good quality one-stage trigger is preferable to a poor two-stage model.

Triggers are usually adjustable for length and weight of pull, often in the first and second stages. This adjustment can often be carried out by simply following the manufacturer's instructions. If you are in any doubt, leave it alone and consult your local gun shop.

The final, and arguably most important, component I am going to discuss in this chapter is the safety catch. In a hunting situation, the shooter will often be carrying a gun that is loaded and cocked — a potentially very dangerous tool indeed. The safety catch is a vital means of making the gun safe by deactivating the trigger should it be accidentally pulled, snagged, hit or whatever. Once the shooter is ready to take a shot, it should be possible to easily and quietly disengage the safety catch as part of the final preparations.

It amazes and disappoints me that some otherwise excellent, and certainly expensive, air rifles aren't fitted with a safety catch. The shooter should ensure that his gun comes with this potentially life-saving feature — better still, opt for a gun with a safety catch that engages automatically every time it is cocked and loaded.

Even when the safety is engaged, and even when the gun is unloaded, always treat it as if it were loaded and never point it at anyone. The best way to avoid a life-wrecking accident is to ensure that the gun is never pointed anywhere it shouldn't be.

Choosing your gun

Even when equipped with the knowledge of how an airgun works, making the final choice can still be bewildering. My recommendation to the absolute beginner is to go for a good quality new or second-hand spring-and-piston air rifle, depending on what you can afford. A decent springer is all the gun you need to start out in air-rifle hunting; with practice it will enable you to become an accurate and effective shot and will give you a starting point from which to choose your next, presumably more expensive, gun as you advance.

The best advice I can offer is to try before you buy. The air rifle that ticks all the technical boxes and looks beautiful on the pages of a magazine may not actually suit you, and you won't really know until you give it a try.

The best thing you can do is join a club so you can get your hands on all sorts of air rifles before you arrive at a decision – one of your new air-gunning friends might even be able to line you up with a second-hand bargain. If you don't have a local club, then any good gun dealer should be happy for you to try air rifles out on the range so you can gauge how all the components work together and how a particular air rifle performs in your hands. A good gun shop should also have a compressor to charge diving bottles (or at least a large diving bottle to recharge customers' guns for a small fee) if it sells PCPs. Nothing frustrates me more than a gun dealer who is happy to take the cash for an expensive pre-charged air rifle but can't be bothered to offer the necessary service to keep it charged. A good gun shop should also provide a sound after-sales service including maintenance, repair and advice as and when you need it. Look after your local gun dealer and he will most likely look after you.

Gun maintenance, storage and transportation

When you have your own air rifle, you'll want to take pride in it and take care of it. Most experienced shooters will know exactly what I mean. Shooting is your hobby so you should take pleasure in it, and a large part of that pleasure comes from the joy of owning a good-looking gun that performs well.

Fortunately, air rifles don't need an awful lot of maintenance. In fact, my guns get little more than a wipe-down with a lightly oiled cloth after each outing. Although fairly minimal, this wipe-down is vital to protecting and preserving the surface of the gun because things like rain, sweat from the hands and blood from shot quarry will soon corrode metalwork. Springers need a little more care – though not much more – and will benefit from an occasional dab of grease around the exposed moving parts of the cocking mechanism. Of course, they will also need the spring to be replaced every couple of years or so.

More attention is required when an air rifle gets a proper soaking during a sudden downpour in the field. My initial advice is don't panic because the bluing or whatever finish your gun has is designed to protect the metalwork from a certain amount of moisture. My guns often get drenched to the point of having water running out of every imaginable crevice – including the expensive ones that incorporate circuit boards and sophisticated electronic triggers. The ordeal has never done them any harm because I have taken the appropriate steps on my return home.

First of all, if your air rifle gets really wet, try to avoid putting it back in the gun bag, except, of course – when the law dictates it must be – on your journey home. Apart from soaking your gun bag, packing the gun away for any amount of time will enable the moisture to seep deeper into the action. It's far better to leave it where some air can get around it so that it can breathe.

As soon as you get home, give the gun and sights a thorough wipe-down with kitchen roll to soak up all of the surface water from the exposed parts. If your gun is a pre-charged pneumatic, the next job is to dry fire it (firing it unloaded) a few times to blow out any water. Of course, firing an unloaded springer can cause serious damage, so if your gun is of the spring-

The electronic internals of this high-tech pre-charged air rifle can easily be seen as it's stripped for cleaning after a heavy downpour. Rain poses no threat to your gun as long as you take proper care of it.

and-piston variety you'll need to put a few pellets through it (safely into the ground, on the lawn or suchlike) to achieve the same result. Next, remove the action from the stock so you can repeat the kitchen roll treatment on the hidden parts. Leaving trapped water between the stock and the action will result in rust, and water trapped between a silencer and the barrel or a magazine and the action will have the same effect, so remove them too.

The gun and removed parts will now need a couple of hours to dry naturally in a reasonably warm (but not hot, so please don't get the hair-drier out) and well-ventilated environment. Once the gun has had a thorough airing, it just needs a light wipe-down with oil before replacing all the parts and fixing the action back in the stock. Your airgun is now ready to store

until your next outing.

One maintenance job that is sometimes required, and is perfectly easy to do for yourself, is barrel-cleaning. After firing hundreds and hundreds of pellets, the barrel can become fouled with lead deposits. Some barrels are more prone to fouling than others, but it can result in a loss of accuracy. If your gun's grouping of pellets starts to deteriorate, it's a good idea to clean the barrel with a simple pull-through device that can be purchased fairly inexpensively from your local gun shop. The improvement is often drastic enough to necessitate re-zeroing, and it usually takes a few shots to get a freshly cleaned barrel sufficiently leaded to shoot consistently.

Your airgun's stock – if it's of the wooden variety – will benefit from an occasional application of oil. The unvarnished woodwork finish often associated with better quality air rifles can become a little dry without such treatment and, although unlikely, splitting along the grain can result if this is overlooked. Purpose-made stock oil is available from gun shops, although I have occasionally raided a dab of walnut oil from the pantry and it seems to do the job perfectly well.

At the time of writing, English law does not necessitate the installation of a secure gun safe for the storage of sub-12ft.lb (non firearms-rated) air rifles. However, the government has recently suggested that rules for airgun storage might be tightened but what this might entail and when, or even whether, this might become law has not been confirmed.

Nonetheless, a secure gun cabinet comes highly recommended. Keeping your guns under lock and key provides ultimate peace of mind that they will not fall into the wrong hands – be it at the hands of intruders or of inquisitive young people in your household. If you can't afford a gun safe then a lockable wardrobe, cupboard or cabinet is the next best thing; I would certainly suggest that airguns are kept in a locked room, out of sight from casual visitors, at the very least. Leaving guns leaning in the corners of rooms is far from advisable both from a safety and security point of view and because of the simple fact that they could very well get knocked over and damaged. Wherever you decide to securely store your air rifle, make sure it is a place that is free from damp so your coveted gun stays in tip-top condition.

As well as keeping within the law, it is also important to ensure that sufficient measures are taken to ensure that your gun is properly protected when in transit. An airgun is a precision instrument; it takes time and effort to get one properly zeroed, so the last thing you want is for that to be undone by careless handling.

A padded gun bag should offer enough protection in normal circumstances but it could be worth considering the purchase of a hard case with foam lining if you are going to be doing a lot of travelling with your air rifle. Even when your gun is in a bag, care should be taken to ensure that it is handled properly; the way some shooters throw their guns around is enough to make me cringe, and I can't imagine how they expect them to still be zeroed at the end of it. I try to be mindful not to bash or jolt my gun whenever I move it, especially when getting it in and out of the car. I'm also very careful not to allow the barrel to bear too much of the rifle's weight whenever I lean it against something. Please, please don't try to lift your gun from the barrel end when it's in a bag – I've seen an airgun heaved out of the boot in this way on more than one occasion. As well as placing you at the dangerous end of the gun, it also puts far too much strain on what is, after all, just a hollow tube of metal that you really ought not to bend.

My final word on gun care is to leave any major work to the experts. Don't be tempted to tinker unless you really know what you're doing. Have-a-go engineering can turn an expensive air rifle into a useless piece of junk, and can also be very dangerous. If you think there's a problem with your air rifle, and you don't know what it is, take it to a gun shop where the necessary work can be carried out by experienced hands. It will probably work out a lot less expensive in the long-run.

CHAPTER 2

Sights, mounting and zeroing

Whatever accuracy your air rifle is capable of producing, you'll need a decent sighting system to enable you to consistently put the pellet in the right place. Sights for air rifles come in two main guises: open sights and telescopic sights (also known as scopes or tele's). The night-vision scope is a variation on the telescopic sight, which we will look at in more detail later. Apart from that, the only other sighting arrangement an air-rifle hunter is really likely to encounter is the laser sight.

Open sights

Open sights are the most basic aiming tool, but that's not to say they aren't effective. Although they lack the magnification of a scope, open sights enable fast target acquisition because your eye does not have to become accustomed to the sight picture. Consequently, opens can be particularly useful in situations where you need to get shots off quickly – when targeting fidgety rats, for instance.

Many guns come with open sights fitted as standard. The usual arrangement features a post (the fore-sight) at the muzzle end of the barrel which is lined up in the grove of the rear-sight element situated behind the barrel. When the post and groove are aligned, they are placed over the target to take aim. Adjustment is usually carried out via two knobs on the rear-sight. One

The rear element of conventional open sights. This simple sighting system works perfectly well at close to medium range.

of the knobs is for windage (left and right) adjustment and the other is for elevation (up and down) adjustment – both turn through a series of calibrated 'clicks' until zero (the correlation between the impact point of the pellet and the placing of the sights) is achieved. The elements of good open sights should be cleanly machined with no rough edges so the sight picture is crisp and the point of aim easily distinguished. Some versions feature glowing fibre-optic elements that provide a really clear aim-point.

Telescopic sights

Although open sights are a great starting point in terms of becoming a competent shot, a telescopic sight is the best way to fully exploit the potential accuracy of your air rifle for hunting at longer ranges of 20 metres and beyond.

As with buying an air rifle, I would advise the novice to opt for a scope at the lower end of the price scale at the outset. Experience gained with this optic can then be used to make your choice when you decide to upgrade, at which point I would suggest that you go for the best you can afford. Consider it as a long-term investment that will pay off in terms of performance over the years.

The large lens at the front of the scope is known as the objective lens. The size of this lens is important because it gathers light to create the sight picture so, by and large, the bigger the lens the brighter the sight picture. A scope with a larger objective lens is likely to give better performance and extend your effective hunting time, in low-light conditions at dawn and dusk. A lens of 40mm or 44mm is about average; 32mm is about as small as I would go, and 56mm is on the large side. Objective lenses usually feature layers of coating that help to prevent light from bouncing back out of the scope and,

Telescopic sights are the choice of most hunters when long-range precision is required.

therefore, improve the brightness of the sight picture. The colour of the coating can be seen in the light reflected from the glass.

Scopes that are adjustable for parallax usually feature a focusing ring, or collar, in the casing around the objective lens, although the recent trend is for a parallax adjustment knob further down the scope on the side by the windage and elevation knobs (known as turrets).

Parallax is an optical phenomenon that can affect the point of impact depending on the angle at which you look through the scope, and is most apparent at the shorter ranges that airgun hunters tend to shoot over. The effect of parallax is not easy to put into words, though it's probably best described as the way the relationship between two objects appears to shift when viewed from different perspectives. Close one eye and point your finger at an object in the room so that it is perfectly aligned. Move your head to the left and you'll notice that your finger appears to shift to the right of the object. Now move your head to the right and your finger will appear to shift to the left, although we know that neither your finger nor the object has moved at all. This apparent shift can also occur with the crosshairs of your telescopic sight if your line of sight is not centrally aligned. If your head is slightly off to the left, the reticule will appear to be to the right of the target. You'll compensate by aiming a little more to the left and will consequently miss to that side of whatever you were aiming at.

Wherever your parallax adjuster is situated, it will be marked with various ranges – usually from ten metres to infinity. By using the adjuster to dial-in the correct range for the shot being taken, the reticule and the target are viewed in almost the same plane, so the effects of parallax are minimised. Focusing-in the parallax adjuster also sharpens the sight picture so it can additionally be used as a means of estimating range. All you do is adjust the parallax until you achieve a crisp sight picture and then read off the range on the dial. This is the reason why side-focus parallax adjustment turrets have become popular; they are easier to reach and easier to read.

Some scopes are not adjustable for parallax and are already set at a specific range – 30 metres is the norm for air rifle scopes. This arrangement is perfectly adequate for the needs of the hunter. The solution is to remember to look straight down the scope whenever you take a shot, just as you should with any sight.

Moving further along the scope, we reach the main tube. These tubes generally come in either one-inch or 30mm diameter. One-inch is the standard size but the bigger 30mm tube is better at transmitting light. The tube, and whole of the scope body for that matter, is usually filled with nitrogen and sealed to keep it from fogging-up when it gets wet.

Halfway down the tube is the saddle on which the windage and elevation turrets sit (and the parallax turret if it's located on the side of the scope). The top turret adjusts elevation (up and down) and the side turret adjusts windage (left and right). The elevation turret usually has arrows indicating which way to turn the dial to move the point of aim upwards; obviously, the opposite direction will shift it down. Likewise, there is usually an arrow on the windage turret showing which way shifts the point of impact left.

The windage and elevation dials are accessed by either unscrewing the waterproof caps or, if they don't feature caps, by pulling the knob outwards into the adjustment position. The adjustment dials usually come in ¼ MOA (minute of angle) or ⅛ MOA variations. At ¼ MOA, one click will move the point of impact one quarter of an inch at 100 yards, which equates to four clicks for a quarter of an inch shift at 25 yards – a good starting range for zeroing an air rifle. To the same token, at ⅛ MOA one click causes a shift of one eighth of an inch at 100 yards so four clicks will cause a shift of just one eighth of an inch at 25 yards.

At the back of the tube behind the turrets is the twisting ring that adjusts magnification on scopes with a zoom feature. Most of the scopes I use have variable magnification from around four-times to 14-times and I use them at around eight-times magnification for most of my hunting. Light transmission is better at lower magnification so I'll often wind down the zoom to four- or five-times when shooting in low light.

To the beginner, high magnification and a huge target sounds like a dream come true but it isn't that simple. As well as reducing light transmission and closing down the field of view – which can make it hard to locate your target in the first place – the higher magnification will also magnify all of your movements. The effect of your pulse, your breathing, your quivering muscles and other slight movements will be increased to the point that the sight picture can be akin to looking out of a boat's porthole on a rough sea. This exaggerated wobble can be ruinous to your confidence and composure when trying to take a steady aim, so think twice before cranking-up the mag. The only time I go much over ten-times is when shooting off a rest at long-range. If you opt for a fixed magnification scope, six-times is a good all-rounder.

Some scopes have illuminated reticules (the reticule is the aiming point, which is also known as a crosshair). If so, the switch is usually located either behind the magnification collar or on a turret. This illumination makes the reticule glow red or green and can prove very useful when shooting against a black background (particularly at night) when the crosshairs might otherwise get lost in the gloom of the sight picture.

There is usually a collar by the eyepiece at the back of the scope to focus the optics to suit your eye. To do this, unlock the collar's locking ring and point the scope at a plain surface (a blank white wall is ideal) so there is nothing for your eye to focus on other than the reticule. Twist the ring until the reticule is as sharp and black as possible, tighten up the locking ring and the job is done.

Reticules come in all sorts of variations on the classic crosshair. Some have lots of lines and denominations for gauging range and working out where to aim at various distances and wind conditions. The final choice really does boil down to personal preference. I don't like my

sight picture to be too cluttered so I prefer the standard mil-dot arrangement, which features equally spaced dots on the reticule either side of and above and below the centre of the crosshair. With practice, these mil-dots should provide all the reference points you need to quickly work out where to aim in various situations.

The lens at the back of the scope is the ocular lens. The space between your eye and the ocular lens is known as 'eye relief' and is critical if the scope is going to work properly. Correct eye relief is usually around 10cm – you can work it out exactly by moving the scope back and forth until you achieve a sharp, round sight picture which fills the whole of the scope as you look straight down it.

Night-vision

Over recent years, the use of night-vision (NV) scopes has become increasingly popular. The big advantage they give the hunter is the ability to ambush quarry in complete darkness because they require virtually no illumination to work. They have disadvantages too – they are expensive and quite heavy.

NV optics really score when nocturnal vermin species like rabbits and rats begin to associate lamplight with danger after persistent shooting over the same patch. With night-vision, there is no lamplight to alert animals to your presence – you can sit and snipe under a cloak of darkness.

Night-vision scopes gather ambient light from the stars and the moon, and even from distant streetlights, through their objective lens. The electronic wizardry happens when that light hits a photocathode at the front of the image intensifier behind the lens. High-energy electrons produced by the photocathode create an image on the phosphor screen at the back of the scope tube, and it is this enhanced sight

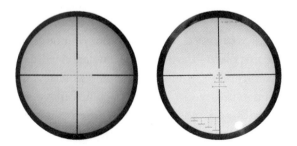

Left: The popular mil-dot format of scope reticule.
Right: A Multi Aim Point variation.

picture that the shooter sees through the eyepiece. The intensified image can be tens of thousands of times brighter than what you would see through a conventional scope. One important note: the delicate internals of night-vision scopes are easily damaged (literally burned-out) by bright light, so always keep the front lens cap on until after dark.

Most NV optics come fitted with an infrared (IR) illuminator. This illuminator is like a little torch and casts a beam of virtually invisible infrared light to enhance the sight picture if there is not enough ambient light for the optics to work.

The effective range of a night-vision scope depends on how sophisticated it is and how much you pay for it. First generation (Gen-1) NV scopes are not as technologically advanced as Gen-2 and Gen-3 optics, which cost significantly more. Gen-1 NV optics are good enough for close-range rat shooting but expect to pay at least £1,000 for something that provides suitable image quality to tackle rabbits over greater distances.

The image through a night-vision scope is nothing like the sight picture you see through a conventional scope. The phosphor screen creates a grainy, green picture. The image is ghostly pale, although light reflected from the eyes of your quarry glows a bright silvery/green. The NV sight picture is strangely flat, almost one-dimensional, and this can make range estimation rather tricky – this is easily overcome by establishing fixed range markers where you expect to be shooting.

Night-vision scopes also tend to be lower magnification than conventional telescopic sights. This makes spotting pellet holes in paper targets very tricky, so it's difficult to judge the necessary adjustment when zeroing. The windage and elevation adjustment turrets, or

Using a telescopic sight with a night vision attachment to shoot rats. These optics are bulky but provide a high degree of stealth after nightfall.

knobs, on NV scopes are also usually a lot smaller than those on normal scopes, and messing about with them in the dark can be a very fiddly business. So, keep your night-vision hunting as stress-free as possible by zeroing in daylight. As explained, you'll have to keep the front lens covered to prevent damage but the cap has a tiny aperture that lets in sufficient light to generate a clear, bright image when the scope is switched on.

With the scope switched on, NV hunting is quite a revelation. The behaviour of nocturnal quarry can be quite different when there's no light to disturb it. It is fascinating to watch the snowy green image of usually very timid creatures as they go about their business completely oblivious to your presence.

Night-vision scopes are bulky and make for a very hefty combo when fitted to an air rifle of average weight. This isn't really too much of a problem because these optics lend themselves to ambushing from a fixed position so you're unlikely to be traipsing great distances with your NV outfit. However, one very important consideration is the fact that night-vision scopes aren't really suitable for daytime hunting, which means it's best to have a dedicated airgun for NV hunting unless you want to constantly be swapping and re-zeroing sights. So, as well as needing expensive optics, you may also need two guns. Night-vision optics that fit to your normal telescopic sight are one solution to this problem, although it is a bit of a compromise. These add-ons provide phosphor screen image intensification through your everyday scope so there's no need to re-zero. Early clip-on NV attachments fitted to the rear lens of the telescopic sight and, while they work well enough, they result in a very uncomfortable shooting position because the additional length pushes your head back towards the rear of the rifle's cheek-piece. Fortunately, front-mounted night-vision image intensifiers that fit to the objective lens of the scope via an adjustable collar are becoming increasingly popular, and I find these much easier to use. Unsurprisingly, they affect gun handling by making the rifle feel somewhat front-heavy, but at least the eyepiece of your scope is in the right place.

Night-vision equipment lends itself to certain rat- and rabbit-shooting scenarios. The NV hunter can take large numbers of rats by lurking in a dark corner of a farm building and picking-off the unsuspecting rodents as they slink out from their hiding places in search of food. For rabbiting, NV can be put to good use by sitting or lying within range of a busy warren as night starts to fall. You'll be able to see the bunnies as they hop out to feed on the dew-covered grass but they won't be able to see you.

In my opinion, night-vision optics are a great luxury if you can afford them but be prepared for a serious amount of faffing around before you get fully accustomed to using this equipment. Ultimately, the hunter whose budget can only stretch to conventional lamps for night-time shooting shouldn't feel particularly disadvantaged. In fact, he can rest assured that his after-dark forays will most likely be a lot less complicated than those of the NV hunter.

Laser sights

The greatest benefit provided by laser sights is very fast target acquisition. These sighting systems project a precise beam that can be seen as a small red dot on the target. Zero the sight so the dot coincides with the impact point of the pellet and you have a fast and effective means of aiming in low light.

Laser sights can also be used to estimate range when used in conjunction with other sighting systems. This is particularly useful when using night-vision, when range-finding can be tricky. The laser sight is mounted to the scope or barrel so that it is offset to the side and then zeroed so the red dot coincides with the aiming point of the scope at zero range; for the sake of argument, we'll say 25 metres. Assuming the laser is offset to the right, the red dot will be seen to the right of the aiming point of the sight picture until the two overlap at 25 metres. Beyond that range, the red dot will appear to the left of the aiming point. The shooter can make range estimations based on how far to the left or right of the 25-metre overlap the dot is. Similarly, if the laser were mounted straight on top of the scope, the dot would appear above the sight's aim point until the overlap and then fall beneath it.

Either fitted directly to the gun or mounted to a scope, lasers are most effective at short range when used as sights. Therefore, they tend to be used for indoor rat-shooting at extremely close quarters. I hardly ever use them but some shooters have great results with this sighting system.

Laser sights project an incredibly bright, concentrated beam that can damage your eyesight. Never point them at your eyes, at anyone else or at a moving vehicle.

Mounting a telescopic sight

It is essential to mount a telescopic sight properly if it is going to perform as it should, and it is surprising how many people manage to get this seemingly simple task wrong. There's a bit more to it than simply clamping mounts to the rifle, slapping the scope on and tightening up the screws.

When mounting a scope to an air rifle, the first thing to check is that you have all the necessary tools to hand. You will need a plumb line (a piece of string with a stone tied to it for weight will do the trick), a helper, Allen keys that fit properly (because mangled screws don't look nice and will soon rust) and, of course, a scope and a suitable set of mounts.

With regard to choosing mounts, you'll need the right diameter to fit the scope (either one-inch or 30mm) and the right height. As regards height, I like to mount my scopes just high enough for the objective lens to clear the gun by anything between 1mm and 5mm. Keeping it low means the line of sight is as close as possible to the pellet's line of trajectory when it leaves the barrel. Two-piece mounts are usually adequate for pre-charged air rifles, but if you use a springer go for a sturdy one-piece mount with an arrestor block behind to stop the recoil from shaking things out of position.

Start by fixing the gun in a horizontally upright position. A purpose-made gun vice is great if you have one; if you use a more conventional vice make sure you use something soft to buffer the clamps so they don't mark the rifle stock. If you don't have a vice, prop the gun between a few cushions on your sofa – it sounds a bit desperate but it's certainly the kindest option for the gun.

First remove the screws at the top of the mounts so you can take off the piece that clamps down the scope. Then loosen the screws at the base of the mounts so they open enough to slide them onto the rifle's scope rails. Locate the mounts into the rails and tighten the screws, leaving them just loose enough to slide up and down along the rails without too much effort. Next, place the scope, with the elevation turret pointing upwards, into the cradles of the mounts. Depending on the length of the scope, the mounts should be about 20mm either side of the saddle at the centre of the tube – you may have to be a little flexible with this distance depending on the arrangement of the rails on your rifle. Place the clamps back onto the top of the mounts, replace the screws and tighten them just enough to stop the scope slipping.

Make sure all screws are tightened enough to keep everything from falling off. Then pick up the rifle, close your eyes and mount the gun into your shoulder. When you open your eyes you will see the exact sight picture for this arrangement. If you had mounted the gun with your eyes open, you would most likely have adjusted your hold or the position of your head to make for a better sight picture but this way you see exactly how the scope works when you hold the gun properly. The chances are that the sight picture will not be perfect because the eye relief (the distance between your eye and the scope) is not right. This is when you need your helper. Keeping your head exactly where it is, get your assistant to take the weight of the gun so

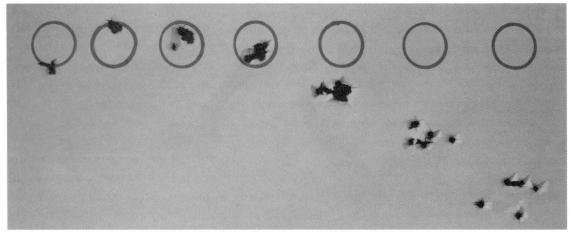

Groups of shots on paper enable the shooter to determine the pellet's point of impact at various ranges and to estimate the compensation needed to hit the mark.

you can use your free hand to slowly slide the mounts backwards and forward until the eye relief is just right and you have a large, clear picture filling the scope. When the eye relief is spot-on, tighten up the bottom screws to securely fix the mounts to the rails.

Now you've got the mounts locked where you want them, its time to ensure that the scope is exactly upright. The vertical element of the crosshair should be perfectly upright so that the pellet remains aligned throughout its flight path. If, in still conditions, the pellet rises and falls exactly in line with the crosshairs, you will be able to make exact adjustments to your aim to correlate with different ranges. Now is the time to set up that plumb line – all you need to do is hang it from a tree in the garden and you've got a perfect vertical line.

Mount your gun in your shoulder again, make sure you are holding it upright with no cant (cant is leaning to the left or right and should be avoided at all times to keep your aim true) and look at the vertical plumb line through the scope. Get your helper to take the weight of the rifle once more and this time use your free hand to twist the scope in the semi-tightened mounts

until it corresponds exactly with the plumb line. Once you are happy that the reticule is exactly upright, tighten the screws to fix the scope in the mounts – you want the screws to be secure but don't go too mad because you'll risk crushing the scope tube. The whole operation sounds quite a rigmarole but you now have a perfectly mounted scope that should never need to be moved again.

Zeroing and range estimation

Mark an A4 sheet of white card with a black pen to create a bulls-eye of about 20mm diameter and place it against a safe backstop. Starting from about 10 metres, fire a group of five shots at the bull from a steady shooting position – firing groups is preferable to making adjustments based on single shots as it allows you to make allowances for wide misses (also known as fliers). Adjust the windage and elevation dials on your sights depending on where the group struck the target – if it fell low and to the left, you will need to adjust your sights up and to the right. Repeat the process until your groups of shots are hitting the bull.

Now that you know your rifle and scope are more or less zeroed, move the target back to 25 metres – the typical range for setting sights on an air rifle. Because you started at 10 metres, the pellet is likely to strike the further target a little too high. This is because when the pellet leaves the barrel it is below the line of the scope. At 10 metres, it still hadn't risen up to the line of sight so you would have adjusted the scope to make up for that. Repeat the original zeroing process to set the sights for 25 metres.

Now you have the sights zeroed, you can try targets at various ranges to work out the amount of aim you need to give over the target (hold-over) or below the target (hold-under) – try five-metre spacings from 10 to 40 metres or more. Hold-over and hold-under will vary depending on rifle calibre, power, scope height and the angle of the shot. Typically, with a rifle zeroed at 25 metres, you can expect shots to strike low at 10 metres so you will need to aim a little higher to make a direct hit. The point of impact and line of sight will meet at what is known as the primary zero at around 15 metres; from here out to just beyond 20 metres you can expect the pellet to rise above the line of sight so you would need to aim a fraction below your target to hit it squarely. At 25 metres, you reach the zero you dialled into your sights, and beyond that the pellet will start to fall lower and lower. By interpreting the point of impact at various ranges into the mil-dots or whatever points of reference your scope reticule features, you will be able to work out exactly where to aim depending on the distance of the shot.

Of course, knowing where the pellet is likely to strike at various ranges is useless unless you are able to estimate range with reasonable accuracy. Very accurate, and fairly expensive, electronic laser range-finders will quickly tell you the distance between you and wherever you point them but I think they are an unnecessary outlay and encumbrance. Due to the air rifle's limited range, you only really need to be able to work out ranges from about 10 to 50 metres, and this is fairly easy to learn. I taught myself to estimate range by constantly testing myself as I strolled around the fields and the woods. By trying to guess how far away trees, fence posts and the like are and then pacing it out as you walk around your shoot, you'll soon be able to work out hunting distances with reasonable accuracy. I still pace out the distance to every kill I make to check just how accurate I was when I estimated the range prior to pulling the trigger. When you become proficient at range-finding, you can start working out what happens when shooting at different angles and in the wind. You are now on your way to becoming an accomplished shot.

The effect of elevation

The rules of hold-over and hold-under are affected by the angle of the shot. The most obvious example is when shooting directly upwards – the sort of shot you might sometimes be presented with when hunting in woodland. One would assume that a pellet flying straight up into the air would strike lower than usual as it is faced with more resistance from gravity. The reality, however, is quite the opposite. This is because the sights have been set to compensate for gravity pulling down against the near-horizontal path the pellet usually takes. Because the pellet emerges from the barrel below the line of sight, it rises up to the primary point of zero somewhere around 15 metres and continues to rise a little above the line of sight before gravity drags it back down to the secondary zero at around 25 metres.

But when you fire directly upwards, gravity is pulling straight back on the pellet from behind the line of flight, not below it. As a result, the pellet will still cross the line of sight somewhere around the primary zero but, without gravity pulling along the flight path, it won't be pulled back to the secondary zero. The consequence is a wide miss above the target, or, more specifically, behind you, so you'll need to aim low when making this kind of shot.

However, if you ease the angle – shooting towards the top of a tall tree from a distance or up a steep hill, for instance – the effect of gravity is stronger than when shooting flat so you will miss low. The answer is to aim slightly high depending on range. Shooting down a steep hill reverses the effect as the pull of gravity is reduced. This sort of shot can be regarded as being assisted by gravity and consequently the pellet doesn't slow as quickly and will miss higher than expected.

Bearing this basic theory in mind will set you on the right track but you'll have to master it in practice for yourself before you tackle live quarry. The only way to get to grips with it is to set up targets at various angles and see for yourself where shots land and where you need to aim to bring them back to the mark. There are all kinds of natural targets available for practising high shots; apples, conkers and dead branches can be used to simulate a shot at a lofty pigeon.

CHAPTER 3

Ammunition and calibre selection

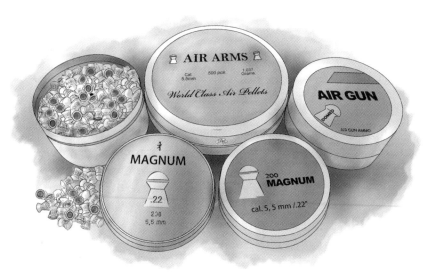

Your choice of ammunition will greatly affect your air rifle's accuracy, and there's a vast selection to pick from.

It is a peculiar fact that slight variations in pellets can have a tremendous influence on an airgun's performance. Seemingly very similar designs can produce very different results when fired through the same gun, and even variations in size of a fraction of a millimetre can make a surprising difference to the grouping of shots. Some guns show more variation between different brands of pellets than others; such guns are often referred to as being 'pellet fussy'. That said, you could probably couple a decent air rifle with any reasonable pellet and achieve sufficient accuracy to kill rabbits out to 20 metres; but find the perfect combination and you'll be able to more than double that range in calm conditions.

To understand the basis of pellet selection, it makes sense to have a grasp of the make-up and components of the projectile and what you want it to do.

The easiest question to answer is what we want our ammunition to do. Because the power of air rifles is comparatively low, it is vital that we, as hunters, are able to land our shots in exactly the right place to strike a vital organ. Therefore, consistent accuracy is critical. Once we've put the pellet right where we want it, our next demand is that it does the maximum damage possible to ensure a clean and humane death for our quarry.

Now let's look at the pellet's design. Starting at the top, the main front section is known as the head. Behind the head is a narrowing which is called the waist (this narrowing provides the axis through which the pellet rotates as it cuts through the air) and the back section of the pellet is called the skirt.

Lead is the most common and, in my opinion, best material for air rifle pellets. This

The four main designs of airgun pellet (from left) domed, flat-head, hollow-point and pointed.

soft metal is excellent for hugging the rifling along the inside of the barrel as the pellet travels along its length after the blast of air has been caught by its skirt. The softness of lead also helps it to do its job when it connects with the target; mangling and mushrooming to deliver maximum shock energy as opposed to disintegrating or drilling straight through as a harder material might.

Head shapes vary greatly, and the marketing patter used to promote the different brands states the merits that each shape has to offer. Unfortunately, most of this waffle is untrue. The sad fact is that, over the years, the constant droning about matching a pellet to the hunting job in hand has actually convinced many air-gunners that the marketing drivel is true. It isn't.

For longer than I can recall (probably since long before I even picked up a gun) pointed pellets have been touted as being great for hunting, especially at long range, because they offer improved penetration. There isn't much truth in this. In fact, pointed pellets are generally very bad for hunting because they are usually very inaccurate. The problem is that the noses of pointed pellets are inclined to get knocked off centre either during production or distribution, or when you and I put a handful in our pockets for a trip into the field. A pellet with a damaged nose will not fly straight and true and,

as a result, down-range accuracy will be poor. As accuracy is our ultimate goal, I suggest that we disregard pointed pellets.

Another variation on the standard design is the flat-head pellet. The hollow-point pellet is quite similar in shape and performance so we'll consider them both together.

This type of pellet has, as the name suggests, a flat head or, in the case of a hollow-point, an indented head. The blunt shape of these pellets makes them excellent in terms of their ability to deliver maximum shock and damage to the target. The trouble is that their shape causes a lot of drag through the air so they slow-down rapidly and aren't very accurate over longer ranges. Nonetheless, flat-head and hollow-point pellets can be very effective for close-range vermin control, such as rat shooting.

My favourite design of pellet for all-round performance is the classic domed head, also known as the roundhead. A decent, consistently made, domed pellet will provide good accuracy out to extreme range and deliver plenty of clout when it hits its mark. There are lots of great brands available so you're sure to find one to suit your air rifle.

Frustratingly, guns that rolled off the same production line can favour different pellets, so the final choice is a little trickier than just asking what ammo brand suits your model best. The only way to find out is to experiment, so I would recommend trying three or four kinds of good quality domed pellets made by the leading manufacturers – the initial outlay will pay off. Find which one is most accurate in your gun and stick with it.

The great calibre debate

The air rifle calibre debate has rumbled on for decades and filled countless pages of airgun magazines. The fact is that the debate concerning the two main calibres, .177 and .22, will most likely never be settled because, in all honestly, they are both equally good and equally bad in different ways.

When I started shooting with air rifles, the larger .22 calibre was in vogue – probably just because it was bigger. There is no denying that the bigger, heavier round will do more damage when it hits home; it is impossible to argue against the basic physics. The downside with .22 calibre is that, being heavier and slower, the pellet falls through the air more rapidly as it travels down-range so you have to give it a lot of hold-over at longer ranges. Experienced hunters who are familiar with the down-range performance of their hardware use .22 to devastating effect in the field.

More recently, there has been a distinct trend towards hunting with the .177 calibre. At legal-limit, sub-12ft.lb, power levels the smaller calibre has a much faster, flatter trajectory than the .22 and consequently necessitates less calculation for hold-over. However, because the smaller, lighter .177 round delivers less of a whack than the .22, you really do have to ensure that you land your shots in exactly the right place.

A third option is the more recently developed .20 'compromise' calibre. As far as I'm concerned, this middle ground just further complicates the issue. The choice of ammunition for the .20 is limited compared with the two major calibres and I have never been convinced by the benefits it is supposed to offer.

If you want to deliver a real wallop, the .25 is an absolute sledgehammer of a calibre. The trouble is that this round is so heavy that it's not really any good for anything much beyond 20 metres when fired from a sub-12.ft.lb airgun, and there isn't much of a choice in terms of brands. Still, it's certainly worth considering if you want mighty stopping power for close-range vermin control.

Personally, I favour the .177 for most or my hunting with non-FAC air rifles. The flat flight-path gives me a wider margin for error when working out ranges in the heat of the moment but the lesser clout means that I strictly limit myself to head-shots virtually all of the time. That said, I usually opt for the .22 when hunting rats at close- to mid-range. At close quarters, the zippy .177 can sometimes drill straight through without making an instant kill – even with head-shots – but the heavy round kills rats cleanly every time as long as it is delivered to the skull.

Of course, many shooters will want one gun that can be used for various hunting applications – and who can blame them? In this case, final calibre selection really does boil down to personal choice, and the .177 or .22 will serve you well as long as you put in the practice. If you're an experienced hunter who is already enjoying success with a specific calibre, my advice is to stick to what you know and don't allow yourself to be influenced by anyone else's ramblings.

CHAPTER 4

Shooting stances, technique and practice

When practising, it's easy to always opt to shoot from the position that produces the best results. It's human nature to want to stick with the formula that equates to the tightest groups on the target paper, which means that most of us do the majority of our practice from the sitting position.

The trouble is, opportunities have a habit of presenting themselves at the most awkward times in the hunting field. If a rabbit lops out from cover within range when you're mid-stalk and up to your elbows in thistles and nettles, you're going to want to shoot it – but certainly not from a sitting position.

To be an effective hunter, you need to take time to become familiar and competent with all shooting stances: standing, kneeling, sitting and lying – and probably a few variations on these main ones. Try out all these positions when shooting paper targets on the range and it will soon become apparent that your capabilities vary from stance to stance. As accurate shooting

starts with stability from the ground up, you'll most likely notice that you can achieve the accuracy required to tackle live quarry at greater ranges when lying than when sitting; similarly, you'll be more accurate sitting than kneeling, and more accurate kneeling than standing.

The free-standing position is by far the most difficult to master, and I know few hunters who are able to tackle live quarry at much beyond 25 metres from this stance. Nonetheless, the extra elevation of the standing position can be very useful for clearing obstacles such as the aforementioned thistles and nettles, and it is certainly one to familiarise yourself with – even if you have to limit yourself to closer ranges.

When adopting the standing stance, start by thinking about your feet. They are your point of contact with the solid earth, your only connection with absolute stability, so make sure that they are planted firmly and comfortably. Weight distribution is important, so your feet should be a little way apart with your left foot pointing forward towards the target if you are right-handed. The body should be turned in the direction of the left foot. I am often asked whether the left elbow should be kept down to provide support against the body or stuck out when taking standing shots. My answer is to try both and stick with whatever suits you best. What is important is that the fit of your gun allows you to shoot with your head in a relatively relaxed, upright position rather than having to stoop down to peer through the sights.

Moving on to the kneeling stance, contact with the ground is again the priority. I am right-handed so I kneel with my left foot pointing forward and my right foot tucked under my backside. If I can, I sit back onto my right foot for extra stability. The elbow of my left, leading arm then hangs over my left knee, which provides support under my arm. A lot of shooters make the mistake of trying to rest their elbow right on their solid knee bone. This is ruinous to stability because the round, hard surface of your elbow just rolls around on the hard, flat surface of your knee. Again, I try to keep my head as upright as possible.

When shooting from a sitting position, I place my feet apart with my left foot pointing in the direction of the target. The elbow of my left, leading arm then rests behind my left knee and the elbow of my right, trigger arm rests behind my right knee – resting and not leaning, in order to avoid the wobbles previously mentioned.

The lying or prone position sounds fairly straightforward, and it is, but there are ways of improving it. Feet should be placed a little way apart, and instead of just having them straight behind you, swing both legs around slightly to the left (as ever, just reverse this if you are left-handed) in the direction of the target and your leading, left hand. This results in a more comfortable shooting position.

This is just the way I prefer to adopt these stances but if you are more comfortable and, above all, more accurate with a different variation, then my advice is to do it your way. Of course, it is unlikely that you'll always be able to get yourself into a textbook stance when opportunities arise in the field, so adaptability is the key to success.

Taking the shot

The conclusion of the shot involves much more than just snapping at the trigger when the sight picture looks right. Good trigger technique, controlled breathing and the all-important follow-through combine to make for consistently accurate shooting.

Starting with the trigger, the blade should be sitting against the sensitive pad at the end of your index finger. This allows the shooter to feel exactly which point the trigger is at as the tension is gradually taken-up, enabling the point of release to be easily predicted. Many shooters make the mistake of wrapping their finger around the trigger with the blade in the crease on the inside of the last joint of the finger. This is poor technique and should be avoided.

Preferred breathing patterns tend to vary from shooter to shooter. The most commonly recommended technique is to breathe gently as the sights gradually settle on the target then, as the shot comes good, exhale lightly before holding your breath just prior to taking the shot. A lot of shooters hold their breath a bit longer; usually for several seconds as they compose the shot and on until after they've pulled the trigger. I'm one of these shooters and this technique works fine for me. One thing to be aware of is the effect of holding your breath for extended periods. Often, the shot takes longer to make than we would like – perhaps because that

1 2

3 4

1. Standing shots are the hardest to master and therefore require the most practice.

2. Often used when ambushing quarry, the sitting stance provides the hunter with a stable platform.

3. The kneeling stance is a stable and versatile shooting position.

4. The prone position provides optimum accuracy unless the shot is obscured by low vegetation.

A gentle grip is the key to achieving consistent accuracy with a recoiling air rifle.

pigeon in the treetops won't keep its head still or maybe because the stance doesn't feel quite as steady as it should. Whatever the reason, the time occasionally comes when you've just held your breath too long to take the shot; the trembles start to kick-in and it's difficult to think of anything much other than the fact that you're running out of air. At this stage, you've gone beyond the point of making a reliably accurate shot and the simple, and only, solution is to take a few breaths and start again.

Follow-through can make or break a good shot and in order to master it you have to get past the common assertion that pulling the trigger is the final act of shooting. In essence, follow-through is the habit of maintaining composure until you see the pellet strike its mark but it actually starts a lot earlier than that.

I suppose there is an element of psychology to this but, as I start to take up the trigger, I am already imagining a positive result – I'll be visualising the squirrel being whacked from its lofty perch or the rabbit slumping into the grass. The trigger is softly nestled on the point of the second stage as my breathing settles and the crosshair comes to rest on its mark. When the shot is right, I'll gently touch off the trigger and remain on aim, keeping the crosshairs steady, until the pellet hits home. This disciplined approach of seeing the shot right through makes the action of taking a shot smooth and fluid, rather than concluding with an erratic snatch at the trigger when the time seems right.

In the written word, the process of taking a shot sounds like an overwhelming checklist of complicated procedures. Fortunately, it's much simpler in practice. Be mindful of your trigger technique, breathing and follow-through from the outset and good shooting quickly becomes an instinctive, subconscious habit.

Consistent shooting with recoiling air rifles

As previously mentioned, achieving consistency with recoiling air rifles is not as easy as it is with recoilless pre-charged guns. The movement of the spring and piston creates a jolt or kick, which is more than enough to throw the pellet off aim unless it is properly managed.

I have watched countless shooters trying to strangle the kick out of a spring-and-piston or gas-ram air rifle by gripping it with all their might, but the result is quite the reverse. The only way to properly manage the movement of a recoiling air rifle is to let it recoil, and do so in a way that keeps it consistent.

The best way to achieve this consistency is to hold the gun as lightly as you can. Place the butt pad in your shoulder, support the gun gently (and don't try to squeeze it) with your leading hand, and just cradle your trigger hand loosely around the pistol grip. Held in this way, your gun is allowed to recoil quite freely, and will always follow the same path as long as you allow it the same freedom of movement. By enabling the recoil to continually follow this course of travel, the effect will always be the same and shots will travel consistently to the desired mark.

Solid rests are to be avoided if you shoot a recoiling air rifle. Whereas the dead, recoilless action of a pre-charged air rifle allows it to be shot from the steadiness of a solid support, the moving parts of a springer rule out this option. When I was a youngster, I was often bemused and disheartened to shoot horribly erratic groups while resting my gun so securely that the crosshairs sat unmoving on the bull's-eye every time I took a shot. What I didn't realise was that when I pulled the trigger, I was setting off a series of movements inside the gun that caused my spring-and-piston air rifle to bounce harshly off the hard surface I was leaning on. This inconsistent and uncontrolled recoil manifested as a series of wild misses by the time the pellet had reached my target.

You can take rested shots with a springer or gas-ram air rifle but you have to make sure that the gun is cushioned from whatever you are leaning on. The trick is to use whatever you are resting against (maybe a tree, gate or fencepost) to support you rather than the gun. So, use the rest to prop your arm or hand but ensure that you are still holding the gun in the way previously described. This way, you are taking advantage of the extra stability but the gun is still able to follow the consistent path of recoil. Consequently, shots will land wherever the crosshairs settled when you pulled the trigger and not where the jolt of the exaggerated recoil flings them.

Practice and garden plinking

One common desire shared by everyone who has been bitten by the shooting bug, however experienced or whatever age, is the urge to get out and shoot their gun – especially if it's a new gun. Shooting is a very addictive pastime, and there's nothing wrong with that because any type of shooting amounts to useful practice that is of immeasurable value when we come to tackle live quarry.

Although the open countryside makes for the most beautiful of venues, the quietness and limited power of air rifles means it is perfectly acceptable to shoot them in a moderately sized garden, as long as you exercise common sense and follow a few basic guidelines.

First and foremost, shooting must be done within the law. No pellets should ever be allowed to stray beyond your boundary; the second a single pellet crosses to the other side of your garden wall or fence, you will be liable to prosecution. Safety and noise nuisance are other very important considerations.

Air rifles are very quiet in operation, and it's easy not to notice the sound of a pellet whacking into a backstop when you're engrossed in the challenge of ripping a bull's-eye to pieces. However insignificant the plink of a pellet hitting home sounds to you, it could be quite irritating – and disconcerting – to a neighbour who is out trying to enjoy a quiet afternoon on the sun lounger, so consideration must be shown. You are, after all, an ambassador for our sport so let's all try not to ruffle anyone's feathers.

The best way to maintain good neighbourly relations is to pay a visit next door and explain your intentions. Assure your neighbour that you will be sticking rigidly to the letter of the law and going out of your way to ensure absolute safety and minimal disturbance, and it is unlikely that they will be able to find anything to reasonably object to. This open and honest approach is better than leaving it to the constant 'phut, whack, phut, whack, phut, whack' soundtrack of a target-practice session to rouse your neighbour's curiosity sufficiently to prompt them to take a peep over the fence, only to be greeted by the sight of you sitting behind what, to the uninitiated, can look like a pretty fearsome weapon.

Once you've paved the way for garden target practice, you'll need to set up a safe, orderly range and follow a strict code of conduct.

The first priority for anyone who intends to shoot in the garden is to ensure that there is absolutely no chance of people and pets straying into the line of fire. The people who share your home should be told that the garden is out of bounds; pets and children in particular should be kept indoors. You can't just assume that a cat or a dog won't run in front of the gun, and the same goes for children – keep them well out of the way. It is also wise to put up signs stating something along the lines of 'SHOOTING IN PROGRESS – KEEP OUT' anywhere where people could enter the garden. These signs can be easily and cheaply printed off from your home computer.

In terms of range layout, no shots should be made past any blind corners or gateways from which people could possibly enter the garden. The best direction for shooting is towards a good, solid backstop like a wall of brick, stone or

When done responsibly, practising in the garden is a great way to hone your airgun shooting skills.

A knockdown target set up in the garden with concrete slabs as a backstop.

concrete. These materials obliterate lead pellets and stifle all their energy, sending them tumbling harmlessly to the ground with no chance of a ricochet. Never, ever consider using a wooden backstop. The fibrous nature of wood means it is liable to bounce pellets back at you, rather than harmlessly absorbing the impact. I witnessed this catapult effect when I was a youngster. Luckily, the rebounding pellet struck me in the body and not in the eye but the mark it left served as a reminder not to make the same mistake again. That was the first and last time I used a wooden backstop.

If you don't have a wall at the end of your garden, large paving slabs can be used to create an equally effective backstop to place behind your targets. The only problem is that an effective backstop does tend to make a bit of a noise when it's struck by a hurtling pellet so it pays to pop something in front of it to dull the sound. A discarded telephone directory will catch a pellet with minimal noise, and an old cereal box stuffed with rags is equally effective. Attach paper targets to either of these, using paperclips or tape, and you should be set for some quiet target practice. Just remember that these mufflers must still be placed in front of a suitable backstop as pellets will eventually rip right through them.

Shooting in company makes practice more enjoyable and a lot more satisfying. Good shots are all the more gratifying if they are witnessed by someone else, and an element of competition will encourage you to shoot to the best of your ability. However, the presence of another shooter means a strict code of conduct must be established, understood and adhered to.

The most important thing when shooting in company is to ensure that all people on the range are safely behind the guns. Sitting side by side on a wooden bench is a great way of ensuring that you know exactly where your shooting partner is at all times. It is also a wise move to establish a shooting order so shots aren't just being let-off at random. If, at any point, someone needs to travel down range – perhaps to check or reset a target – then a clear call to stop shooting should be made. Before anyone moves, ensure that all guns are unloaded, magazines are removed and muzzles pointed in a safe direction. This routine should be followed whenever you go down range, even if you are shooting on your own.

Leaving a gun unattended in the garden is asking for trouble and should never be allowed to happen. If I'm practising and I have to go indoors (perhaps because the doorbell or phone is ringing) then I'll unload, remove the magazine and take the gun in with me. Following this routine means that I miss the occasional phone call and guest but it is a sacrifice I'm prepared to make to avoid the chance of a tragic accident.

Punching paper is the best way to work out exactly how you and your rifle/scope/pellet combo is performing. Paper targets are unforgiving because they clearly illustrate exactly where a pellet has struck; you can easily read and interpret the effect of factors such as ammunition selection, wind and range have on the point of impact. I've been shooting air rifles for more than two decades but I still learn something every time I nip out to the garden bench to try out a new combo. The trouble is, even when you have company and a never-ending supply of hot tea, paper-punching can get a little boring. Luckily, there are all sorts of target variations available to the airgun shooter.

Practice shooting is often referred to as plinking, because of the sound the pellet makes when it hits the backstop, and the variety of targets available to the inventive plinker is virtually endless. Some targets may be a bit too noisy for shooting in more confined situations where neighbours might become irritated, so show consideration and base your choice on the situation specific to your home range.

If you have a fairly large garden and can get away with making a bit of noise, knock-down metal targets are great fun because they provide a visual response. Hit the circular kill area on a knock-down and, as well as the smack of the pellet against the metal, you'll be rewarded by the sight of the target falling over. These targets reset by the pull of a string so one quick yank and you're ready to whack it down again. On other variations, you have the added challenge of having to strike a secondary kill area to reset the target. Spinning targets are equally fun and reset automatically thanks to gravity. Hard mints are another entertaining and reasonably cheap target that offer some visual excitement. They're also useful because their size is more or less equal to a head shot on most air rifle quarry. So pick up a couple of tubes of mints next time you're in a sweet shop, line them up in front of your backstop and watch the dust fly as you smash them to pieces with well-placed shots. All of these targets provide an enjoyable way of becoming more familiar with your hunting outfit once you tire of shooting at paper; and, of course, if you can't shoot in your garden, you can always practice at a club or on the ground where you have permission to shoot. Just remember to ensure that there's always a suitable backstop in place.

CHAPTER 5

Clothing and accessories

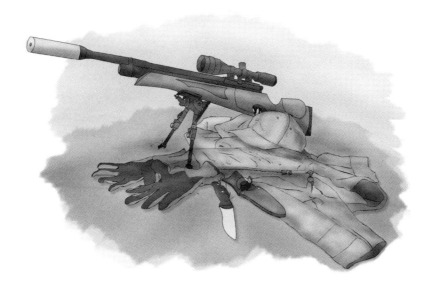

Hunting wear

Outdoor clothing is big business and the air-rifle hunter is faced with a massive, and sometimes bewildering, choice of styles, materials and camouflage patterns. Fortunately, most of the shooting clothing on the market is well up to the task, but some brands are certainly better than others.

Let's start by looking at camouflage patterns, because the variety now available really is staggering. First of all, I want to dispel the myth that you have to wear the latest, most expensive tree-print camo pattern to get anywhere near your quarry. I have to admit that, in the right situation, the degree of concealment provided by modern camouflage is quite astounding but, in all honesty, you could probably achieve similar results wearing a drab pair of trousers and a brown jacket once you've learned the basics of field craft.

The most important job that camouflage clothing has to do is to conceal the human form; an outline that, quite understandably, has struck fear into most wild creatures since our ancestors first picked up a spear. A good camouflage pattern produces a break-up effect that confuses prying eyes and makes it difficult to distinguish the hunter's outline against whatever background he is trying to use as cover. In most circumstances, this can be achieved with a fairly basic, mottled camouflage pattern and I would advise any beginner who is trying to kit himself out on a fairly limited budget to look to army surplus. For just a few pounds, you should be able to get yourself a rugged pair of trousers and a jacket that will survive several years of abuse in the field. And don't worry about how well tailored it is because baggy clothing will do a much better job of that all-important outline break-up than a slinky fit that hugs your body.

Another alternative to expensive specialist clothing is the net suit. These loose-fitting,

37

lightweight, affordable cotton suits come in most camouflage patterns and simply fit over whatever clothing you need to keep out the weather. On most occasions you'll probably just want a tough pair of jeans and a sweater underneath but the versatility of having a camouflage shell under which you can wear whatever clothing the day's conditions dictate can be very useful. In the winter, you can wrap-up with plenty of warm layers under your net suit and in the heat of summer you can get away with just shorts and a T-shirt yet still wear a full suit of camouflage without overheating.

If you can afford to spend a bit more, waterproof, tree-pattern camouflage with realistic foliage prints does provide an impressive degree of concealment and has certainly established itself as the basic uniform among air rifle hunters over recent years. Shooters from other branches of the sport often tease air-gunners about our fetish for dressing like trees; look through the pages of the monthly airgun press (and I'm as much to blame for this as anyone) and you'll see that they've got a point.

I usually opt for modern camouflage patterns because I genuinely believe that they improve my chances of going unnoticed – albeit only by a very slight degree over conventional camouflage. To get the most from this sort of clothing, and from any camouflage clothing for that matter, you have to appreciate that it doesn't work by magic – it's not an invisible cloak. For optimum effect, camouflage has to be matched to the surroundings, and you have to make the absolute most of existing natural cover to get the best from it.

So, when you choose a camouflage pattern, think about where you shoot and the kind of backgrounds your clothing will be seen against. If you shoot mostly in the woods, for instance, your quarry will usually be looking down at you from the trees so you'll want something that blends in well with the leaf litter. If you shoot mostly in the summer, it might pay to opt for a

You don't have to spend a fortune on branded clothing to blend in with the countryside.

pattern with more of the greens and yellows associated with that season rather than the greys and browns more often encountered in a winter landscape. Be wary of the very pale patterns with colours that look better suited to the desert than the British countryside. I like a pattern with plenty of contrast too – most people would be surprised by the amount of black and white created by the play of light and shade on branches and foliage.

Be careful when you wash your camouflage clothing because a lot of detergents contain a cleaning agent that can leave a trace that really stands out in the vision spectrum of some wild animals when it catches the light. The perfume in soap powders and liquids will also leave an unnatural odour that will spook your quarry if it catches a whiff. For these reasons, I don't use any cleaning products when I put my shooting clothes in the washing machine; they just get cleaned in plain water. And I actually wash them as little as I can get away with because I believe that the natural smells my clothes pick up when I'm sitting in the woods, sloshing through ditches and lying in wait in the grass helps to conceal the odour of the human being wearing them.

Returning to the matter of fit, the aim is not just to distort the human outline but also to be able to move comfortably, and loose clothing scores points in this regard too. As well as allowing you sufficient mobility to go through all the contortions of a difficult stalk (which might even involve crawling on your hands and knees) your shooting clothes should also provide enough freedom for you to comfortably adopt any stance. When you try trousers, make sure that you can squat and kneel in them and when trying a jacket ensure that the shoulders are generous enough not to restrict you when you raise your gun. Also remember to check that the

sleeves are long enough not to ride halfway up your arms when you lift the gun to your shoulder.

In terms of what you actually need, the main garments are a fairly durable jacket and pair of trousers that will act as a weather-proof shell, helping you to blend in with the natural surroundings and enabling you to add other layers as the weather dictates. I like a jacket with a decent hood that will keep out any sudden downpours, and plenty of spacious pockets to carry my hunting essentials. It's also handy to have a jacket that is long enough to keep your backside dry when you sit on damp ground.

One very important consideration that a lot of people overlook is making sure that your clothing is quiet. Modern materials mean it is possible to buy clothing that will protect you from the foulest of weather but doesn't rustle like old-fashioned waterproofs. But, however quiet the fabric is, jingling zips and clinking poppers still sometimes create sounds that could arouse suspicion when you're trying to get close to your quarry. The best way to find out how noisy your hunting clothes are is to wait up until everyone has gone to bed and the distant sounds of traffic and the like have died down, then slip on your hunting clothes. With the rest of the family sound asleep and the television turned off, you'll be surprised how quiet your house is; you'll also probably be surprised to hear just how much noise your shooting clothes make when you try to creep around in the still of the night. These little sounds won't go undetected by the finely tuned hearing of a rabbit.

Apart from clothing to keep you warm and dry, the hunter also needs appropriate footwear, and this should be matched with the conditions. Ideally, I like to wear the lightest footwear I can possibly get away with, particularly for stalking. When you are trying to creep up on a rabbit,

By matching camouflage clothing to the surroundings, the hunter can disappear into the landscape.

you'll need to get past its sensitive hearing and its ability to detect vibration through the ground. The best thing to wear on your feet in these conditions is a worn-out old pair of trainers. Apart from being quiet, shoes of this kind also provide great freedom of movement and enable you to feel the ground as you slowly shift your weight from foot to foot. Unfortunately, old trainers aren't very good at keeping your feet dry in long, wet grass so I usually opt for a more robust shoe that is a cross between a trainer and a lightweight walking boot.

A lot of air rifle shooters like to wear bulky, military-style, lace-up boots that come halfway up to the knee but I can't think of less appropriate footwear. These boots certainly protect against the elements, keeping your feet warm and dry, but they restrict the movement of your ankle and produce heavy footfalls that are likely to alert rabbits to your approach. I had a pair of these boots and soon got rid of them after some very clumsy and frustratingly unsuccessful stalks.

If conditions are really wet under foot, then I will wear welly boots. Admittedly, these don't offer much finesse for stalking but they certainly keep the water out. Some rubber boots are certainly better than others; go for the ones with a good fit around the ankle and heel, and couple them with a decent pair of long, thick socks, and they'll slop around a lot less than an ill-fitting pair. Of course, if you're shooting from a static position, the lack of finesse doesn't really matter.

One thing that is worth checking when you choose footwear for hunting is that the sole has a tread pattern that provides plenty of grip. There are few things worse than trying to scale steep grassy slopes in slippery conditions while wearing boots that don't provide adequate traction – as well as making stalking difficult, it's also quite dangerous.

There are a few small and relatively inexpensive items of clothing that can make a real difference to a hunting session. A lot of hunters are happy to splash out on expensive jackets and trousers but forget about covering-up their face and hands – and there's probably nothing that spooks wild animals more than a human face. Camouflage clothing does a great job of blurring your outline and hiding you from your quarry, but its effect can be greatly enhanced by ensuring that every last patch of flesh is concealed.

Covering your hands is easy; all you need is a pair of cotton gloves. These don't cost very much and are available in camouflage patterns from most good gun shops. I would certainly recommend the type that have a stippled rubber grip in the palms as they certainly help when it comes to gripping your gun – the ones without can make a polished wooden stock feel precariously slippery. Also, some types of shooting gloves come with fingers that fold back, which is great for improving grip and enhancing your feel of the trigger. Being able to feel and accurately predict the break point of the trigger through your gloves is paramount for accurate shooting, and I actually go as far as to cut off the end of the trigger finger on my gloves if they aren't made to fold back.

There are several ways to keep your face concealed, and I don't think camouflage paint is one of them. This stuff is greasy, messy and gets all over your clothing and equipment, and a camo'ed-up face is also likely to strike terror into any dog walkers or ramblers you might happen to bump into. A peaked cap is a far more practical solution. Although the cap won't physically cover your face, the peak will cast enough shade to greatly improve concealment. The peak will also improve the picture through your telescopic sight by preventing sunlight from spilling onto its rear lens.

I must admit that I don't like wearing hats unless I really have to because they tend to make my head itch. For this reason, I usually opt to wear a camouflage head net in hunting situations that require me to keep my face concealed. A lightweight head net provides complete cover, won't get itchy, and is about the best way to avoid spooking wary crows and pigeons when you're peering up into the trees. The only downside with a head net

is the narrow field of view that can hamper stalking, for which you need to be able to scan all around. Fortunately, rabbits don't have great eyesight, so you can usually get away without wearing a head net when stalking them. As well as hiding the patches of flesh that can betray your presence, hats, gloves and head nets will also help to keep you warm in the winter and, very importantly, help to keep biting gnats and midges off your flesh in warmer weather.

My recommendations on clothing are geared towards swinging every last possible percentage in the favour of the hunter and, as a result, probably sound quite elaborate. The preceding paragraphs are, however, only intended as guidance. I spent my first years as a hunter slopping around the fields in ill-fitting rubber boots, blue jeans and an old waxed jacket, and I still managed to shoot my fair share of pigeons and rabbits. There's more to getting close to your quarry than wearing the right clothes; field craft will always be the hunter's greatest asset.

Coping with the cold

When hunting in really cold weather, you have to think very, very carefully about your

The hands and face can attract unwanted attention from quarry species – covering them up makes the shooter less conspicuous.

Soup, hot from the flask, is one way to maintain your core temperature and your morale when the weather is cold.

A decent pair of gloves is essential for hunting in sub-zero temperatures.

clothing – not just for keeping you concealed but, most importantly, for keeping you warm and keeping you alive. At the very least, it's no good feeling cold when you're out hunting because you won't be able to perform to anything like your optimum. You won't shoot accurately when you're shivering and your hands are numb, and you'll most likely end up going home early once you start thinking about a warm house and hot food. At worst, you could be risking your life; shooting often takes place in remote places so who's going to find you when you're gripped by hypothermia? It's no laughing

matter; I've felt the early stages of hypothermia so I know what I'm talking about. It came on very quickly and before I knew it I could hardly see, I couldn't think straight and I could barely stand up – fortunately I was with a friend or the situation could have been dire.

The best advice when shooting in extreme weather is to keep on the move. It's surprising how much heat your body will generate when it's burning off calories. Eating a decent meal before you set out will help too, and it's also worth stowing a flask of hot tea or soup in your backpack. A mobile phone is useful on any hunting trip; you never know when you might need to ring for assistance, and a phone is just as useful for damage limitation so you can call home and brace your better half for a late arrival when the pigeon roost is particularly productive. I keep my phone on silent so there's no chance of it ringing and spooking my quarry at the end of a particularly tough stalk.

In terms of winter clothing, layers are very good at trapping the warmth. Wear plenty of layers and you can always remove one or two if you work-up some heat when you're on the move. Another important thing is to prevent heat from escaping from those all-important extremities. A hat is a must in really cold weather; most heat escapes through the head so remember to 'lag the loft' with a warm hat. Your feet need to be well insulated too, so opt for a couple pairs of thick socks. If it's really cold and I know I won't be moving about very much, I'll wear thermal moon boots. These boots are worn by cold-storage workers and they really will keep your feet toasty in even the rawest of weather – they aren't much good for stalking in, though. You'll probably want to upgrade your usual lightweight hunting gloves for something more substantial when the temperature really plummets. There are lots of great gloves available that keep out the cold while still enabling you to shoot properly; the neoprene ones with fold-back fingers are particularly good. You'll also appreciate being able to carry your gun on your shoulder with a sling on bitterly cold days. The sling will keep your hands free, enabling you to stuff them in your pockets, snugly away from the elements.

Useful accessories

Apart from the essential and obvious gun, scope and ammunition combination, there are a few extra bits and pieces that will come in handy on a shooting trip. I don't like to be too bogged down with kit when I'm hunting on the move but even I usually carry a few basic accessories.

At the top of my list of equipment comes a good quality hunting knife. A sharp blade will come in handy for all sorts of jobs in the field, from preliminary game preparation to the minor pruning tasks that often accompany the construction of a hide. Ideally, you really should have two knives: a small one with a blade like a surgeon's scalpel for cutting quickly and cleanly through flesh and fur, and a bigger one with a thicker, stronger blade for hacking through branches. However, few hunters are going to want the burden of carrying two knives, so most of us compromise on one all-rounder that can make a reasonable job of most tasks.

Forget the big commando knives, and settle for something you'll be able to wield with a bit more finesse – one with a blade of around three inches should be about right. Also, try not to be seduced by the apparent benefits of an all-singing, all-dancing, gadget-packed knife. As a hunter, you really don't need to carry a knife that features a selection of tools. While some people might think it would be nice to have a screwdriver handy if they noticed a loose screw in their gun, this really is highly unlikely to

happen if you take proper care of your air rifle and check things like screw tightness from time to time when you're cleaning it.

Look at a knife as a long-term investment and be prepared to spend a few pounds on one. While I wouldn't recommend spending so much on a knife that losing it would amount to a serious disaster, it is a fact that the more you spend, the better quality you will get. Cheap knives are a false economy as their blades don't usually keep their edge for very long at all whereas a knife made of decent steel will take a good edge and stay sharp for longer. On the subject of sharpening, make sure you use a good, smooth stone and not the old chunk of carborundum you use for your gardening tools – a coarse stone will make mincemeat of the fine edge of a good hunting knife.

Hide netting is another useful piece of kit for the air rifle hunter. These days, you can buy all sorts of pop-up tent-style hides but you still can't beat a good piece of hide netting for value and versatility.

For a few pounds, you can buy a large piece of hide netting that can be used to create a screen wherever you like. This netting is available in various colours and even in modern camouflage patterns but any drab colour will suffice because you can always weave vegetation into it to help it blend in. Gun shops also sell extending hide poles. Although these poles make a useful support for hide netting, you can always hang your net from bushes, sticks and fences if you're on a tight budget.

Your hide netting can also double-up as a useful carry-all. Shot quarry, decoys and the like can be placed in the middle of the net, which can then be gathered up from the corners and flung over your shoulder like a sack.

Better still, a medium-sized backpack can prove to be an invaluable accessory for carrying

Simple accessories can make a big difference. A backpack is useful for carrying essentials, and a sling makes it much easier to carry a gun over long distances.

A sharp, sturdy knife is useful for all kinds of tasks in the field, from trimming branches to preparing shot quarry.

essential pieces of kit, especially during longer trips in the field. I tend to use the main compartment of mine for carrying shot quarry and stow things like my flask and sandwiches into the large side pockets. If you come across a real bargain rucksack in a camping store, check the colour before you buy. The fluorescent tones favoured by the camping, hiking and rambling fraternity might undo the effect of your camouflage clothing somewhat, so make sure it's a drab colour.

Owing to the nocturnal habits of some of the air rifle hunter's quarry species – rabbits and rats, for example – hunting after dark can be incredibly effective. In these circumstances, you're going to need a light source and, although sophisticated and expensive night-vision gear can be very effective, a lamp will always prove to be a useful accessory.

For rabbit-shooting, where you need to pick out your quarry in the lamplight over greater ranges, it's best to opt for a large, powerful lamp with a decent-sized rechargeable battery pack. You'll want something that can cast a good, tight beam

a hundred metres or so, enabling you to spot rabbits long before they are spooked by your approach. That tight spot-beam is important because you really don't want a lamp that spills light, revealing you to your quarry every time you switch it on. Combined with the power pack, this sort of lamp can be a fairly heavy piece of kit and, as you'll need your hands free to do the shooting, it's useful to have a companion who can act as your lamp man.

When targeting rats over shorter distances, a compact scope-mounted lamp really does take some beating. Best of all, they're totally hands-free so you don't need to rely on a helper to operate the lamp for you. These nifty – and relatively inexpensive – little lights simply clip to the scope tube via a quick-release mount. They usually have an on/off switch that attaches to the stock of your rifle so you can operate it with your leading hand. Simply flick on the switch and you've got a nice pool of illumination wherever you point the gun, allowing you to scan through the scope in search of rats. The light is also useful for little night-time tasks such as reloading and picking up shot quarry. Most scope-mounted lamps come with a rechargeable battery pack that either attaches to your belt or sits in your jacket pocket; some even clip to the butt of the rifle. Although quite compact, these power-packs provide sufficient running time for a typical hunting session after an overnight charge. It's also worth buying a set of filters to fit to your hunting lamp. These coloured filters dim down the light, attracting less suspicion from quarry that might have become lamp-shy following persistent shooting over a particular area.

A gun sling is an accessory that will quickly prove its worth if you have to walk long distances with your air rifle. Even a comparatively light gun is a fairly heavy piece of kit, especially after you've been holding it for any length of time. Fit a sling and you've got a shoulder strap that makes your gun much easier to carry.

When choosing a sling, look for one that is soft and supple and sits comfortably and securely against your shoulder – the last thing you want is a sling with a shiny finish that causes it to slip. Also, you don't want a sling with buckles, swivels or catches that rattle or click when you are walking, because the sound will alert quarry to your presence. My favourite sling has quick-release swivels, which means I can fit it to my gun for ease of carrying when I'm on the move, then quickly unclip it so it doesn't get in the way when I reach my hide or ambush point.

Slings usually fit to the gun via studs located at the fore-end and butt end of the stock. The front stud can also be used to fit a very useful accessory – a bipod.

Bipods support the front of the gun, providing a rock-steady rest for lying and, if you get one with long legs, sitting shots. Most air-gunners just use the more compact bipods, or pods, for shooting prone, and the results are very impressive. However, in my experience, bipods, like most rests, work well with the recoilless firing cycle of a PCP but make for unpredictable shooting when coupled with a recoiling springer or gas-ram.

The support provided by a decent bipod virtually eliminates all of the wobbles you usually encounter when trying to hold the gun still. As a result, you can expect a PCP's group sizes to be greatly improved and hunting ranges consequently increased. Of course, hold-over and hold-under, along with the effects of wind, will still affect accuracy, so consider all factors and get plenty of practice on the range before attempting longer than usual shots off a bipod.

You can buy cheap bipods that clip to the barrel of your air rifle but I don't like the thought of the barrel bearing the weight of my gun – there's too much risk of it being pushed upwards. The best bipods have adjustable legs and a swivel action that enables you to keep the gun upright even if you're set up on a slope. They aren't cheap but a good one will last you a lifetime as long as you give it the occasional wipe-down with oil.

When shooting off a bipod, you don't need to use your front hand in the usual way, as the weight of the gun is already supported. What I do is place my left hand under the butt of the rested rifle so, by clenching and rolling my fist, I am able to adjust my aim by tiny increments as I prepare to make a shot.

A stock-mounted stud enables the attachment of numerous useful extras. They aren't difficult to fit, as long as you follow a few simple guidelines.

Fitting studs

Some guns come fitted with studs to accept slings and bipods but you often have to fit them yourself. This is a fairly straightforward job, as long as you do it properly and don't try to rush. I've mangled one or two stocks by hastily trying to fit studs before a hunting session, so I know what I'm talking about.

The first thing to do when preparing to fit studs is to make sure you have all the right tools to hand. You'll need a power drill and a selection of drill bits as the screws that fasten the studs to the woodwork are usually tapered in stages. What I then do is have a test run on a lump of old wood, marking each of the drill bits with masking tape to indicate exactly how deep I have to drill to snugly accommodate each stage of the screw as it bites into the wood.

Make sure you remove the action when you're ready to move on to the stock. This point cannot be stressed enough; not only do you risk damaging the gun with the drill, you also risk a dangerous explosion of compressed air. Mark exactly where you want to fit the studs to the stock (centrally, and in far enough to prevent the wood from splitting) with a bradawl, and then begin by making the narrowest, deepest hole before making the wider ones. The fit should be quite tight so you'll probably need to use the shaft of an Allen key to tighten the stud into place. If it does not align exactly when tightened, use one of the plastic washers usually provided with the metal studs to achieve alignment. The tight fit of the screw thread should be more than adequate to hold everything in place, but I usually squeeze a drop of wood glue into the hole for added peace of mind.

CHAPTER 6

Legal matters and permission to shoot

If you are going to shoot and/or own an airgun, it should go without saying that you must do so within the law. Whenever shooting gets a bad press, it is invariably a foolish minority spoiling things for the responsible majority. As a shooter, it is important to acknowledge that your actions will be scrutinised and, as a representative for all shooters, you must ensure that you always conduct yourself in a safe, responsible and law-abiding way.

Airgun law

UK laws for airgun use are among the toughest in the world. Punishment for misuse of airguns is in line with that for firearms offences and can result in a prison sentence.

In the UK at the time of writing, you do not need a licence to own an air rifle (you do in Northern Ireland). However, certain strict conditions do apply. First and foremost, your air rifle's muzzle energy must not exceed 12.ft.lb

which is equivalent to 16.2 joules. It is your legal responsibility to ensure that your air rifle is within this legal limit at all times. If your air rifle produces more than 12ft.lb energy at the muzzle, it is instantly classed as a Section 1 Firearm. Should this happen, and you do not have a firearms certificate (FAC) with specific provision for your air rifle, you will be committing a serious criminal offence. The power of air pistols must not exceed 6ft.lb. Air pistols are, therefore, not suitable for pest control or hunting.

Muzzle energy is a calculation of the projectile's speed and weight. The speed of the pellet is measured with a device called a chronograph. Inside a chronograph are two optic sensors which record the passage of the pellet and calculate its speed by working out how long it takes to travel the fixed distance from one to the other. Most gun shops and shooting clubs have chronographs.

It is your responsibility to ensure that the power level of your air rifle remains within the law.

Some chronographs can work out muzzle energy for you once you have tapped-in the weight of the pellet and fired your shot through the sensors. Less sophisticated models require you to do the sums for yourself – with the help of a calculator.

There's a sum for calculating muzzle energy once you've determined muzzle velocity and the weight of your chosen pellet. Simply multiply the square of the muzzle velocity (feet per second) by the weight of the pellet (grains) and divide by the magic number 450,240 and you'll arrive at muzzle energy (ft.lbs). So, to find the power produced by an air rifle recording a muzzle velocity of 600 feet per second with a pellet weighing 14 grains, the sum would be: 600 x 600 x 14 ÷ 450240 = 11.19ft.lbs

The weight of most pellets can be looked up online and some websites even feature muzzle energy calculators, into which you just need to input pellet weight and muzzle velocity. A simple internet search should point you in the right direction.

Most manufacturers ensure that their guns leave the production line with an in-built margin for error to ensure that muzzle energy is within the law. Therefore, most legal-limit air rifles in the shops are actually producing a muzzle energy of somewhere just above or below 11ft.lb off the peg. However, there are several factors that can lead to an accidental increase in muzzle energy.

Heavier pellets usually produce higher energy, so it is well worth testing the power of your gun if you change from one brand to another. Changing the spring of a spring-and-piston air rifle will affect its power. Ensure that the new spring is suited to your make and calibre of gun and check muzzle energy after fitting a replacement. Dieseling (an explosion resulting from excess oil or grease in the chamber of a spring-and-piston gun) can also cause a rise in energy.

Some irresponsible shooters fit over-sized mainsprings or deliberately cause dieseling in an attempt to get more power from their air rifles. Apart from being illegal, this is also likely to damage your gun and ruin shot-to-shot consistency.

There is no restriction on anyone aged 18 years or over buying an air rifle or ammunition, and you can use it wherever you have permission to shoot. Commercial sales of air rifles must be conducted face to face by a registered firearms dealer (RFD). This restriction only applies to airguns and silencers and does not apply to pellets, scopes or other accessories. You do not need to be an RFD to privately sell your used air rifle.

People aged between 14 and 17 can borrow an air rifle and ammunition and use it without supervision on property where they have permission to shoot. At this age, you cannot buy or hire an air rifle or receive one as a gift. Your air rifle must be bought and looked after for you by someone aged 18 or over – usually your parent, guardian or some other responsible adult.

If you are aged under 14 you can use an air rifle under the supervision of someone aged 21 or over on land where you have permission to shoot. The law states that parents or guardians who buy an air rifle for use by someone aged under 14 must exercise control over the gun at all times, even in the home or garden.

You must ensure that you are properly authorised by the landowner or whoever controls the sporting rights of wherever you are planning to shoot – ideally, this authorisation should be granted in writing. Make sure that you know where all boundaries are as well as any areas that could present a hazard. It is an offence to allow pellets to stray (either directly or by ricochet) beyond the land where you have permission to shoot, or to fire your air rifle within 50 feet of the centre of a public highway, bridleway or footpath if this could be deemed as causing anyone danger, injury or interruption.

People aged under 18 cannot take an air rifle to a public place unless they are supervised by somebody aged 21 or over. Anyone carrying an air rifle in a public place should have a reasonable excuse for doing so (taking the gun to a shop for repair or to a shooting ground, for example). Whenever carrying your gun in a public place, and this includes your car, it should be in a fastened case, unloaded (this means emptying or removing the magazine) and de-cocked. Although it is difficult to see how this can be any more dangerous than carrying a tin of pellets, it is technically illegal to carry a magazine loaded with airgun pellets in a public place.

As a shooter, it is your responsibility to ensure that you understand and follow current airgun law for the place where you live. If in any doubt, consult the relevant authority.

What you can shoot

As a hunter, it is essential to know what species you can legally shoot. It is also essential to have a good reason for shooting them. To kill for the sake of killing is nothing short of loutish and shows a serious lack of respect for wildlife, the countryside and yourself. The decision to take an animal's life is not a decision to be taken lightly, so make sure it is based on sound reason and not just the impulse to tackle a live target.

The ability to quickly and clearly identify quarry species is also vital. Killing an animal that is not recognised as legitimate quarry is illegal and utterly unacceptable. As a serious hunter, you should quickly develop an interest in the finer workings of nature and the countryside, and your bookshelf will consequently feature several volumes on wildlife. Books provide a good basis for quarry identification, but the only way to learn accurate recognition is in the field and that takes time. The best thing an aspiring hunter can do is befriend a knowledgeable countryman who can guide and assist in learning how to identify and understand the habits of your quarry. If at any time you are unable to positively identify the animal in your sights as legal quarry, don't pull the trigger. It's too late when the shot has been fired, so don't run the risk of making an embarrassing, illegal and downright stupid mistake.

The main vermin species the UK air rifle hunter can target all year round with no restriction are the brown rat, the grey squirrel and the rabbit. Others, including the mink, may be targeted with FAC-rated air rifles.

Authorisation to shoot avian quarry (birds) with an air rifle is currently granted under general license by the government body Natural England. Bird species listed under the general licence that can be regarded as legitimate quarry include woodpigeon, feral pigeon, collared dove, crow, magpie, jay, rook and jackdaw. Two species of parakeet – ring-necked and monk – have recently been added to the general licence in England, though not the rest of the UK. Escapees have formed large colonies in the wild that are causing considerable crop damage, particularly around Hertfordshire. It will be interesting to see whether air rifles have a significant part to play in the control of this introduced species. The English general licence goes on to include the Canada goose, Egyptian goose, ruddy duck and lesser black-backed gull, but these are not generally considered as air rifle quarry species.

You do not need to apply for a general licence but you are required by law to act within its terms and conditions. In basic terms, the licence permits authorised persons (landowners and the people to whom they grant permission to shoot) the right to control the above-mentioned bird species in order to prevent the spread of disease or serious damage to livestock, foodstuffs for livestock, crops, vegetables, fruit, growing timber, fisheries or inland waters. Under the general licence, the feral pigeon is the only avian pest that can be shot using artificial lighting. It is, therefore, illegal to shoot any of the others by lamplight.

It is also a requirement of the general licence that avian pests should be killed in a quick and humane manner. This is, of course, the prime intention of any responsible hunter targeting any live quarry. It is common sense that a shot that risks causing injury or a lingering death should be left.

Natural England's general licence also states that people acting under it must be satisfied that non-lethal methods of resolving the problem are ineffective or impracticable. This caveat suggests that scaring tactics should be attempted before resorting to shooting. It is, however, something of a grey area and this advice has been much criticised by official bodies representing countryside sports, not least because it is difficult to gauge exactly which alternative methods are 'ineffective or impracticable'. Nonetheless, failure to comply with the requirements of the licence can result in a fine of up to £5,000 and/or a six-month custodial sentence, so be warned.

The list of species defined as pests varies from country to country and is frequently reviewed – annually for England, Scotland, Wales and Northern Ireland. The list quoted above applies to England at the time of writing. To be sure of current legislation on the control of pest birds in your locality, check on the website of the relevant government agency.

It is the responsibility of anyone who intends to shoot live quarry to make their own decision on what constitutes legal, necessary and ethical pest control based on the above guidance. My advice is to read and digest what the law states and then apply it to the pest-control situations you encounter.

Acquiring permission to shoot

One of the biggest challenges faced by the would-be air rifle hunter is finding somewhere to shoot. Some people are fortunate in that they have friends or family with farmland over which they can hunt, but most of us have to work hard to secure a place to shoot.

I can still recall the frustration of the constant knock-backs from farmers when I sought permission as a young shooter. The best piece of advice I can offer is to not be too disheartened and to persevere. The satisfaction of acquiring your first piece of hunting ground will more than make up for the effort.

When trying to gain shooting permission it is important to think along the lines of the landowners you are approaching. If you owned hundreds of acres of land and depended on it to earn a livelihood for yourself and your family, would you let a complete stranger roam freely with a gun after a casual request? Probably not.

The best way to convince landowners that you are a responsible person and serious about your shooting is to obtain insurance. An annual payment will insure you against damage or injury to machinery, buildings, livestock and people. Of course, as an ambassador for our sport, it is every hunter's responsibility to ensure that an accident is never allowed to happen, but insurance provides peace of mind and will help

to convince your host that you have a professional attitude.

Different insurers offer different premiums and my advice is not to automatically opt for the cheapest. I have been a member of the BASC (British Association for Shooting and Conservation) for many years and happily recommend their services. This organisation works hard to protect country sports and promote their benefits to the natural world. As well as including comprehensive insurance cover, membership of the BASC entitles you to free advice from the organisation's numerous experts in every imaginable field of shooting, and you get their regular magazine too. Also, the BASC is a respected and trusted organisation, so most landowners will have heard of it when you mention your insurance.

The best initial approach to landowners about hunting permission is to write to them. Send a simple letter outlining the fact that you are fully insured and wish to offer a free pest-control service, showing absolute respect for property and livestock. Suggest a meeting to discuss the farmer's requirements, remembering to include your contact details. Expect to be disappointed and don't go chasing-up your letters with impatient phone calls. Farmers are busy people, so if you don't get a reply you can assume that your letter was ignored. It may sound futile but letter-writing is always worth a try. If you send out 20 letters and just one results in shooting permission, you've succeeded.

Should your letters fail to secure you shooting rights, you'll need to think about paying a visit – but not until a few weeks after you wrote, because you do not want to come across as being pushy. Before you head for the farm, think about your appearance and the sort of impression you want to create. Turn up on a farmer's doorstep wearing your camouflage clothing with your gun

Winning the trust of a landowner in order to secure shooting permission can be one of the greatest challenges faced by the air rifle hunter.

PRIVATE PROPERTY

slung over your shoulder and you should expect a rude reception.

Dress tidily but don't overdo it (a suit and tie probably won't impress most farmers) and remember your manners. When the door opens, refer to the letter you sent, reiterate your intentions and remind him or her about that all-important insurance. Also remember to point out that you are looking to provide a useful

service because, like the rest of us, most farmers like to think they're getting something for nothing. When considering who to ask, look out for the fields that are overrun with rabbits or being hammered by wood pigeons when you're out and about – you might receive a very warm welcome from a farmer who is plagued with vermin. If nothing else, a face-to-face meeting should enable your potential host to get a feel for whether or not they would trust you on their land. As ever, expect disappointment and remember to be polite and gracious if you are refused permission. Countryside communities are usually close-knit and word will soon get around if you offend someone.

This close community is probably the key to securing shooting rights, and if you're already a well-known and trusted member of your local community, you've got a head start over new arrivals. Think about your friends and family and anyone they might know who owns some land and might appreciate some free pest control. A recommendation from someone who knows you counts for a lot in terms of trustworthiness and will certainly put you on the fast-track compared with a surprise request on the farmhouse doorstep.

If you're new to your locality, then you'll need to tap-in to the community. The pub is a good place to start, and if you've got children they could come in useful too as one or two of their school friends could be from farming families. It sounds a little devious but it's just about expanding your social network and enabling you and your friends to help each other.

When you do find yourself talking to the right person (be it in the pub, the school playground, the church, the village hall or wherever) don't go straight in with the big question. Hopefully the conversation will drift to their farming background and you might be able to ask if they ever have any trouble with vermin. If they have, generously offer your services – you'd be doing them a favour, after all.

When you do get permission to shoot, make sure you get it in writing. This is a prerequisite to validate your insurance and could also come in handy if anyone ever questions your actions or your right to be there when you're out hunting. Also remember that you are there to carry out a service, so let the landowner explain how he or she would like you to operate – you might have to fit around farming activities. Some parts of the farm might be no-go areas because of livestock, workers or walkers. Remember as well to make sure that you know exactly what your host wants, and doesn't want, you to shoot. They are on the official quarry list but jays may be a personal favourite of the landowner's – and it's too late finding out after you've shot one. You also have to respect your host's wishes when it comes to just how hard you hit the vermin. It's their land, and if they want you to try to eradicate the rabbits then that's what you must try to do; it is no good thinking you can leave a few for next year. Between you, you should be able to work out an agreement that is beneficial and realistic for both of you.

That first permission will put you firmly in the local farming loop so remember to act responsibly at all times. Your host will, no doubt, discuss your activities with friends and colleagues, and a few positive comments could soon open up more opportunities. Offer to lend a hand with jobs on the farm if you are ever able to, alert the landowner to any fencing, hedging or gates that may need repair, and notify them of any suspicious activity on their land – as well as keeping down the vermin, you also have an important role to play as an extra pair of eyes around the farm.

CHAPTER 7

Hunting and field craft

A word on ethics

The decision to pursue and kill an animal is not one to be taken lightly. As well as acting within the law and targeting only the pest species that are regarded as legitimate air rifle quarry, the hunter should also have a good reason for his actions.

As game species such as pheasant, partridge and hare are not usually considered as being air rifle quarry, the species typically shot by air-gunners are all classified as vermin. These pest species, therefore, all have habits that conflict with man's activities and it is consequently accepted that their numbers need to be culled in certain circumstances. Some species, such as rats and magpies, are controlled purely because they are vermin and pose a threat either to people's livelihoods, to human health or to more sensitive populations of less common wild birds or mammals. Rabbits and pigeons, although a serious agricultural pest that can cause ruinous

damage to a farmer's livelihood, also have the added bonus of providing delicious, free meat for the table.

Meat harvested from wild rabbits and pigeons is absolutely free-range and about as organic as you can get. And, because the animal's wild lifestyle has enabled it to live and feed as naturally as possible, it is very lean as well as very tasty.

I would argue that it is virtually impossible to eat meat that has been reared to higher welfare standards than that harvested by the air rifle hunter. Our quarry was born in the wild, it lived, grew and fed in the wild and is usually completely oblivious to the fact that its life was going to end right up to the point that it was cleanly killed with a well-placed shot.

Maintaining that high level of welfare right to the end is absolutely imperative. It is a little-known fact that wild animals usually come to a miserable end – dying as a result of either

It is a hunter's responsibility to ensure that all quarry is killed humanely, and with good reason.

disease, hypothermia, starvation or predation – but it is totally unacceptable for any animal to suffer unnecessarily as a result of the actions of an irresponsible shooter. Every hunter's top priority should be to show absolute respect for his quarry and to ensure that it is despatched as swiftly and humanely as possible.

In most instances, the only way to be totally confident of ensuring a clean kill with an air rifle is to take quarry with a shot to the head. There are a few exceptions when heart-and-lung shots can be equally effective which I'll discuss later, but by and large, head shots should be regarded as the norm. The damage inflicted by an air rifle pellet smashing through the skull and brain of our comparatively small quarry is almost always enough to ensure instant death. Also, when aiming for the head, a misplaced shot will usually result either in a complete miss or a lethal impact to the neck; the result of a misplaced shot when aiming for the heart or lungs can be quite different.

To the novice, the demand of making head shots on all quarry – even pigeons – must sound like a very tall order. It is, and that's why all the time taken to ensure your gun, scope and pellet combo

The magnificent colours of a magpie are far from black and white when viewed close-up.

The jay's striking blue wing feathers are prized by the shooter and the fly-tyer.

Waiting patiently at the pigeon
roost on a still winter evening.

Retrieving the first pigeon of the evening from the woodland floor.

Hunting with air rifles is a sport for all seasons – whatever the weather.

Safe gun handling is important at all times, and especially when crossing obstacles.

Shooting pigeons in summer as they flit beneath the canopy.

Setting out pigeon decoys on the summer corn stubbles.

Targeting grain-robbing grey squirrels around a pheasant release pen.

Pest control on the farm as the
nocturnal rats venture out at sunset.

Softening lamplight with a red filter makes it
less likely to spook skittish rats.

This little chap might be too young to shoot but he can join in
and enjoy the countryside while learning about hide building.

is set up and performing to its optimum, and all the time spent punching paper on the range to get yourself up to scratch, is so important. And beginners needn't worry about trying to make head shots at 30 metres or more; it's all about knowing your limitations and shooting within them. If you want to shoot rabbits but can't hit a target the size of a walnut consistently at more than 20 metres, then 20 metres will have to be your maximum hunting range until your shooting improves. There are plenty of ways to get yourself very close to your quarry and I'll explain a few of them a little later on.

However much we practise and however mindful we are of shooting within our abilities, there will be instances when the shot doesn't find its mark as cleanly as we would like. Every hunter has a responsibility to make sure every effort is taken to avoid wounding, but it would be a lie to suggest that it will never happen. From time to time, a misplaced shot may result from an unexpected gust of wind, from an unnoticed twig striking the pellet slightly off course or because your quarry moves at the split second you decide to touch off the trigger. Rather than trying to ignore the unpleasant fact that wounding might happen (albeit very rarely) the vital thing is to know what to do to finish off your quarry as quickly as possible when it does happen. First of all, don't panic; it's no good flapping, because you need to get to the animal so you can end its life immediately.

A lot of hunters ask me: 'What is the best way to kill wounded quarry?' Well, you're holding a gun so I would suggest the best way to finish the job is to shoot it. Don't try taking panicked shots from a distance, though. What you need to do is quickly walk up to the animal, reload, make sure there is no chance of a ricochet, place the muzzle of the gun an inch or two from its head and, depending on the angle, make a shot

either into the back of the skull or just behind the eye.

In instances when a close-range shot would be unsafe, the best way to finish off wounded quarry is with your hands. If it's a rabbit, pick it up firmly with the hind legs in your left hand and your right hand around its neck. While holding tightly with your left hand, stretch it across your right knee, head down, by pushing down swiftly and giving a slight twist with your right hand. Breaking the spine or neck in this way will instantly end the animal's suffering. Left-handers will probably need to reverse the hold.

The method for birds is even faster. Pick them up by the head and give a flick so the body swings around the neck, windmill-style. The weight and momentum of the body will instantly break the neck

If you are disturbed by the thought of wounding a living creature, you should be. It is a thoroughly unpleasant experience and the unease it causes shows that you have respect for your quarry.

Similar unease is often caused by making one's first kill. Taking the life of an animal is an alien experience for most people because they have grown accustomed to buying meat from the supermarket. These days, meat is often packaged in a way that removes it far from the realities of what happened on the farm, at the abattoir and on the butcher's table. Unfortunately, the fact that shop bought meat is so remote from the animal from which it came means that many people buy it and it eat without showing any regard for animal welfare. Much of the meat bought from supermarkets comes from animals that lived miserable lives, reared indoors in hideously cramped conditions with no exercise or stimulation, being fed a dull diet of pellets until the day came to be forced into crates or trucks to take them to where they would queue up to die. I am afraid that I regard people who take no interest in the welfare of the animals that are reared to provide them with food as being unacceptably ill-informed. It frustrates me very much that many of the people who regard harvesting your own meat with a gun as being cruel are the same ignorant fools who buy cheap meat from a supermarket or fast-food shop, yet have no concern for the suffering of the animals they eat because they leave it to someone else to do the killing.

To get back to the original point, the emotions stirred by the first kill never go away entirely. However well we know our quarry has lived and although we know it died with the minimum possible suffering, taking an animal's life should always have some subtle effect on the hunter. There is nothing soft or foolish about this emotional response; it shows you are human and, above all, it shows that you have respect for your quarry.

Every hunter has a duty not to take shots that pose a serious risk of wounding. As previously explained, unforeseen circumstances can sometimes result in a shot that lands wide of the intended mark, but there are also times when it's simply too risky to fire. Perhaps you've had no luck all day and that out-of-range rabbit you would usually try to stalk closer to looks more tempting than usual, or perhaps there is a woodpigeon in the tree right above you and the shot looks good apart from a couple of fine twigs that might deflect the pellet off its course. Either way, if the shot looks risky, leave it. There will be other opportunities on other occasions.

Taking chancy shots smacks of cruelty. A person who takes a shot that presents an obvious risk of causing suffering is a lout and not a hunter. There's no place for such mindless individuals in the world of shooting, or anywhere else for that matter.

Rabbits

The rabbit (*Oryctolagus cuniculus*) is the mainstay quarry for many air rifle hunters. It is a notorious agricultural pest, breeds rapidly and provides excellent meat for the table.

Wild rabbits, sometimes called coneys, need to consume around a pound of fresh green food every day, so large colonies can quickly eat into farmers' profits. But their munching isn't confined to grass, and these small mammals are also partial to root, cereal and salad crops. With the British rabbit population estimated at around 45 million, the national bunny herd munches its way through more than 20,000 tonnes of farm crops every day, costing the farming industry an estimated £100 million every year.

Rabbits also do extensive damage to young trees by gnawing their bark and nibbling fresh shoots. This bark-stripping will often kill trees, and those that survive often end up deformed. Consequently, rabbits can be ruinous to stretches of newly-planted hedgerow shrubs.

If the rabbit's eating habits aren't enough to upset farmers, its burrowing certainly is. Rabbit excavations cause serious damage by undermining hedge banks and field margins.

The decline of the British farming industry has coincided with a rise in 'horsey-culture'. More and more farms are being broken down into small paddocks for equestrian use, and rabbits are not welcome. Cherished horses and ponies have been known to break legs when a misplaced hoof goes down a rabbit burrow. The worst-case scenario for an injured horse is euthanasia; at best its owner is going to have to pick up an expensive bill from the vet to get the beast on the road to recovery.

Even the best fencing in the world is eventually breached by rabbits. Most equestrians know how important it is to take swift action when this destructive pest moves in and will probably appreciate the offer of some quiet, safe and effective pest control from an air-gunner.

Rabbits love to raid vegetable patches and they'll devour most crops found in the garden or allotment. Their burrowing and scraping can wreck a well-kept lawn and cause unimaginable destruction to a golf course. Green-keepers won't tolerate the costly damage inflicted by rabbits so it could be worth getting in touch with your local golf club if you're looking for somewhere to harvest rabbit meat.

Rabbits are social animals, who live in underground colonies. They establish their warrens anywhere where the digging is easy; sandy soil is their favourite terrain but they will burrow into embankments and similarly disturbed soil virtually anywhere from sand dunes to mountainsides.

The numerous jokes surrounding the rabbit's breeding capacity are not exaggerated. A doe can produce a litter of up to six kittens every other month from the age of about 16 weeks. Peak breeding time is from late January through to June, but rabbits can breed throughout the year and rapid population explosions are common, especially after mild winters.

It is thought that rabbits were introduced to Britain sometime around the twelfth century when they were highly valued for their fine meat. Since then, they have established themselves as a pest species, but man's efforts to eradicate them have not been successful.

The attempt to eliminate rabbits saw its darkest and most desperate days with the deliberate introduction of myxomatosis in the 1950s, which almost wiped out the entire population.

This hideous disease is spread by blood-sucking insects such as fleas and mosquitoes, and causes rabbits a pitiful, lingering death. Symptoms include a watery discharge from the eyes and swelling and sores around the eyelids and nose. Infected rabbits quickly lose their natural alertness and can take weeks to die.

The deliberate spread of myxomatosis was made illegal half a century ago but the disease still flares up from time to time. Rabbits seem to be building-up a tolerance to the disease and its effects are not so devastating as they once were.

There is no threat of humans contracting myxomatosis by eating properly cooked meat, although the symptoms make infected animals far from appetising. I don't eat rabbits that display any sign of the dreaded myxy.

Rabbits have a grey-brown coat and a silver-white underbelly, but their most distinctive features are their long ears and a fluffy white tail known as a scut. Their colouring varies depending on their habitat, and white and black individuals are sometimes encountered.

In the hunting field, rabbits are only likely to be confused with hares – a game animal that is not recognised as suitable quarry for legal limit air rifles. Hares are much larger than rabbits and have black-tipped ears.

All sorts of different tactics can be used to control rabbits with an air rifle, and a basic ambush on a warm summer's evening is the simplest. If you want more of a challenge, stalking them can be very satisfying – and very frustrating when the rabbits are being particularly twitchy. Rabbits are most active after dark and emerge in great numbers to dine on tender, dew-drenched grass come nightfall. Consequently, lamping tactics can be very effective when the days start getting shorter in the autumn.

Rabbits are well equipped when it comes to natural defences – the result of featuring on the menu of a wide range of predators, including humans. Although their eyesight is nowhere near as sharp as that of a crow or pigeon, they have

An ambush from a discreet hiding place is one of the simplest and most effective ways to hunt rabbits.

Sniping rabbits from a bipod on a summer's evening – a fine way to amass large bags.

incredibly acute hearing, a tremendous sense of smell and an amazing ability to detect vibration through the ground.

The best way to approach rabbits is from downwind, so that your scent and sound is blown away from them. Footfalls have to be feather-light, otherwise alarmed rabbits will soon be stamping on the ground to warn their mates of approaching danger before they disappear into the hedge.

When you do manage to creep within range, a head shot is essential. Some hunters boast of being able to cleanly dispatch rabbits with well-placed (but rarely witnessed) heart and lung shots, but I'm not convinced. Rabbits are relatively big quarry for air rifles and, as far as I'm concerned, a head shot – preferably from the side and just between the eye and ear – is the only option when using an air rifle producing power within the legal limit. The rabbit has a relatively soft skull and a direct impact from either .177 or .22 calibre will deliver a clean kill.

Shooting rabbits

One of the simplest ways to hunt rabbits is to ambush them as they emerge from their burrows to feed at the end of the day. As a youngster, I spent countless unproductive days in the field trying to stalk within range of wily rabbits. Back then, my hunting skills weren't very well honed and I simply couldn't creep close enough to the rabbits on my patch to get a shot. Then one day it occurred to me that it might be just as well to sit and wait rather than put myself through the ordeal of another failed stalk. Sit-and-wait tactics, sometimes referred to as static hunting, soon accounted for my first rabbit, and I've gone on to shoot hundreds more by adopting this very basic approach. The simple fact is that it's very difficult to go unnoticed when you're on the move, but it's surprisingly easy to blend in with the countryside just by keeping still.

Sitting in wait is particularly productive through the summer months when rabbits are at their most abundant. This is the season when rabbits are best to eat too. From June through to September, there are usually plenty of half to three-quarter grown bunnies about. These young animals are only a few months old and their meat is far more tender than those which have over-wintered.

The first thing the hunter needs to do when ambushing rabbits is to establish where his quarry is likely to emerge. The most obvious things to look out for are rabbit burrows in the hedge bank or around the margins of the field. There are several indicators that confirm whether a burrow is part of an active warren; these include fresh droppings (these are round, dark in colour and shaped like raisins) and recently excavated soil. If a rabbit hole is obstructed by dry, dead leaves then it is probably not occupied. Other signs of the presence of rabbits include runs worn through the grass and undergrowth, scrapings in the ground and very short grass resulting from nibbling around the edge of the field. Of course, the best indication of the presence of rabbits is actually seeing one or two out enjoying the evening sun.

When you've located a spot that is frequented by rabbits, the next thing to do is work out where to position yourself. The distance you opt to set up from the emerging rabbits is dictated by your shooting ability. If you can only achieve the required accuracy out to 20 metres, then you'll

Rabbits leave various calling cards that reveal their whereabouts. Droppings and holes are obvious signs of their presence.

just need to sit 20 metres away from the target zone.

In terms of concealment, you don't need a vast amount of cover for ambushing rabbits because their eyesight isn't great. I don't go to the trouble of building a hide for this kind of hunting but I do wear full camouflage, often including a head net and gloves. Once clad in head-to-toe camouflage, it's surprising how little natural cover you actually need to keep yourself hidden. Get right against the hedge where patches of nettles, thistles, brambles and cow parsley will help to keep you out of sight, and try to keep on the downwind side of the rabbits so your scent isn't blown towards them. A beanbag seat will keep you comfortable while you wait for the unsuspecting bunnies to emerge, and will prevent you from getting a wet backside if the ground is damp.

Sometimes, if you can't get the right angle from along the hedgerow, you'll need to target rabbits from a position out in the field. Because of the obvious lack of cover out in the open pasture, it's usually best to lie on your belly. When shooting from a lying position, you hardly need any cover to keep you concealed – a clump of thistles or a thick tussock of grass is often adequate. In this position, your beanbag will make a useful rest for your gun; a rolled-up coat is equally effective or, if you use a recoilless rifle, fit it with a bipod and enjoy some truly rock-steady rabbiting.

Some of my best tallies of rabbits have been made by sniping from out in the field, with the added support of a bipod. The extra stability provided by a bipod improves accuracy considerably and, in experienced hands, converts the humble air rifle into a lethal killing machine, particularly in calm conditions.

Rabbits are quite nocturnal in their behaviour and are also very active at dawn and dusk. When ambushing them, I usually aim to arrive an hour or so before sunset to catch the best of the action. After a long, hot summer's day, hungry bunnies can't wait to leave their burrows to feed on the grass as it's softened by the evening dew.

After deciding which particular area to target (usually some spot along a hedgerow or old railway embankment) I then take about 25 paces out into the field and find a suitable place to lie in wait. This distance allows me to cover a reasonable stretch of hedge, given the extra range provided by the bipod on a still evening. Hopefully there will be a few longer tussocks of grass or a patch of docks to hide amongst and the ground will be dry and fairly flat. I get myself down into the prone position, tuck my trousers into my socks (it's always worth doing this to avoid picking up ticks when static hunting) and then slip on my head net and gloves. There's usually a fair amount of shuffling at this point while I try to get myself as comfortable as possible before I pop out the legs on my bipod and make sure I can cover all the rabbity spots without the threat of nettle stems, long grass stalks and the like getting in the way of my shots. With the preparations made, all that remains is to wait and hope that the bunnies oblige.

As you lie in the pasture at the end of a summer's day, your nose will be filled with the rich, sugary smell of crushed grass. The fading sun starts to sink and the misty evening haze gives all the colours of the countryside a dusty blue-grey haze; there really isn't a more peaceful place to be – though it's probably not quite such an idyllic setting if you suffer from hay fever.

The first arrivals of the evening are a pair of tiny little rabbits, so young their ears are still short and round. This is quite typical; older, wiser rabbits are sensible enough to let the gullible youngsters venture out first while they hang back until they are convinced that the coast is clear. The baby bunnies are within range but they're hardly big enough for the table; as the landowner just wants the rabbits thinned-out rather than completely eradicated, you decide that these ones can wait until there's more meat on them.

Suddenly a movement catches your eye a little further down the bank. There's a perfect pan-sized rabbit sat grazing about ten metres out in the field. You were so absorbed by the antics of the two undersized bunnies that you failed to notice this one slip through the brambles and trundle out onto the grass. It's off slightly to your right so you lift the gun, very slowly and very quietly, and shift yourself a few inches until you're on aim. Looking through the scope, you focus the parallax dial until the image is sharp and then read off the range at just over 30 metres. There's no wind and you've been practising a lot on paper so you're confident of making the shot. You flick off the safety catch with your thumb and the rabbit hears the click. It's sitting up on its hind legs, its ears pricked as it tries to locate the source of the sound. This is no disaster, though; the rabbit stays put and it's now presenting you with a much clearer target than when it had its head down feeding. You place your left hand under the butt of the rifle to make fractional adjustments to your aim until the crosshairs sit absolutely motionless just on top of the rabbit's head – you've given a little hold-over to compensate for the extra distance. Instinctively, you touch-off the trigger and the pellet hits home with a smack that shatters the calm of the still evening and sends the two little ones running into the nettles. The rabbit springs forward into a somersault and lands on its back, unflinching. Check through the scope to confirm that the rabbit is cleanly killed. It is, without a shadow of a doubt, so you hold your position, reload and wait for the next opportunity.

It's surprising how much wildlife you see when waiting motionless in a field as darkness begins to fall. Foraging badgers are a common sight, and it's not unusual to see the occasional fox slinking along the hedgerow as he sets out on his hunting rounds. You might even be fortunate enough to catch a glimpse of a barn owl ghosting across the darkening meadows. Some of my friends insist they can add wild boar and big cats to the list.

Ambushing rabbits can be very effective but hunting doesn't get much more exciting than stalking. Pitting your wits against your prey in an attempt to creep within range is tremendously challenging, and incredibly satisfying when it goes to plan.

In my opinion, stalking is the pinnacle of hunting with air rifles because it is undeniably tricky and will certainly put your skills to the test. Although it can be difficult, and sometimes very frustrating, most people should be able to stalk reasonably proficiently by following a few simple pointers, and by trying to think like their quarry.

The obvious disadvantage of stalking is the fact that you are on the move. Movement is the worst enemy of anyone who is trying to avoid detection so it is vital to exploit every possible opportunity to conceal your approach; this needs to be considered even before you leave the house.

To start with clothing; as well as enabling you to blend in with the countryside it also has to be quiet because rabbits will soon flee if they catch the sound of a jingling zip or a flapping collar. In my opinion, a head net is rarely necessary for stalking – firstly because rabbits aren't too sharp-eyed, and secondly, and more importantly, because the limited field of vision is a hindrance to the hunter on the move.

Choosing the right footwear is very important, and I'm sure a lot of people get this

The deciding moment: taking the shot after stalking to a predetermined firing point.

Gateways and gaps in hedgerows are useful 'windows' through which the stalker can catch quarry unawares.

wrong. Heavy, clumpy, army-style boots are not appropriate; I've tried this footwear but found it almost impossible to creep discreetly around the countryside when I could barely bend my ankles. The hefty soles of these boots also make it difficult to feel your way around the terrain with your feet, and their heavy footfall is bound to send alarm signals to edgy bunnies.

As I mentioned earlier, my favourite footwear for stalking is an old, worn-out, pair of trainers – or something more like a lightweight hiking boot if it's likely to be a bit wet underfoot. If it's really wet, I'll opt for wellies, but I know this will put me at a disadvantage.

When it comes to getting past the rabbit's finely-tuned nose, be mindful not to head out smelling like you're on the pull. Aftershave and deodorant are designed to get you noticed, and that's the last thing you want when you're hunting. Give your favourite fragrance a miss whenever you're in pursuit of rabbits, because one whiff will be enough to send them running, and they'll be able to catch that whiff a mile off with the help of the wind. The same goes for smoking, too – wary rabbits won't hang around if they smell even a hint of cigarette smoke.

The best time to encounter rabbits above ground is either side of their nocturnal feeding spree, so I usually head out stalking at dawn or just before dusk. The countryside is usually very quiet at this time so noise must be kept to a minimum from the outset. Even a little thing like car keys will spoil a stalk if you have them jangling in your pockets – on some shoots I stash mine in a secret place on my way out, on others I leave them in the farmhouse or farm office. Excess baggage will also rustle, clunk and flap, as well as restricting your movements as you try to weave through the undergrowth, so don't take anything you don't really need. Pellets and a sharp knife are the only real essentials.

It is also beneficial to have a planned route in mind before you set out. This way you should have some idea of what terrain you're going to encounter, when to expect to see quarry and what cover you might be able to utilise to get yourself within range for a shot. It is also an advantage to approach your quarry with the wind in your face so the human smells that strike terror into wild things are wafted away from their nostrils. However, don't get too hung-up on wind direction – if you can spend an entire stalking session with the wind in your face, you're a better hunter than me.

When stalking, my movements are slow and steady from the start, and I keep close to hedgerows and any other available cover that might help me to avoid detection. Once I have seen a rabbit or group of rabbits, I stop walking and weigh-up the situation I am presented with. During this brief pause, I want to catch my breath, work out what my quarry is doing and whether it is aware of my presence, before establishing the best possible way of getting close enough to make a kill.

As I've already stated, a stealthy approach is important from the very beginning, but it's even more important when you've spotted quarry or expect to see it at at any moment. Fortunately, the farmland environment usually includes all sorts of features that can be exploited to help the hunter go unnoticed as he closes in on his prey.

You'll need to take advantage of every scrap of natural cover you possibly can. Think about how the long nettles or overhanging branches could be used as a screen, and how contours in the lie of the land can be exploited to keep you out of sight. Shade is an often neglected form of concealment that can easily be utilised to keep you from prying eyes. Simply keeping within the shade cast by a tall hedge will make it much harder for your quarry to spot you, especially if it's out in full sun. Think about your shadow too. Shadows are long at either end of the day and, if the sun is behind you, could send an advance warning of your approach many yards in front of you. Your backdrop is also a very important consideration because, although rabbits aren't blessed with the sharpest eyesight, they'll soon

spook if they spot your silhouette moving against the sky. You may have to crouch very low or even resort to a belly-crawl to prevent yourself from being sky-lined. And while you're going through these contortions, remember to keep your movements quiet and soft on the ground.

It pays to set yourself a predetermined firing point before you embark on the final stages of a stalk, and your quarry will let you know how you're doing in your bid to get there. If rabbits are aware of your presence, you should be able to notice. Signs of alarm include raised ears, a raised head and even the stamping of a foot to warn their fellows. If a rabbit displays any of these signs, stand dead still until it relaxes, then proceed with absolute caution until it gives you another sign to stop.

A stalker on the move needs to place his feet softly and quietly – hence the need for light, flexible footwear. Rather than walking normally and landing your foot heel-first, it pays to walk with your toes pointing downwards so the front tip of the foot makes first contact with the ground. Your toes are more sensitive than your heels, and walking in this tip-toe fashion will enable you to 'read' the terrain for potentially noisy clutter like leaves and twigs. By slowly distributing your weight onto your foot, starting with the toes, you should easily be able to lift back up if you feel something other than soft ground. This isn't so easy once you've loaded the majority of your weight onto your heel.

Another thing that can be used to your advantage when stalking is background noise. Sounds like passing traffic, aircraft and even the wind in the trees are generally accepted by rabbits if they occur frequently enough. If you do need to move across terrain that is likely to make some noise – maybe through a squelchy patch of wet ground – it can pay to wait until there's some background sound to help mask any disturbance generated by your approach.

One sound the hunter really doesn't need is the alarm call of a blackbird. This shrill, piping call is recognised as a sign of distress – an indication that something isn't right in the countryside – and usually sends rabbits, and most other wild animals, dashing for cover. Sometimes there's nothing you can do about it; you'll be stalking along completely engrossed in the behaviour of your quarry, and watching where you're putting your feet, when suddenly a blackbird whizzes out of the hedge uttering a screech that nearly stops your heart. If you're lucky, you'll notice the blackbird going about its business, either in the bushes or on the ground, before it spots you. My advice is to keep still and stay put until it moves on.

There is one very useful dodge that many shooters often overlook, which is a pity because it often yields some great rewards without the usual hassles of stalking. Whenever hunting on the move, be mindful of gateways, blind corners and gaps in hedges – and any other 'windows' that might allow you to happen upon your quarry without being noticed. Rather than strolling up to the gate between fields, try creeping up to it instead; you'll be surprised how often you spot rabbits within range as you peep through after a cautious approach.

Whichever methods you have to utilise to creep within range or rabbits, you should eventually find yourself close enough to take a shot. The chances are that you have worked hard to earn this prize so make sure you don't blow it by fluffing the final preparations.

If the stalk has been a tough one, then the chances are you will be at least a little out of breath. After a strenuous stalk on the hills, I can often hear and feel my pulse pounding through my head and my heart drumming in my chest.

It's virtually impossible to hold a steady aim in this state so the best thing to do is keep still and rest for a moment; if your quarry failed to notice your approach, then it's unlikely to rumble you when you're resting. While I'm recovering, I'll weigh-up the scenario before me and think about the best way to make a telling shot. If the ground is dry and free from obstructions, I'll often lie down for a really stable shot. Sometimes long grass will make a kneeling shot the best option, or nettles and docks might even mean that I have to stalk close enough to take a "stander" to get the right angle.

Occasionally, you'll be presented with more than one rabbit to choose from. The obvious choice is to go for the closest and easiest shot to ensure that the stalk ends in success but it's sometimes possible to muster more than just a single kill. A ruse originally suggested to me by my friend and accomplished air rifle hunter, Ian Barnett, has helped me to round off numerous stalks with more than one bunny to show for my efforts. What Ian recommends is to ignore the closest rabbit or rabbits and go for the furthest one – assuming it is within your competent range, of course. The crack of a pellet smashing a rabbit's skull is significantly louder than the muzzle blast of a moderated air rifle, so the remaining rabbits will frequently turn and stare at the shot rabbit. Because you went for one of the further ones, the puzzled bunnies will be looking in the opposite direction from you as they try to locate the source of the sound. This means there's less chance of you being spotted and, therefore, a good chance of you getting a second shot before the rabbits bolt for cover.

After a successful stalk, most of us will want to plod on in search of one or two more rabbits for the pot. Carrying shot bunnies is a hindrance the stalker can do without and this can either be remedied by placing them in a backpack or, better still, hocking them. If you feel the part of a rabbit's hind leg behind the long foot, you'll notice a bone and a tendon running parallel. Make a slit between the bone and tendon with your hunting knife and the rabbit is ready to hock from a discreet branch or hedge ready for collection on your return. All you do is hold the rabbit upside down with its hind legs either side of whatever you intend to hang it from, then thread the foot of the uncut leg through the slit in the other until it pops through to create a secure fixing. Remember to hock your bunnies somewhere where they'll be out of sight of walkers and out of reach of foxes.

The rabbit's nocturnal lifestyle means that hunting after nightfall can be very effective. Lamping is a great way to harvest rabbits; so effective, in fact, that I tend to limit my season from early autumn to late winter. As most of the rabbit control I do is to limit numbers to a sensible level, absolute eradication is not my intention, so I lamp fairly lightly. However, there are instances (such as when rabbits pose a danger on equestrian holdings) when the landowner will expect a thorough extermination job. In these situations, frequent and indiscriminate lamping, whatever the season, is the most effective option. Lamp rabbits hard during the warmer months when their breeding cycle peaks and you'll really knock them back, often for a very long time. When hunting for the pot, this is counterproductive, but you have to respect the landowner's wishes and remember your role as a pest controller. Another consideration that makes me reluctant to venture out rabbiting after dark during the spring and summer is the fact that nightfall comes so late, and I can think of better things to be doing in the small hours – sleeping, for one.

Lamping is productive but it isn't easy. There are nights when it can be an absolute waste of

Hocking rabbits by making a cut through one hind leg and popping the other one through to create a 'handle' is a useful way to lighten the load when hunting on the move.

Hunting after dark is much easier with the help of a companion.

even if there are, they'll hear you crunching across the frozen grass long before you get close enough for a shot. If the sky is clear enough for you to cast a shadow on the ground (and this happens more often than you'd think) my advice is not to waste your time heading out.

When the conditions are right, I wait until a couple hours after nightfall to ensure that the rabbits have had adequate time to venture right out into the fields. If you're planning a lamping session, it's wise to call the landowner, and even the local police, to let them know of your intentions – people can get rather suspicious when they see beams of light shining around the countryside in the middle of the night.

It is possible to lamp rabbits on your own with a scope-mounted light but I prefer to have some company when hunting at night. Apart from making the procedure a whole lot easier, it's wise to have someone with you just in case something goes wrong – accidents happen, and you don't want to be stuck in the middle of nowhere, on your own, with a broken leg on a cold winter's night. I would also recommend that you take a mobile phone and a hand-held torch as a backup light; a headlamp is even better, and will come in very handy when it's time to gut the rabbits. If you do venture out on your own, let someone know where you are going and when you intend to return. I never go lamping over unfamiliar ground; it's just too risky. On a new shoot, a few hours' daytime reconnaissance will enable you to plan a safe route around your hunting ground, and to earmark any potential hazards that might be encountered.

If you have a lamping companion, you'll be able to opt for a bigger, more powerful, hand-held lamp with a separate, rechargeable battery that either sits in your jacket pocket or straps around your waist; you may even be able to share the cost. Although you need to be able to cast a

time, and I've never witnessed the often talked-about rabbits that sit obligingly, dazzled by the lamplight, as the hunter nonchalantly stomps within range for the shot. In my experience, rabbits aren't much less wary at night than they are during the day – there's just usually more of them about – so all the rules for getting past their defences still apply.

The best nights for lamping rabbits during autumn and winter are the really dark ones with plenty of cloud cover. A bit of a breeze will create some useful background noise to hide the sound of your approach and, hopefully, blow your scent away from your quarry. And light drizzle is no bad thing; it softens the grass, making it even more irresistible to rabbits. Rainfall also releases all sorts of natural, earthy smells that will help to mask your human odour. The worst nights for lamping are cold, clear, frosty ones. Rabbits don't like extreme cold so there won't be many out in the first place and, reasonably long beam, power isn't as important as some people would have you believe. What is important is to ensure that your chosen lamp doesn't spill too much light. You don't want a lamp that floods light all over you, just a tight pool of light where you point it. Coloured filters that clip to the lens are inexpensive and can be useful. It is thought that some colours of light are less visible to animals than others. I am not convinced, but I do use filters to dull down the beam if rabbits become 'lamp shy' after frequent lamping.

Successful lamping needs a quiet approach, so be mindful not to make too much noise slamming car doors on your arrival and, assuming you have a companion, keep talk to a minimum. If you shoot with the same person, you should quickly establish a set routine without the need for too much chatter and deliberation. One of you will have the role of shooter and the other will be lamp man. As well as shining the light, the lamp man also has the duty of carrying the rucksack loaded with shot rabbits, as the burden is likely to compromise the shooter's ability to take accurate shots. You can always swap roles halfway through the night if you're both capable of shooting accurately with the same set-up.

A multi-shot air rifle is a great asset for lamping because reloading in the dark can be a fiddly affair. You shouldn't carry loaded magazines in your car, or even in your pockets or gun bag in a public place, so wait until you arrive to fill up with ammo. Avoid creating unnecessary disturbance by using the light of the car or your lamp to fill your mag, and a spare if you have one, before you head into the fields.

When everything is ready, give your eyes a few minutes to become accustomed to the darkness and make your way quietly to the fields; – the shooter should always walk in front with

his gun pointing to the ground and the safety catch set. If you can, it pays to make your way around without using the lamp, so as not to alert the rabbits.

As you enter the first field, the lamp man switches on with the light pointing downwards and then casts the beam gradually away from you, making slow, steady sweeps from left to right. There's no sign of anything as far as the beam can reach, so you switch off and move on.

You stop further along the hedge and the light goes on again. As the beam reaches out into the cold darkness, plumes of your warm breath swirl like smoke in the red filtered light. You stare into the spot of illumination, willing a rabbit to appear among the drifting shadows of the grass tussocks. Your heart races as you think you've spotted the shine of an eye but it's just an amber droplet of water reflecting the light back at you. The lamp sweeps further into the field and you're greeted by the sight you'd been hoping for. At first, you can just distinguish a pair of rabbit's eyes glowing in the gloom but, as your mate steadies the light, you can make out the rest of its form, and three others close to it. The group of rabbits is about 100 metres away, close to a large patch of gorse on a steep hillside. They're much too far away for a shot, so the light goes off and the pair of you creep closer, as quietly as you can, until you're 50 or 60 metres away from where you spotted the rabbits.

The lamp goes back on, pointing at the ground again, and is swept slowly outwards until it catches the bunnies. They're still there. The sound of the wind in the trees was enough to mask your footfalls but one of the rabbits is sitting bolt upright, probably alarmed by the strange beam of light cutting through the darkness. This time the light stays on, and you both hold your position until the rabbit relaxes and resumes feeding. The lamp man stays put, keeping the beam fixed on the rabbits, while you carefully creep closer, remembering to keep wide of the light. As you stalk along the outside of the beam, the rabbits can't see you but you move as stealthily as ever so as not to spook them with a clumsy footfall.

After a short but strenuous hike, you're about 25 metres away. You stop, catch your breath and mount the gun but you decide not to take the shot. Up on the hillside, the wind is buffeting your body to the point where it's impossible to hold a steady aim, so you try to move in closer. An intricate scramble along the slippery slope and you've closed in another five metres but the nearest rabbit has sat up again, clearly agitated, so you daren't proceed any further. You drop quietly to your knees and settle yourself into a steady shooting position as you raise the gun into your shoulder. The improved stance and shorter range make for a better looking sight picture, so you push off the safety and the crosshairs gradually come to rest on the head of the closest rabbit, which is now sitting bolt upright. The trigger is subconsciously slipped as the shot looks right and a loud crack signals success. The other rabbits dash for cover and you're plunged into darkness as the lamp man tries to follow them with the beam, but they're not stopping. The fleeing bunnies disappear into the scrub and your companion swings back the lamp, illuminating your way as you collect the first addition to the night's bag.

When shooting at night, it's usually better to carry shot rabbits in a backpack rather than hocking them for collection later on – mainly because it can be difficult remembering where you've left them after two or three tiring hours yomping around the hills in the dark. When the load starts to get a bit heavy for the lamp man, you can always lose some ballast by stopping to gut the haul. As well as being a good way to lighten the load, paunching in the field is favourable to carrying out the messy job when you get back home, so it's wise to carry a sharp knife for the task. I also try to remember to keep a bottle of water in the boot of my car so I can give my hands a quick rinse before I drive home – my wife doesn't like the steering wheel and gearstick getting too rabbitty. And don't worry about leaving heaps of rabbits' intestines out in the fields – the resident foxes and badgers will have devoured the lot long before daybreak.

Paunching is a job best done in the field. Foxes and badgers will devour all evidence by daybreak.

Woodpigeons

Woodpigeon (*Columba palumbus*) is usually the first quarry species to spring to mind whenever I think about shooting for the pot. The woodpigeon, or woodie, is an agricultural pest and is abundant in most parts of the UK. It is a large, plump bird with rich, dark breast meat that provides a great reward for time spent on crop protection duties.

The woodpigeon is a heavily built bird with grey/blue plumage. Colouring is darker on the back, fading to pale grey on the underside. The chest is a rich pink colour and the blunt tail has a bold black tip. The woodie has conspicuous white wing bars, white patches on each side of its mauve neck and a long yellow beak which darkens to an orange/red at the base.

The hunter must be able to distinguish the woodpigeon from the stock dove (*Columba oenas*), and rock dove (*Columba livia*). These birds are both much smaller than the woodpigeon and do not have its distinctive white wing bars. The stock dove has black-tipped wings and has a distinctly shorter tail than the woodie.

The woodpigeon has established itself as an enemy of the farmer as it is particularly partial to ripening corn. Peas, rape, kale, sprouts and numerous other crops are also prone to decimation by pigeons. The UK woodpigeon population is estimated at around three million breeding pairs, and that amounts to a heck of a lot of crop damage – especially when that number is bolstered by an army of young birds towards the end of the summer.

Pigeons are flocking birds and gather in their hundreds when a rich feeding opportunity arises. Woodies have an uncanny ability to spot their companions from miles away, as the flapping of those white wing bars signal flock mates swooping in and out of the feeding zone. Hordes of ravenous pigeons soon home in, leaving farmers with ruined crops. The hunter can exploit this flocking instinct by using decoys to attract pigeons; good bags can be made over a pattern of imitation birds.

Woodpigeons have also established themselves as a serious garden pest. They're just as happy grubbing up seeds as dining on ripening vegetables, and Brussels sprouts are a real favourite – especially if they're sticking up through a covering of snow that's keeping the birds from foraging on the ground. Of course, the limited power of the air rifle makes it ideal for garden pest control applications, and there's nothing more satisfying than smacking down a bird that's stealing the fruits of your toils on the vegetable patch. Knowing that a pigeon was helping itself to your vegetables makes it taste all the sweeter when it's on the table too.

True to their name, woodpigeons are often encountered in woodland where they feed on acorns, beech mast, ivy berries and other fruit. During the winter months, they often gather to roost in large flocks in the more sheltered parts of the woods. As the weather improves from the arrival of spring and onwards, pigeons spend much of the day flitting around in the canopy. Targeting them when the trees are in full leaf can be frustrating because they're hard to spot. Often, all you can hear is the pigeon's distinctive coo-coo-cooing followed by the clatter of wings as a spooked bird erupts from the trees (often much closer than expected) before you even manage to spot it.

Woodpigeons often nest through all but the coldest months but peak breeding tends to occur around late summer when food is most abundant. They build their flat nest of twigs in dense trees, often favouring hedgerow species such as hawthorn, blackthorn and holly. Pigeons usually lay two white eggs and are the only bird to produce milk similar to that of mammals.

This rich protein appears as a rich, cheesy substance in the bird's crop.

Woodpigeons are equipped with finely tuned senses that make them a worthy and challenging adversary for the hunter. They have sharp eyesight and an uncanny ability to spot the movement of a gun being raised to the shoulder – however slowly and discreetly you try to do it. Woodies also have very good hearing, and the sound of twigs cracking underfoot is usually enough to send them flapping off over the horizon.

Some shooters advocate chest shots for woodpigeons but I don't. Their thick plumage, dense breast muscle, solid breastbone and food-stuffed crop make them virtually bullet-proof unless you're using an FAC-rated air rifle. With a legal-limit gun, stick to head shots, or take low pigeons from the back, between their shoulders, where there is less tissue in the way of the vital organs.

Shooting woodpigeons

Some of the finest pigeon shooting coincides with the approach of harvest time. Large flocks of woodies descend on ripening corn crops during this season and the air rifle hunter can gather large amounts of fine meat for the table while out on his crop protection rounds.

There are usually two windows of opportunity for making really good bags of pigeons. The first arises when strong winds and heavy rainfall flatten large areas of corn crops, creating landing areas for hungry woodies to exploit. The birds soon identify these flat spots and swarm to them to feed on tender grains of ripening corn. The other time to catch pigeons feeding in great numbers is just after the crops have been harvested. Woodies will flock to the dusty fields to forage spilt grain and flattened corn stems among the stubbles soon after the combines have moved out. That said, decoying opportunities arise throughout the year, depending on local farming activities. Whatever it is that's attracting them, be it clover, peas, beans, corn or something else, the principles for decoying pigeons are much the same.

You need to act fast when you notice pigeons gathering on their feeding grounds on your shooting patch. Similar crops ripen at much the same time so the birds could well be presented with numerous opportunities to gorge

Woodpigeons quickly descend on the leftovers when the combines roll off the cornfields.

Although decoy birds should face roughly into the wind, some variation will make them look more lifelike.

themselves at countless locations across the locality. The wise hunter will set up an ambush to make the most of the situation before the birds move on to pastures new.

The best way to capitalise on the opportunity presented by this type of feeding situation is to use decoys to exploit the pigeon's flocking instinct. Contrary to popular belief, decoys don't work by magic and birds won't come flying in just because you've scattered a few plastic imitations around a field. Decoys will convince pigeons that it's safe to return to an established feeding ground but you need to put some thought into how you use them if they're going to work properly.

Time is of the essence, but don't be too hasty; a few minutes' reconnaissance at the outset can save hours of wasted time in the long run. When I embark on a pigeon-decoying session, I begin by sitting back and watching so that I can establish where the all-important flight lines are.

Flight lines are the paths that woodpigeons use to fly in and out of their feeding grounds, and their roosting sites, too. They are like invisible highways in the sky with clearly distinguished entrance and exit routes in and out of the area the birds are occupying. Pigeons use features of the landscape – such as hills, valleys and prominent trees – to help them navigate, and it is surprising how rigidly they stick to their established flight lines. Once you've worked out where the paths are by watching the birds from a distance, you'll be able to ensure that you set up your decoy pattern right under an incoming route – and the birds are far more likely to be deceived by the decoys if they're located in the right place.

With a target area in mind, gather your hide-building equipment, your gun and your decoys and find a discreet place to set up within comfortable shooting distance of where you intend to place your decoy flock. Construct a hide and remember to dress it with weeds from the surrounding area to help it go unnoticed.

Once the hide is in place, all that's left to do is put out the decoys, and the way this is done can make or break your efforts. I begin by pacing out 15 metres from my hide and then position what will be the closest decoy to my shooting position there. Next I place the furthest decoy 30 metres from my hide. These two imitation birds are my range markers, and I know that any pigeon that lands within the decoy pattern is somewhere between 15 and 30 metres from me – this estimation can be refined depending on which decoy they are closest to.

The next job is to add more decoys to the group to create a wide U-shaped pattern. This horseshoe shape gives incoming birds plenty of room to land among the decoys. The bottom of the U should be facing into the wind, as should each of the decoys. Birds generally face the wind to land and take off; they also remain facing this direction for most of the time because they don't like the breeze ruffling their feathers. Although your decoys need to be facing roughly into the wind to look natural, they don't need to be lined up like soldiers. Some can be tilted off at a slight angle, and the distance between individual birds can be varied to give the plastic flock a more natural appearance. You can also make your decoy pattern look more convincing by buying various designs of decoy rather than a whole flock of the same type. How many decoys you have in your flock depends on how many you can afford and how many you can carry. A general rule of thumb is the more the merrier, and I usually use a dozen or so decoys for pigeon shooting.

I use a mixture of plastic pigeon decoys, including full-bodied patterns and the open-bottomed 'shell' variety that pack neatly into each other for easy transportation. Over the years, I have acquired various brands, all with slight variations which I am sure help to give the overall flock a more natural appearance. I tend not to use the elaborate 'flapper' systems, powered either by the wind or a battery. While the movement generated by these arrangements can grab pigeons' attention sufficiently to secure a crossing shot for the shot-gunner, a convincing pattern of static decoys is the best way to encourage pigeons to land and settle while the airgun shooter takes aim.

One or two crow decoys can improve your chances of success. Pigeons know that crows are the most cautious of birds and their presence will help to convince in-comers that all is well.

However, it is not normal for crows to feed right among pigeons, so place your crow decoys a little way from your flock of woodies, further out in the field. As well as encouraging pigeons to settle, this addition to the decoy line-up might also attract the occasional passing crow within range.

When the decoys are set out, it's time to crawl into your hide and make yourself comfortable. A shooter can quickly become parched during long, hot summer days in the field, so remember to take a bottle of water to wet your whistle from time to time.

Waiting in the hide as the pigeons circle overhead can be very exciting. The action usually begins with birds pitching in to parts of the field that are well beyond shooting range, but don't worry too much because they'll help to persuade others that the area is worth visiting.

Watch through the netting, but don't move about too much because pigeons are easily spooked. There's a light sound of flapping and you look up to see a flock of four pigeons gliding into the decoy pattern with their wings outstretched. The birds plop into the middle of the artificial flock and start scratching around the stubbles in search of nutritious kernels.

Having woodpigeons among the decoys at close range is thrilling stuff and you'll need to move very gingerly to avoid startling them. Raise your gun into your shoulder, slowly and steadily, and push the muzzle through the hide net until it is well clear of any vegetation. As you peer through the scope, try to pick out the closest bird. Its distance from the furthest range marker tells you it's about 25 metres away, so you don't have to make any adjustments to your aim. Pigeons are bulky birds and you know that a head shot is required – the trouble is that pigeons have a frustrating habit of bobbing their heads as they peck at the grain. Watch the bird through the scope and get a feel for the way it moves; you'll notice that there's a distinct rhythm as its head dips to and from the crosshairs at a steady beat. Choose your moment and touch off the trigger as the unsuspecting bird's head lingers in front of your aiming point. There's a crack and a fine puff of feathers as your pellet finds its mark. The disturbance sends the other pigeons flapping away with a loud clatter of wings but the shot bird remains motionless on its belly. Pigeons that fall in this way will add to the appeal of the decoys but nothing frightens incoming pigeons more than a bird that flops over belly-up. If that happens you'll need to break cover and remedy the situation.

The finest pigeon decoy of all is a shot pigeon, and there's a way to make them look even more lifelike. I always keep six-inch lengths of stiff gardening wire (the plastic-coated stuff that comes on reels to support roses and the like) to prop up dead pigeons when I add them to the decoy pattern. I use a pair of pliers to strip the top inch of plastic coating from the wire and push this end into the dead bird's chin, just behind the base of the beak. By pushing the other end of the wire into the ground, it can be used to support the bird's head in a very convincing manner. Just remember not to have the head raised too high, otherwise the bird will look as if it is alarmed. Another thing I do when I leave the hide to retrieve shot birds is tidy any feathers from among the decoys. This debris from shot birds can be enough to cause concern among new arrivals.

On some occasions, the pigeons will stream to virtually every corner of the farm apart from within range of your hide. This situation is enough to drive even the calmest of people to absolute distraction – especially after going to the lengths of building a hide and setting out decoys. One way to rectify this irritating behaviour is to use flags to divert the birds away from the areas that they are visiting in preference to your target area. Simple flags can be created by tying white carrier bags to sticks and jamming them in the ground. The sight of a plastic bag flapping in the breeze is usually enough to drive pigeons elsewhere – hopefully right in front of you.

A word of warning to the aspiring pigeon decoyer: be prepared for failure. Setting up an ambush with decoys entails a reasonable amount of work and, although the rewards can be great (bags of more than a dozen birds are not uncommon), there will be times when the pigeons don't oblige. When the best laid plans collapse and the pigeons fly elsewhere in spite of your unstinting efforts, try not to be too disheartened. There will be days when the birds simply refuse to come to the decoys, and usually for no obvious reason. I try to take some comfort in the knowledge that it is the unpredictability of the sport, and the occasional disappointments that this brings, that make the good days all the more satisfying.

A dead pigeon makes for a most convincing decoy. Their heads can be propped up with a piece of stiff wire pushed through the chin.

Ivy berries lure pigeons to the woods when other food is scarce during the winter months.

Their normal woodland habitat provides pigeons with roosting sites and, at certain times of the year, a food source.

Around autumn time, as fruits ripen and the leaves take on their copper tones, pigeons flock to the woods to forage for food. Acorns rate highly on their menu, as does beech mast, and sweet chestnuts are also favoured.

Rather than setting up an elaborate ambush, it can be very rewarding to set out on foot with minimal equipment just to lurk in the woods to see what's about. The abundance of natural food during early autumn usually sends woodland creatures into a frenzy of activity, so expect to encounter more than just pigeons. Jays and squirrels are also likely to be on the forage,

building up their fat reserves and stashing food in readiness for the harsh winter months that lie ahead, so a mixed bag is very much on the cards.

This sort of shooting can be very productive just after first light. At this time of year, the days are starting to shorten and wild creatures wake up with quite a hunger after sleeping through the long dark hours. The woods are a magical place to be on a damp misty morning, as dewdrops drip from the branches onto the carpet of bronze and red leaves below. The best way to hunt in this situation is to make slow, quiet progress, stopping frequently to scan ahead – and remember to look down as well as up because your quarry will be spending much of its time on the ground where acorns and mast are falling. When you spot your intended target, it's useful if you can get a thick tree between you so you can use it as a screen. Ideally, you'll be able to creep to the tree unnoticed and then slip your gun quietly around the trunk to make the shot. As well as providing great sport, this kind of shooting on the move is also a great way to familiarise yourself with your hunting ground and earmark productive looking areas that might warrant further attention on a later visit.

After the autumn glut, nature's larder steadily dwindles until food becomes quite scarce at the end of the winter. At this time of year, ivy berries provide pigeons with precious nutrition when there's not much else about. I've spent some very productive afternoons lurking in the parts of the woods where dense patches of ivy are heavy with bunches of dark, hard berries. Although poisonous to humans, these berries provide woodies with precious pickings when times are tough, and often attract a steady trickle of hungry birds throughout the day during the early part of the year.

Another great way to target pigeons in the woods is to ambush them as they return to roost.

This type of hunting is well suited to the quiet, stealthy approach of the air rifle hunter and it's possible to make good bags when you time it right.

Roost shooting is at its best during the colder months, when the leaves have fallen from the trees, from mid autumn through to early spring. This is for two main reasons. Firstly, woodland shooting is a whole lot easier after the winds have stripped the trees of their leaves due to the simple fact that it's easier to spot the birds and take clear shots when there's no foliage in the way. Secondly, pigeons seem to gather to roost in greater numbers as the weather deteriorates. Some of my best outings have coincided with harsh weather just after the turn of the year.

First of all, you need to identify an active roosting area, and this isn't particularly difficult. The best approach is to sit and watch from a distance, so you can see which areas of the woods the birds fly to as the setting sun turns the sky to gold. You can also locate pigeon roosts when you're hunting in the woods by day; find an abundance of the woodie's calling cards (splats of whitish-grey droppings on the ground) and you've probably found a roost. Pigeons like to roost in sheltered areas, so the lee side of the wood, which is most protected from prevailing winds, is a good place to investigate. Just like you and me, birds don't relish the thought of spending a cold winter's night being battered by the wind and the rain, so they favour the trees that offer the most protection from the elements. Evergreens such as laurels, pines and firs provide much-needed shelter at a time of year when foliage is sparse, as do thick patches of ivy, the waxy leaves of which will keep birds sheltered from all but the heaviest of rain. Roosting pigeons usually fly to the exposed branches of taller trees before they drop down to roost in thicker cover. Try to shoot them when they are in these open areas because it can be impossible to spot woodies, let alone make a shot, once they've snuggled into dense, tangled

Waiting for the pigeons to arrive in the woods as the winter sun sinks behind the hills.

A modest bag of woodies taken during an evening's roost shooting in foul weather.

cover.

When I'm after roosting pigeons, I try to get into position a couple of hours before nightfall. This means that I should be quietly waiting just before the birds start to arrive. Turn up later and you run the risk of disturbing birds that are already settling down to roost and, quite understandably, they can be reluctant to return after the commotion of an approaching hunter crashing through the leaves and twigs.

I choose a place where I can target likely roosting trees from some shady spot. I don't build a proper hide because I might need to shift position to somewhere that gives me a better vantage point if the birds aren't heading to the trees where I expected them to go. The sort of cover I look for is a bush or tree that will help to conceal my human form without hampering my ability to shoot. Put on a head net and gloves to hide light patches of skin, and a tree trunk can be as much of a screen as you need to keep you hidden. If you use a recoilless pre-charged air rifle, a tree trunk also provides a useful support to lean on as you prepare to topple a woodie with a tricky head shot.

When I decide on a spot, I use the side of my foot to shunt any leaves from around where I'm standing. Pushing dry leaves and brittle twigs out of the way will expose the soft, damp leaf mulch of the woodland floor, and this allows the hunter to move silently if he needs to shift his feet or slip around the tree to take a shot.

It's a wonderful feeling, waiting in the woods on a winter's evening when there's a nip in the air. There's something about this scenario – the remoteness of the location, the smell of the woods, the weak golden glow of the setting sun and the chill of the approaching night – that really satisfies the hunter-gatherer instinct and alerts the senses.

On a still evening, the arrival of incoming birds is signalled by the gentle beating of wings. Groups of pigeons usually circle the roost once or twice before opening their wings and dropping into the branches. Sometimes birds arrive in ones and twos, and at other times they arrive in their dozens. However many birds settle above you, you can rest assured they their eyes will be scouring the ground below for any signs of danger, so move with extreme caution.

Keep behind whatever you're using for cover and raise your gun, oh so slowly, to your shoulder. Pick the bird that presents you with the clearest shot and check the view through your scope. Pigeons have a frustrating habit of landing just behind a haze of fine twigs and, as even the finest twig can deflect an airgun pellet way off course, it's important to check that there are no obstructions between the muzzle and the target. If the only bird within range is obscured by twigs, leave it, because the shot is likely to result in a miss or, worse still, wounding. The chances are that the woodie will eventually shuffle or flutter to another branch and present you with a better opportunity. Even if it doesn't, another bird will probably pitch somewhere better before the light goes. Either way, it is far preferable to forfeit a doubtful shot than to risk causing suffering by shooting recklessly.

When the chance does arise, you'll want to hit the pigeon in the head. Take a little time to compose yourself before firing because it's a tricky shot to make. Think about your breathing and remember to make necessary adjustments to your aim to compensate for the pellet's trajectory. Get it right and you'll send that plump pigeon crashing into the leaf litter – they're heavy birds and come down with quite a thud.

If you drop a woodpigeon and it's cleanly killed, it's wise to stay put for a moment before dashing out to retrieve it. Make a mental note of where it landed, but keep still, because although the rest of the flock most likely departed with a clatter of wings when you nailed your bird, there is a good chance that they'll quickly return. Air rifles are so quiet when fitted with a silencer that startled pigeons don't always fly very far away. In fact, they sometimes take to the wing, circle a few times and then fly straight back. Give them a couple of minutes and, if they don't come back, get on with retrieving your shot bird because you don't want to end up rummaging around the woodland undergrowth trying to find a pigeon in the darkness after you've forgotten where it fell. Once you locate your prize, pick it up and quickly return to your position because more pigeons will soon be coming in to roost. Shoot well and you might bag four or five woodies before nightfall.

Weather conditions can influence roost shooting greatly. My favourite evenings are the still, crisp ones early in the year – the sort of evening when there's a hint of frost in the air. These are the most pleasant evenings to ambush pigeons as they fly back to the spinney, but they aren't always the best. Still conditions mean there will be no ambient sound caused by the wind in the trees, so you have to be extra quiet to go unnoticed. The shooting is a little easier when there's a slight breeze. This is not just because it helps to mask any sounds you make as you shuffle about but also because the swaying it causes in the branches helps to make the movement of raising your gun to your shoulder less conspicuous to suspicious pigeons. Also, pigeons tend to fly straight to the lower, and therefore closer, branches when there's a chilly breeze about. That said, you don't want it too windy; blustery weather might force the birds to

land a little lower but it can be very difficult to make accurate shots when your target is clinging to a branch that's being buffeted by a strong wind. In these situations, maximum shooting distances have to be adjusted to suit the conditions.

Rain can also affect roost shooting, and usually adversely. When the weather turns wet, the birds often opt to spend the night huddled in trees close to their feeding grounds rather than flying through the rain to reach their favourite roost. Fog has a similar influence on the behaviour of pigeons. The consequent lack of visibility makes it difficult for them to navigate, so they can be reluctant to fly very far until it clears.

Pigeon shooting gets tricky when deciduous trees turn green with a flush of new leaves in the spring. The biggest problem with woodland shooting during the warmer months is spotting birds through the foliage before they spot you and fly away. There are opportunities for the hunter, though, when courtship pulls pigeons down below the canopy.

When overcome by the urge to mate during peak breeding season, from late spring through to the end of the summer, pigeons spend quite a lot of time swooping from branch to branch lower down in the trees. You can't always see them to start with, but their cooing usually betrays their approximate whereabouts. Simply sitting still and waiting for the pigeons to show themselves is one way to target them during this time. If you're less patient, a pigeon caller can sometimes be put to good effect. It can take a little practice to get it right, but distant woodpigeons can often be persuaded to venture closer by using a caller to mimic their cooing.

Collared doves and feral pigeons

The collared dove (*Streptopelia decaocto*) is a smaller cousin of the woodpigeon and can also be taken with the air rifle. They taste just as good as woodies but are about half the size, so double up on quantities if you're using them in a pigeon recipe.

Originally native to Asia, collared doves have spread over much of Western Europe, including most parts of the UK, over the last few decades. These birds feed mostly on grain (which is why they taste so good) and are often found raiding corn crops and stubbles alongside woodpigeons. They also flock around farmyards, sometimes in their hundreds, where they steal from grain stores and cause problems by fouling feed and water supplies with their accumulated droppings.

Collared doves are a buff/grey colour with pinkish-white chests, a black beak and a distinctive thin black collar on the neck. Their coo-coo, coo-coo call is sometimes mistaken for that of a cuckoo by people who are less adept at identifying bird calls.

Shooters need to be able to distinguish collared doves from the rare turtle dove (Streptopelia turtur). A summer visitor from Africa, the turtle dove is darker in colour with mottled, tortoiseshell plumage on the wings and has a purring call.

The best way to target collared doves is to wait in a farm building and pick them off as they swoop in to raid the grain silos. They aren't half as wary as woodpigeons and certainly don't treat people with anything like as much suspicion. Collared doves lose much of their natural caution and become quite trusting when they become accustomed to the comings and goings of workers on the farm.

You'll usually be able to get close enough to collared doves to make clean head shots without too much difficulty. However, their slight build means that heart-and-lung shots are equally effective but, rather than being tempted to go for the big target offered by a straight aim at the chest, take them slightly from the side and aim to place your pellet just below the elbow of the wing.

The other member of the pigeon family that air rifle hunters may encounter is the feral pigeon *(Columba livia)*. Ferals are sometimes referred to as flying rats because they often carry disease. Apart from that, they can also pose a serious health risk by littering buildings with their droppings – it's not uncommon to find barns and warehouses with piles of feral pigeon faeces that are several inches thick. As well as fouling feed and water put out for livestock, this filth poses a threat to humans when ferals flock to buildings used to store food crops.

Feral pigeons are descendants of the true rock dove, which has the same Latin name and was domesticated and bred for food in the Middle Ages. Nowadays, feral pigeons are birds of town parks, derelict buildings and farm units, and come in all colours. As these birds can carry disease they should not be eaten.

The shooter should be most careful not to confuse racing pigeons with feral pigeons. Disorientated racers occasionally drop in to the farmyard to recuperate and get their bearings, so you may encounter them from time to time. Pigeon fanciers can get rather attached to their birds and shooting one can be compared with shooting somebody's pet. By and large, racing pigeons usually look brighter, leaner and more alert than ferals. They'll also have a ring on their leg so make sure you check before pulling the trigger.

Feral pigeons can become very tame and are usually shot at close-quarters in disused industrial buildings and barns. This type of cull is far from

The farm is a workplace and shooters must always be aware of the hazards that might be encountered.

sporting – it's a job, simple as that. The usual approach with feral extermination is to get in and bag as many as possible before the rest of the flock wises up and makes an exit. As this sort of shooting is done at very close range, heart-and-lung shots are effective, especially if you've got the clout of a .22 or even .25 calibre gun. Fast target acquisition is the name of the game and open sights or laser sights tend to be favoured over teles. Nonetheless, time should be taken to ensure that shots result in clean kills, and a quick dispatch made when they do not. Feral pigeons may be regarded as little more than vermin but,

just like any other animal, they are entitled to a swift, humane death with minimal suffering.

It is important to clear away the corpses at the end of a feral pigeon cull; mainly because leaving slain quarry lying around is utterly loutish and also because they will create a serious hygiene risk if left to decompose. Check with the landowner how best to dispose of the bodies – incineration is the most effective option – and remember to pack a pair of gloves because you should not pick up feral pigeons with your bare hands, especially if they've fallen onto a floor carpeted with festering droppings.

Shooting collared doves and feral pigeons

As collared doves and feral pigeons tend to flock to farmyards, it's likely that you'll be shooting them in close proximity to, or even inside, buildings. It is in situations like this that the limited power of the air rifle really scores.

There are times when the relatively low power of airguns might seem like a disadvantage but, in the confined shooting environments often encountered around the farm, it is actually a huge advantage. Shooting around the confines of agricultural buildings presents the shooter with a long list of potential hazards that must be considered and overcome before you even think about pulling the trigger. A gun with too much grunt just wouldn't be safe to use in such a situation, but with a little forethought and the safe use of backstops, the air rifle is perfect for close-quarters farmyard vermin control.

Nonetheless, a reckless shot still has the potential to cause expensive damage or serious injury, so absolute care must be taken to stay safe. The shooter must always be aware that the farm is, first and foremost, a place of work, so expect there to be people around and ensure that all necessary precautions are taken.

Whenever I arrive for a farmyard shooting session, I begin with a visit to the farmhouse or a chat with whoever I find working on the farm. As well as allowing me to glean useful information regarding the vermin and its whereabouts, this conversation also enables me to find out who's working and where they are. If there are farm workers anywhere near where I plan to be shooting, I'll then talk with them to establish exactly what they're up to and whether I'll be able to safely incorporate my plans around that. It's common sense really, but farming operations must always come before shooting activities.

Because people depend on the farm for an income, and often live on site, it should go without saying that all livestock, buildings and machinery must be treated with the utmost respect. Whenever shooting in the vicinity of farm animals or machinery, the safest option is to keep fairly close to them and shoot in the opposite direction. Keeping near to hazards means they're unlikely to escape your attention in the heat of the moment and makes it a lot easier to ensure that shots are made away from them.

With regard to backstops, it's a very fortunate coincidence that most farm buildings feature a lot of concrete and iron in their fabric. A square impact into these materials will obliterate a lead pellet, stripping its energy and sending it tumbling harmlessly to the ground with no risk of ricochet. Be wary of wooden surfaces – even something as solid as a railway sleeper – because their fibrous nature means they have a habit of bouncing pellets back at an alarming speed. Care must also be taken when shooting towards the roof (which is fairly likely given the fact that you are targeting avian quarry). Limit yourself to shots at targets that are either perched in front of steel joists or sitting with nothing but clear sky behind them. You might be doing a useful pest control job but farmers won't consider it great value if you leave a trail of leaking roofs. In fact, they'll probably tell you to go away and never come back (only not as politely) and then go and tell the rest of the local farming community not to let you on their property because you're a liability.

Although shooting feral pigeons is usually a fairly straightforward and unchallenging pest control procedure, collared doves often prove a little more wary, so the hunter has to work harder to outwit them. The attractions that lure them to the farm often draw crows, magpies, jackdaws and woodpigeons too, so a mixed bag is on the cards if you get it right. Areas to investigate include grain and feed stores, while silage clamps are also recognised as a food source and you'll often encounter doves and other avian quarry scavenging spilt feed close to livestock. Sport around farm buildings is usually consistent throughout the year, although activity tends to peak in the colder months when the birds struggle to find food on the open fields.

One of the best ways to target collared doves and other avian pests around the farm is to establish the path they are taking in and out of the buildings and try to ambush them en route. Pigeons and corvids usually have favourite vantage points – maybe a tall tree or a grain silo – where they perch to scan for danger before committing themselves to land on the ground. Get within range of one of these lookouts and you should set yourself up for a steady trickle of activity.

You don't need to go over the top with camouflage when hunting around the farm because quarry species will have become accustomed to humans. The constant presence of workers and the noise of machinery mean that even usually wary species like crows and magpies are less suspicious than they are in the open countryside. You certainly won't need a head net, and a pair of old jeans and a drab jacket should be just as effective as the latest camouflage patterns – possibly even more so – when you're against a backdrop of farmyard clutter.

There should be no shortage of cover. Most farms are fairly ramshackle and offer all sorts of shady hiding places from which you can observe likely looking spots. Parked tractors, piles of feed sacks and stacks of hay bales provide useful screens to keep you hidden from sight.

Although they aren't the most beautiful places to shoot, farmyards are a useful retreat for the air rifle hunter. Farm buildings provide a welcome sanctuary on the days when horizontal rain, biting cold wind or even scorching hot sun makes more exposed places somewhat less appealing. It's likely that quarry species will be thinking the same so they'll most likely be heading to the barns to dodge the weather, too. And, even if action is a little thin on the ground, at least you should be able to find a warm, dry place to sit down and enjoy a flask of tea while dodging the domestic chores. And of course, you're providing a useful service. I've secured some of my best shooting permissions by first winning the landowner's trust by thinning out feral pigeons, collared doves or crows around farm units. Even when you're allowed to wander the pheasant coverts in pursuit of woodpigeons for the pot, your host will still expect you to keep the farmyard free from uninvited guests.

Grey squirrels

Like virtually all introduced species, the grey squirrel (*Sciurus carolinensis*) has caused problems for native wildlife.

Released in Britain from sites including Woburn Park during the late nineteenth and early twentieth centuries, the grey squirrel has made an undeniable contribution to the demise of our native, and protected, red squirrel (*Sciurus vulgaris*). The UK grey squirrel population is currently estimated at around 2.5 million, a figure that eclipses the remaining 150,000 native reds.

The grey's seemingly unstoppable rampage is not so much down to physically pushing out the native species, as many people wrongly assume, as through being more adaptable, and through the spread of disease. Grey squirrels can carry squirrel pox but, unlike red squirrels, are immune to the virus. The grey is also less fussy when it comes to food and habitat; their diet is very broad and they are just as likely to reside in deciduous woodland as coniferous woods whereas the red favours conifers. In a nutshell – pardon the pun – the grey is simply a more successful species.

Admittedly, grey squirrels are bigger, stronger and more aggressive than reds. This, combined with the fact that greys live in greater densities, (three or more pairs per acre compared with just one pair for reds) means they are unlikely to be ousted once they have taken over a territory.

Grey squirrels are, as the name suggests, grey in colour, but their coat does vary from locality to locality and from season to season. By and large, their winter coat is silvery grey with a brown tinge along the back. In the summer, they often take on a more reddish colour. The underbelly is white and the long, bushy tail is mostly grey, though often has a distinctive white band around the outer edge.

Although the red squirrel is usually considerably redder in colour, the potential for variation means this is not a sure means of identification. There are, however, other features that distinguish the grey squirrel from the red. Primarily, grey squirrels have small rounded ears whereas red squirrels have long tufts of fur that give the impression of long pointed ears. The red is also very slight in build compared with the comparatively bulky grey.

The grey squirrel's nest (known as a drey) is often the first indication of its presence in the woods. You'll often see tatty-looking, football-sized summer dreys, which are made from twigs and lined with leaves and moss, high up in the trees. Bigger winter, or maternity, dreys are usually constructed in the fork of a large branch or even inside hollow trees. Squirrels usually give birth to two litters, typically of three or four young. The first litter arrives in early spring and the second follows in mid to late summer.

Apart from the obvious threat they pose to the native red squirrel, greys have a few other character traits that enforce their pest status, one of these being their habit of robbing eggs and chicks from nests. Although nuts and berries make up a large part of their diet, they won't pass up the opportunity of a protein boost in the shape of an egg or young bird. The impact of grey squirrels on populations of songbirds (including some very scarce species) is thought to be considerable. The grey squirrel's nest-raiding antics have also made it very unpopular with gamekeepers. Keepers work hard controlling marauding foxes, stoats, mink and corvids to protect precious wild broods of pheasants and don't like the thought of a bunch of greedy squirrels scoffing the fruits of their labours. The squirrel's tendency to steal grain from pheasant feeders serves to cause further aggravation. Squirrels can also cause a nuisance in the garden. As well as decimating the nests of wild birds they are also adept at breaking into bird feeders and making off with their contents.

The case against the grey squirrel goes on, as they also pose a problem to foresters. Squirrels are very fond of stripping the bark from trees so they can feed on the sweet sugary sap beneath. If a complete ring of bark is stripped from the base of a sapling, the tree will die, as its supply of nutrients is cut off. In less severe cases, bark-stripped trees grow to be stunted and deformed, which results in a reduced timber value.

Grey squirrels are most active around dawn and dusk and tend to follow the same established routes through the woods. They are incredibly agile animals and are capable of moving through the treetops at great speed, often making impressive leaps and landing on the flimsiest of twigs. In spite of their acrobatic ability, grey squirrels also spend a lot of time foraging on the ground. Contrary to popular belief, they don't hibernate through the winter but do become noticeably less active when the weather is very cold, and they don't like to venture out during particularly wet weather. Squirrel activity tends to reach a frenzy in the autumn when there's an abundance of nuts and seeds for them to forage and store. Grey squirrels are notorious for burying caches of nuts and for struggling to remember where they left them. These forgotten stashes of nuts can play an important part in the propagation of new saplings.

Commercial forestry enterprises tend to use poison to control squirrel numbers, though many would argue this is not the best option. Poisoned grain is placed inside species-specific, L-shaped tunnel feeders deigned to be accessible only to squirrels in order to prevent other animals from entering and ingesting the bait.

The damage to this field maple is a result of bark-stripping by grey squirrels.

Forestry companies often control squirrels with poisoned bait dispensed from feed hoppers. Hunting with air rifles is more selective and ensures a quicker death.

While the feeders work in this respect, the grey squirrel is a messy eater and I have often witnessed poison hoppers with vast amounts of treated grain spilt around them. This poses a serious risk to native birds and mammals,

A trio of squirrels shot during the autumn acorn frenzy.

including dormice.

Air rifles allow a far more specific grey squirrel cull, and an infinitely more humane end than a lingering death brought about by poisoning. Also, I recently spoke with a Forestry Commission wildlife ranger who made a very interesting point. While this very experienced woodland conservation expert was adamant that grey squirrel populations need to be kept well down because of the undeniable harm they cause to native wildlife, he also felt that a small population can actually be beneficial to other animals. He explained that the dead treetops resulting from squirrel damage create an important habitat for insects, which in turn provide food for woodpeckers. The holes bored by woodpeckers then create habitat for birds and even dormice. So, the possible benefit of tolerating a small, controlled population of grey squirrels is another reason for adopting a selective cull with an air rifle rather than blanket eradication by poisoning.

Grey squirrels are a challenging adversary for the hunter. Equipped with good eyesight and a keen sense of hearing, these artful rodents have a talent for making themselves disappear whenever they detect a suspicious presence in the woods. When hunting with a legal-limit air rifle I strictly limit myself to taking squirrels with head shots. Squirrels are tough little critters and, as far as I'm concerned, a side-on strike between the eye and ear is the only way to swiftly despatch them. Making that telling head shot is made tricky by the fact that squirrels can be fidgety creatures, but the responsible hunter would rather let the occasional squirrel escape unharmed than risk wounding his quarry. Nonetheless, there are one or two little ruses that can be employed to make them keep still.

Shooting grey squirrels

Most of my grey squirrel control takes place through the cooler months, from mid September through to late April. The main reason for this is that it's much easier to spot squirrels from autumn onwards than it is when the trees are in full leaf.

Shooting in the squirrel's woodland habitat is a tricky business during the summer. Thick foliage can make it difficult to locate your quarry before it makes a dash for cover, and the biting gnats and midges that frequent warm, damp woods can be enough to drive a hunter to absolute distraction. Nonetheless, if the landowner who grants you shooting permission expects your squirrel-control service to be a year-round arrangement, then you'll have to keep your side of the deal. Put on a head net and gloves to stop the bloodthirsty insects from eating you alive, and rest assured that the following tactics work more or less the same whenever you apply them.

My favourite season for hunting squirrels is the autumn; the abundance of natural food in the woods sends the greedy little rodents into an absolute frenzy of activity, and the distraction provides the shooter with numerous opportunities to outwit his quarry. At this time of year, I like to hunt on the move, drifting through the woods while scouring ahead for any sign of a squirrel. I take a few steps, stop to scan, and then, if I don't spot anything, carry on for another few metres before stopping to look again. It's important to watch the ground ahead as much as the trees because squirrels spend a lot of time rummaging among the leaves when there's food about. This slow, steady progress can cover quite an acreage in a few hours and yield great results, but you really do have to keep your eyes peeled. Sometimes you'll see the silhouette of a squirrel sitting in the fork of a distant branch with its tail folded over its back, at other times you might just see a head peeping round from behind a tree trunk, or just the flick of a bushy tail. Catch sight of a gently bobbing branch when the wind isn't blowing and there's a very good chance that it's a sign of a squirrel on the move. On really calm days you might even hear the clicking of a squirrel's claws on the bark of a tree as it clambers through the canopy.

When you do spot a squirrel, you'll need to creep within range before it spots you and beats a hasty retreat. Stalking through woods that are littered with leaves and twigs isn't always easy, and you'll have to be very light on your feet to go unnoticed. From time to time, you'll encounter an extremely cocky, or foolish, squirrel that stands its ground and utters a scolding call at you rather than doing the sensible thing and making itself scarce. These plucky little critters inevitably end up in the game bag without too much difficulty, but most squirrels provide more of a challenge.

One of the grey squirrel's favourite tricks is to slip around to the back of the tree as you approach it, and this often turns into a game of cat and mouse as your quarry continues to creep round and round the tree as you follow in

A wary squirrel can often be flushed with help from a companion.

hopeless circles. This frustrating little ruse can easily be exploited if you're shooting with a companion. One of you stands still, ready to shoot, as the other proceeds to follow the squirrel around the tree. The chances are that the not-so-cunning little bushy-tail will be more alarmed by the man on the move than the static shooter and can be guided around the tree until it emerges in front of the gun. If you're on your own, this ploy can be recreated with a white carrier bag – it doesn't always work but it's worth a try. In one pocket of my shooting jacket I keep a head net and gloves and in another I keep a bag for just such occasions – it's also handy for sitting on when the ground is wet. What I do when I have a stubborn squirrel leading me around a tree is slip on my head net and gloves and then take out the bag and spread it open on the woodland floor. I then continue to follow the squirrel around the tree, as quietly as I possibly can. If I'm lucky, the squirrel will be more alarmed by the sight of the bright white bag than by my approach, and will stop and stare while I sneak round and take a shot.

Sometimes, as you make your way through

Grey squirrels quickly home-in on the free meal provided by pheasant feeders during the colder months.

the woods, you'll find the occasional area that warrants more attention. Perhaps a couple of squirrels bolted into a drey as you approached, maybe there are oak or beech trees heavy with acorns or mast, or perhaps there's a large hollowed-out tree or thick tangle of ivy that looks certain to harbour a squirrel or two. Find such a place and it's often worth sitting and waiting in case one or two squirrels venture out.

Later in the year, when autumn has rolled into winter and natural food is running low, there is one particular attraction that can make for a very rewarding ambush, and that's the pheasant feeder. Gamekeepers keep feed hoppers filled with grain to help pheasants through the harsh winter months and to try to stop them from

straying. The hoppers provide a rich food source that squirrels quickly learn to take advantage of, especially during really cold weather. Sit down and wait quietly twenty or so metres from a feed hopper that's being visited by squirrels, and you should be rewarded with some steady winter sport. This tactic works particularly well towards the end of the day, as squirrels become extremely active just before dark. An area of woodland that seemed devoid of squirrels throughout the day can suddenly turn into a hive of activity as the bushy-tails busy themselves gathering food before a long, cold night.

Find a place that offers enough cover to keep you hidden and slip on your head net and gloves for added concealment. After a while you'll gradually become tuned-in to the sounds and sights of the immediate vicinity. The air is filled with the thin tune of the robin and the fluttering of wings occasionally catches your eye as chaffinches fly back and forth to pick at the grain beneath the feeder. Then you notice a rustling in the ivy about thirty metres away and look up to see the waxy leaves trembling as something nudges its way through the tangle that's growing up the trunk of an old oak tree. There it is. A squirrel emerges from the bottom of the ivy and clambers on down the trunk of the tree and onto the ground.

Bold as brass, the squirrel bounds along until it disappears behind the back of the feeder. The next thing you see of it is a bobbing silver tail as it scurries quickly away and slips behind the base of the tree it just descended. This bushy-tail hasn't spotted you, it's just that squirrels are fidgety animals and don't like to hang about in the open. Watch where the squirrel disappeared through your scope and wait until it ventures back out for another helping.

Two minutes later and the squirrel is back on the move and making its way to the hopper. As

Trout flies tied with fibres from grey squirrel tails.

trunk or scuttling across the ground. From time to time, the noise will spook an ultra-wary squirrel and send it running, never to be seen again, but more often than not it works with devastating effect.

What to do with them

Plenty of people praise the culinary qualities of squirrels but I'm afraid I'm not one of them. The squirrel's acrobatic lifestyle in the treetops means that it is a sinuous, wiry creature and this manifests as tough meat, which also doesn't happen to taste too great. A friend of mine once went to great lengths to find a way to make squirrel meat more appetising – even going as far as to cure it in a smoker. In my opinion, if smoking meat can't make it tasty then nothing can, and I'm afraid the smoked squirrel still didn't taste great. Combine the lack of gastronomic pleasure with the fact that, by the time you've gutted and skinned them, squirrels take rather a lot of preparing for very little meat, then you really do have to ask yourself whether it's worth the fuss. If you fancy finding out for yourself, I suggest you try a slow-cooking recipe for rabbit and use squirrel instead. The long, steady cooking time will help to make the meat more tender.

The conscientious hunter tries to make the best possible use of what he shoots. As I don't eat squirrel, I tend to give them to friends who keep ferrets, because these ravenous little hunters certainly appreciate the meat. I cut off the tails before I give them away, though, because the squirrel's most distinctive feature does hold some value. Like the wing and tail feathers of some corvids, squirrel's tails are used by trout fishermen to tie imitative fly patterns. They're only worth a few pence each, but it soon mounts up. See the last paragraphs in the corvids chapter to find out more.

it reaches open ground a few metres from the tree, you purse your lips and let out a squeaking sound (the same effect can be achieved by clicking your tongue in the roof of your mouth) and the startled squirrel freezes in its tracks as it tries to locate the source of the unfamiliar sound. The crosshairs of your scope settle between your quarry's eye and ear, you instinctively push through the trigger and a ringing crack echoes through the copse, signalling a lethal head shot. This ruse is a great way to stop squirrels from fidgeting while you compose a shot, whether they're scrambling through the branches, clambering down a tree

Corvids

The term corvid refers to the crow family. The crow, magpie, rook, jay and jackdaw are all on the quarry list and this bunch includes some of the most cunning adversaries the air rifle hunter is ever likely to pit his wits against.

Carrion crows

The carrion crow (*Corvus corone corone*) is kingpin of the mob and has earned the reputation of being the wiliest of avian quarry. Sure enough, crows are very intelligent birds; they are ultra wary of man and treat more or less everything with suspicion. If you can stalk to within shooting distance of a crow on open ground, then you are a better hunter than I am.

But just because crows are artful, it doesn't mean they are impossible to outwit – it just means your skills will be put to the test. Some hunters make such a fuss about the intelligence of crows that they talk themselves into feeling beaten before they even start. My advice when it comes to hunting crows, or any of the crafty corvids for that matter, is to remember who's smartest. Yes, crows can be very cunning birds, but most of us can lay claim to being further evolved and more intelligent than any bird – it's just a case of identifying and exploiting weaknesses in their defences.

The crow is a large bird and the plumage is entirely black, although it does have a greenish sheen in certain light. It has a strong, thick beak and its call is a harsh kraah-kraah-kraah.

The crow could be mistaken for the protected raven (*Corvus corax*). However, the raven is a much larger bird with a shaggy ruff of feathers around the throat. The raven has a more direct, straight flight which reveals a diamond-shaped tail whereas the crow has more or a loping flight pattern and a wedge-shaped tail.

Crows usually build their nest – a large construction of twigs – high in the trees or among cliffs. Nesting begins in April, when four to seven pale blue-green eggs with brown and grey markings are laid. Although crows are very defensive of their nesting sites, their reputation as being solitary birds is a misconception as they often congregate in raucous mobs at rich feeding grounds and when roosting.

Corvids, particularly crows, have a complex social hierarchy. Members of a crow community frequently work together in defined roles, which are usually dictated by age. These roles often manifest when the birds are faced with something unusual. If there is a hint of suspicion, the older, wiser crows usually have the sense to wait until the younger scouts confirm that the coast is clear before they commit to closer investigation.

The crow is an adaptable bird; an opportunistic scavenger, it will exploit numerous feeding opportunities. The more benign side of their diet includes seeds and worms, and you'll often find them following working tractors to forage whatever has been turned up by the plough. Crows will also scavenge around dustbins and rubbish tips, as well as stealing bread from the bird table. Road kill also features highly on the crow's menu, and they'll raid the farmyard in search of free pickings; this is a bird that has learned to do well when man is nearby. In the woods, hedgerow and garden, crows use that big, powerful beak to good effect, raiding nests and devouring the eggs and young of songbirds. A wily crow will often sit on some lofty perch looking out for parent birds taking food to their young. When the nest site is revealed, the crow will swoop in and devour its contents. The chicks of pheasants and partridges are taken with equal gusto and this predatory streak has made crows an enemy of the gamekeeper. On land grazed by sheep, weak lambs also fall foul of the crow's stabbing beak.

As regards their natural defences, all members of the corvid family have the full set. Their eyesight is razor sharp and they have an uncanny ability to spot the slightest movement – even at a great distance. If you build a hide, expect it to be closely scrutinised by corvids and, if it isn't up to scratch, it will be shunned. The corvid family also possess very acute hearing and they'll usually rumble you and scarper if you make the slightest sound. If that isn't bad enough, they also have a keen sense of smell.

When you do get a crow in your sights which, with a little forethought, can be achieved with surprising regularity – aim to shoot it in the centre of the head. At close range, a whack between the shoulders will result in a clean kill but, being such a large bird, the brain is the favoured target for humane dispatch with a non-FAC air rifle.

Magpies and jays

Magpies and jays are equally opportunistic members of the corvid family. The magpie can be particularly bold, and a gang of these birds will wreak havoc among garden birds with their nest-robbing antics. Jays are more secretive, but frequently supplement their diet with eggs and the young of woodland and game birds.

The magpie (*Pica pica*) is a cheeky and often very comical bird. Their approach is usually heralded by their chattering, clacking calls as they bounce from tree to tree like a mob of rowdy teenagers. Don't be fooled, though, magpies are just as artful as the rest of their ilk – spook them and they are unlikely to return.

Magpies look magnificent and, with their bold markings and very long tail, are unlikely to be mistaken for any other bird. The head, breast and back are black, the belly and shoulders are white, and their apparently black wings and tail reflect iridescent green and purple when viewed closely. You would think that the magpie's bold plumage would make them easy to spot but it blends in with the contrast of dark branches and light sky found in the woods to provide surprisingly effective camouflage.

Magpies nest around the same time as crows but favour dense cover among thick, bushy undergrowth – overgrown hedgerows are a favourite. The nest is a large, globe-shaped bundle of branches and twigs. The hen lays between five and eight eggs, which are pale blue with olive, brown or grey spots.

A woodland bird, the magpie has adapted to exploit feeding opportunities in gardens, parks, farmyards and even around industrialised areas – rubbish tips are a favourite. Like the crow, the magpie knows how to make the most of man's wasteful and untidy habits.

The jay (*Garrulus glandarius*) has similar habits to the magpie but some hunters leave jays undisturbed because they mistakenly believe them to be quite scarce. Although there may be exceptions in some localities, the reason you don't see many jays is not because there aren't many of them around, it's because they are incredibly wary, secretive birds that tend to live in dense woodland and avoid man at all costs. Where I live in Somerset, jays are actually quite abundant and their nest-robbing habits can cause quite an impact on wild broods of pheasants – not to mention songbirds. The jay is also a subject of much folklore, and one or two superstitious shooters won't kill them because they believe it will result in bad luck. Personally, I had plenty of bad luck before I started shooting jays and I don't think my culls around the pheasant coverts have made things much worse . . .

The jay is a beautiful bird, the most striking member of the crow family, and you're unlikely to mistake one for anything else. Slightly smaller than a magpie, it is mostly pink-buff in colour with a black moustache and white throat. On its head is a black and white speckled crest. The white rump contrasts boldly with the black tail and is often the only glimpse you get of a jay as it disappears into the woods. The wings are tipped in black and white but further up are adorned with the most brilliant blue and black bars. These electric-blue feathers are highly prized by fly-tyers as they are a key component of sea trout patterns. The jay has pink legs and a black beak.

Although you seldom see jays, you'll often hear their shrieking call echoing around the woods. It is a prehistoric-sounding screech that you'd more likely associate with a pterodactyl than a relatively small woodland bird. Apart from this rasping alarm call, jays also make squeaky, clucking sounds similar to the magpie.

The jay makes an untidy nest, usually in dense scrub. Breeding begins in late April and a clutch of three to eight eggs are laid. Eggs are glossy pale blue-green or olive colour with buff-coloured speckles.

The jay has a broad diet comprising fruit, insects and even frogs. Like most of the corvids, the eggs and chicks of other birds also feature. Acorns and beech mast are real favourites, and jays become very active, and slightly less wary, around autumn time when food is abundant. Like squirrels, jays are known to stash caches of buried acorns.

In all honesty, the jay's secretive lifestyle makes it a very difficult quarry to deliberately pursue. The jays that I shoot tend to be the result of our paths crossing by chance while I'm out hunting other members of the corvid clan, grey squirrels or woodpigeons.

As with the rest of the mob, jays and magpies are very cunning, and you'll need your wits about you to get past that sharp vision and keen hearing. When you do get one of these birds in your sights, don't be fooled by that grand plumage – magpies and jays are actually very slight birds and among the few quarry species that can be snuffed out just as effectively with a shot delivered squarely to the upper body as with a clout to the head. The hardest part is getting these hyper-active birds to keep still long enough for you to get the crosshairs to settle anywhere on them.

Rooks

The rook (*Corvus frugilegus*) looks quite similar to the carrion crow but its habits are rather different. First and foremost, rooks don't share the predatory tendencies associated with most other corvids and, although they will scavenge carrion, they feed mostly on seeds, worms and insects. For this reason, some landowners see little reason in controlling their numbers. That said, a large flock (the actual collective noun is a parliament) of rooks can do serious damage to agricultural crops. Rooks have a very costly habit of using their long beak to pick freshly drilled seeds from the ground. Another habit that can make them very unpopular with farmers is their tendency to descend on the farmyard in large numbers to scavenge animal feed.

Rooks are very social birds and congregate in large treetop rookeries. A large rookery can be a noisy, messy place and, apart from the din made by the rooks, can be identified by a collection of large, bulky nests made from twigs. Nesting can begin as early as March, and the hen lays between three and eight eggs, which are a pale blue or blue-green colour with dark spots. Pairs of rooks will often renovate the same nests year after year.

Although they are about the same size, distinguishing rooks from crows is fairly straightforward. Whereas the head and beak of the crow is entirely black, the rook has a white mask around the base of the beak, nostrils and chin. The beak is also slightly longer and more pointed than that of the crow. The rook's plumage looks untidy compared with the crow's, especially around the thigh feathers which are often described as looking like a pair of baggy trousers. The croaking waak-waak call of the rook is not as shrill as the shriek of the crow.

Reasons for culling rooks include crop protection and to reduce numbers when rookeries become intolerably noisy – not to mention the filth where droppings accumulate underneath. Of course, the rook is also the staple ingredient of that traditional country meal, the rook pie. I'm afraid I can't bring myself to eat any member of the corvid family, but I'm told that rooks are best to eat just after they leave the nest – before the meat becomes too dark and bitter. If you do want to try if for yourself, don't bother trying to pluck and draw rooks – just remove the breast meat using the technique I describe for woodpigeons.

The season when rooks supposedly taste best happens to coincide with when they are young and gullible enough to let shooters get within range. Young rooks, or branchers as they are sometimes called, leave the nest around 12 May each year and hop from branch to branch around the nest site in the tallest trees before they become proficient in flight. This is the time to reduce their numbers and harvest that tender young meat. Adult rooks can also be targeted from a hide when they are hammering crops on the open farm, and from the cover of farm buildings when they're scavenging food.

I don't do a lot of rook shooting because their numbers rarely need to be controlled in my locality. My advice is to check with whoever owns your shooting grounds to see whether or not they need keeping in check. If you are required to cull rooks, head shots are recommended, even when targeting branchers. Their tendency to reside in the highest of trees, where even the slightest breeze sets the target bouncing, makes for challenging shots, but rooks are large birds and clean kills must always come first.

Jackdaws

Like the rook, the jackdaw (*Corvus monedula*) isn't anything like as damaging to other birds as some of its cousins, and reasons for controlling their numbers should be considered on a case-by-case basis. Some of the farms I shoot over suffer terribly with vast hordes of these little black corvids invading barns to steal animal feed, particularly in the winter. Apart from scoffing expensive foodstuffs intended for livestock, these marauding flocks also pose a threat to hygiene, given the amount of their amassed droppings that end up in the water and feed supplies of resident farm animals. Jackdaws are also notorious for nesting in chimneys. During the nesting season they will drop large twigs down chimneys until one jams, and then drop more and more until the nest almost reaches the top of the cavity. This large blockage of dry twigs and small branches obviously poses a considerable risk of chimney fire, but it has to be said that the problem is usually better remedied by the simple installation of a jackdaw guard on the top of the chimney rather than shooting the culprits.

Jackdaws are adaptable birds and, apart from the farmyard, are encountered in the woods, in the garden, around towns and on open farmland. Their diet is mixed and includes insects, worms, seeds and berries. Being effective scavengers, these versatile corvids are often found in great numbers around landfill sites and they are also adept at bullying garden birds away from the bird table.

Nesting begins in late April and, as well as chimneys, jackdaws will set up home in hollow trees, craggy rock faces and in buildings. Made from twigs, the nest is lined with bark and soil. The female lays four to six eggs, which are pale blue with blackish-brown markings.

The jackdaw is a very social bird and it has to be said that their group antics can be very entertaining to observe. Their call is an abrupt kchack-kchack-kchack sound which is echoed in their name.

At a glance, the jackdaw looks like a small carrion crow, but they are easy to identify on closer inspection. Although mostly black, jackdaws have a greyish nape and shoulders. The eyes are pale greyish-blue and contrast starkly against the black plumage.

Although jackdaws are relatively small, they have a comparatively large head, which makes for a decent-sized target. I would suggest, therefore, that shooters limit themselves to head shots when culling jackdaws.

A decoy owl with piercing yellow eyes can really wind up territorial corvids.

Shooting corvids

Although corvids are quite happy to prey on the eggs and young of other birds, nothing aggravates them more than the threat of other predators. The presence of another predator in their territory literally drives them berserk. You often hear it when you're out in the woods and the fields. When you hear the sound of crows screeching, accompanied by the angry rattles of agitated magpies and maybe even a rasping jay, too, then it's a safe bet the corvid tribe is mobbing a predator. Foxes and birds of prey are often subjected to this barracking, and it's not unheard-of for squirrels to fall foul of it either.

This intolerance of birds and animals that pose a threat reaches its peak around spring and summer time because corvids are fiercely territorial birds and will protect their nesting sites with surprising ferocity. This trait is not shown by rooks and rarely by jackdaws but the rest of the corvid clan really can't resist the urge to let rip on a passing predator. Crows and magpies become completely overwhelmed by the frenzied mobbing and often lose all their usual caution. This trait is something of a gift for the hunter.

The threat posed by an intruding owl or hawk can be recreated by the use of a decoy. Plastic imitation birds of prey are surprisingly lifelike, and usually provoke exactly the same reaction as the real thing. These decoys are available in all shapes and sizes, from giant owls the best part of two feet tall to life-size little owls that literally fit in your jacket packet. Crows and magpies will happily hurl abuse at one when it crops up on their doorstep. When I select a decoy owl for crow shooting, my biggest concern is the design of its eyes. The best sort has large, shiny yellow eyes with bold black pupils. There's something about these piercing eyes that really aggravates corvids.

What you need to do is find a place where the corvids you are pursuing have a nesting site. With crows, this shouldn't prove too difficult because their nests are hard to miss. Magpies tend to hide their nests a little better but don't worry if you can't find one because if there are crows and magpies around, then there are probably nests in the vicinity and that's good enough.

Good starting places for this approach are woodland edges or along overgrown hedgerows that feature one or two mature trees. I try to find a place where I can weave a discreet hide within range of a good, open sitty tree (a sitty tree is a tree that offers the shooter clear, comfortable shots when his quarry alights in it). Sharp-eyed corvids will test your hide-building skills to the full because they really don't miss a trick, so don't be tempted to try and cut corners. Ideally, I like to build my hide a day or two before I intend to shoot because crows and magpies will become suspicious if they see a human messing around with the vegetation near their home.

Another important consideration is the positioning of the decoy. What I look for is a prominent area where it will catch the attention of passing corvids. A clear area of short grass is fine, or sometimes I'll use wire to mount my decoy owl on a branch or fencepost to make it really stand out. Just remember to set it up within your competent shooting range because really bolshy birds will often bypass the sitty tree and swoop in right next to the decoy. I've had crows literally bash the plastic owl onto its back on several occasions, and it's a wonderful spectacle when buzzards drop in for a close

A fine example of a sitty tree; incoming corvids will present clear shots when they land on the dead, leafless branches.

inspection.

If you've been able to build your hide in advance, the best time to arrive for this kind of session is just before first light. That way you'll be able to get yourself in position without the birds rumbling you.

It's a lovely experience being out in the countryside before the rest of the world is awake. Look back over the trail of footprints you left in the dew-soaked grass and you'll see the pale glow of the morning sun starting to seep over the distant hills. Be quick or the birds will be on the move before you're ready. Slip the decoy owl out of your bag and prop it up on the spot you earmarked when you built your hide, then slip behind the net, put on your head net and gloves to ensure you are hidden from those prying eyes, and make your gun ready.

As the first rays of sun start to penetrate the morning mist, you hear the distant clack of a magpie and then a chatter from another one slightly closer. This is exciting stuff – the corvids have started their morning rounds.

Within no time, the inquisitive clucks from the magpies have turned into agitated rattles and it sounds as if there are four or five in the vicinity; one of them presumably within spitting distance it's so close, but you can't see it because it's in the trees somewhere behind you.

Before you know it, a cocky magpie is gliding in towards the decoy with its wings stretched out. The bird is utterly distracted by the plastic intruder so slip the muzzle of your air rifle through the hide netting now while it's distracted. Through the scope you can see the magpie standing bemused just three feet from your owl – it's confused because the decoy is showing no reaction to its presence. Thumb-off the safety catch and allow your breathing to steady as the crosshairs settle on the head of the magpie standing just 25 metres from your hiding place. The time is right; you instinctively push through the trigger to release the shot and the smack that follows the spit from the muzzle confirms that the pellet has found its mark. The magpie is slumped lifeless on its belly – this corvid's nest-robbing days are over.

But your foray is far from over. In fact, it's about to get very hectic because two magpies are now flitting from branch to branch in the sitty tree. They are intrigued by the strange reaction of their companion but too wary to commit to a close inspection. Reload and push the muzzle slowly and quietly through the hide in the direction of the magpies. This time it's harder to make sense of the scope picture; the birds are uneasy and they won't keep still. Stay calm and don't risk a hurried shot. Choose one of the birds and follow it as it hops around the tree –

ignore the other, don't let it distract you. Sure enough, your magpie eventually settles long enough for you to compose a steady aim. Whack! Your patience has paid off and you've made it a brace.

Two losses is too much for the remaining magpies to tolerate and they've wisely decided to beat a hasty retreat. Their calls fade into the distance until all is still again – now is the time to retrieve the bodies. Make your gun safe, slip quietly out of the hide, and quickly gather the shot birds so they don't spook the crows when they arrive.

A long wait follows (so long, in fact, that you've had a welcome cup of tea from your flask) but you soon snap back into hunter mode when you hear the distant croak of a crow. You're lucky, the crows missed the bedlam of the magpies and are starting to drift your way.

Moments later your pulse is racing as two crows circle overhead, eyeing-up the cheeky little owl that has appeared in their territory. Eventually one of them breaks, unable to resist a stand-off with the decoy, and glides into the killing zone. You've slipped the barrel through the net and the bird is in your sights; it's stooped down, head forward and shoulders back, rasping at the inanimate owl. This crow has its back to you but the range is close enough, and the angle just right, for a shot between the wings to strike the vital organs. All that practice is paying off and the third corvid of the morning crumples as the shot hits home.

If you thought the magpies reacted bravely to the demise of their mate, just wait until the crows unleash their less than discreet mourning ritual. When presented with the sight of a fallen comrade, rather than doing the sensible thing and backing off, crows do the complete opposite. In no time at all, the best part of a dozen crows are wheeling overhead, shrieking

A nest made from a twist of dry grass and filled with hens' eggs can pull in corvids when wild birds are nesting.

Good bags of corvids can be made when they fall for decoying tactics.

and bellowing at the scene below. This noisy funeral ceremony is the typical reaction when crows lose one of their number. The raucous antics and complete loss of fear is hard to believe until you witness it, and can also be quite unnerving, but keep your wits about you because this a prime opportunity to add to the tally.

Reload and keep an eye on the sitty tree. It's most likely that crows will take up a seemingly safe vantage point to eyeball the situation before they go any closer. It's like waiting for a bus, and before you know it, three crows swoop into the tree one after the other. They're making a lot of noise but at least they're sitting still. Through your scope, you see the highest of the bunch is presenting you with a clear side profile of its head. Take your time, check the range, compose yourself and allow the crosshairs to come to rest on the crow's brain-box before you touch off the trigger. The dead crow crashes into the undergrowth, adding to its companions' confusion and making them even more flustered.

The pandemonium is at fever pitch now and you can hear the muffled clacks and rattles of distant magpies, unsettled by the din. Even the

blackbirds are uneasy and are uttering their shrill alarm call in response to the screeches and croaks of the crows. The last thing the corvids expect is the shooter hidden in the undergrowth and, if you shoot well, it should be possible to make quite a bag of crows before they wise-up to the danger and vacate the area. The end of the frenzy usually marks the end of the action though, but it's usually worth sitting tight for another half-hour before you break cover, just in case the curiosity gets the better of a particularly gullible crow or magpie. When you do call it a day, and have tidied up and packed away your hide you'll be more than ready to head for home for a proper breakfast.

Decoy birds of prey are not the only way to attract corvids within range. By trying to think like his quarry, the inventive hunter will have a long list of tricks up his sleeve.

As we know, this family of birds has a taste for the contents of other birds' nests and this can result in their downfall. During the spring and summer, when crows and magpies are busy seeking out the eggs and chicks of less aggressive birds, an imitation nest can prove irresistible. All you need to do is construct a nest in a prominent place where it won't go unnoticed – maybe in a field somewhere between the crows' nesting site and their feeding grounds. This sort of nest is easily built from a few twists of straw or long grass; you can even add a few lengths of twine and a couple of feathers to add to the realism. I keep a pair or plastic eggs (you can buy them cheaply from agricultural stores) for just such occasions but a couple of real hen's eggs, preferably with one smashed to show its contents, is even more appealing to greedy corvids. The fake nest can work particularly well when the birds start to wise-up after a couple of pastings with the owl decoy.

When using these tactics, it pays to set out a couple of decoy crows or magpies close to the bait to attract the attention of passing corvids. The decoys will also help to convince incoming birds that the scene is safe – sometimes they'll rush in with no caution whatsoever, completely distracted by the urge to get to the free meal before the imitation birds make off with their breakfast. The rest of the approach is much the same as when using the owl decoy; you'll need a hide, and a sitty tree is useful too. It should work in the same places as the decoy, and I've also had great success using baits set in fields flanking farm building that are being visited by food-nabbing crows.

More substantial baits can also be effective, especially in the winter when natural food is scarce. The classic bait for crows is a dead rabbit with its belly cut open to reveal its guts. It might sound disgusting but, believe me, this is fine dining for corvids – just do your best to shoot them before they manage to peck out the eyeballs because they regard these as a delicacy.

It has to be said that using a rabbit as crow bait is rather a waste of good meat, and there are alternatives. I always keep a few squirrels (which

I feel much less inclined to eat) in the freezer ready to defrost for use as crow attractors. Used in the same way as the rabbit, a squirrel works almost as well. Owing to the fact that corvids are scavengers with a taste for carrion, rabbits' entrails can also be used as bait. This is a great use for the by-product of preparing shot quarry for the table and you can easily bag it up and freeze it. Admittedly, you'll need an understanding partner to tolerate you freezing bags of guts alongside next week's dinners – or you could just keep it to yourself and hope the unmarked bags go unnoticed.

For the faint-hearted, there's a wide variety of less disgusting corvid baits. These birds often sustain themselves by feeding exclusively on scraps of waste food discarded by man, and this scenario can easily be recreated by the hunter. The leftovers from last night's supper might be all it takes to attract crows and magpies with the addition of a decoy or two. Vegetable peelings can also be effective, as can a pile of dog biscuits. I've also had some great days shooting crows attracted by handfuls of flaked white bread scattered over ploughed ground in the middle of the winter. All the thinking hunter needs to do is consider what the resident corvids like to eat and what will catch their eye when viewed from above – there are countless possibilities.

The great thing about using decoys and bait is that you can set them up at whatever range you feel confident of shooting at. Naturally, corvids are reluctant to venture too close to cover because of the threat of an ambush from a lurking fox, so a distance somewhere between 20 and 30 metres is usually about right. Don't just do it by eye; pace out the distance so you can use the decoy or bait as a range marker, enabling you to work out where to aim – you'll need to know the distance to the sitty tree too. I often push small sticks into the ground ten metres beyond the decoy and ten metres my side of it so I can quickly estimate the range and the relative aim-off required when birds land short of or beyond the trap.

Of course, shooting sessions don't always go exactly to plan – far from it – and there will be times when corvids don't arrive *en masse*, or even at all. Occasionally, the birds will fail to notice the decoy or bait and it can pay to use a caller to draw their attention. Crow callers are available from most gun shops and come in the form of a pipe with a reed in front of the mouth-piece. They don't take long to get the hang of, and you'll soon be able to mimic the call of an inquisitive crow with a couple of puffs.

For magpies, you can quickly make your own caller to imitate the chaka-chaka-chak of their rattling cries. Some people use a box of matches as a rattle but I don't think this is quite loud enough so I have devised my own version. All I do is take an empty plastic 35mm film canister and pop about a dozen heavy .22 pellets in there. Shaking this makes a very convincing magpie call that can be heard from a reasonable distance. Just remember not to leave it in your pocket when you head out stalking; wary quarry will hear you rattling around from a mile off.

The most important thing to remember whenever using callers is not to overdo it. More often than not, my crow and magpie callers stay in the bag and I leave it to the decoys or bait to do their job. When I do resort to calling, I start with a couple of rasps or rattles, depending on which one I'm using, and then wait to see what happens. If there is no response at all, or a very distant reply, then I'll give it another go, but I stop as soon as I think the incoming corvids are close enough to see whatever attractor I'm using. If you go over the top, you could end up drawing attention to your whereabouts or even frightening the birds away by mimicking an intruding bird that's looking for a confrontation. The purpose of the caller in this instance is simply to attract the birds' attention so they are drawn to the trap.

From late autumn through to early spring, when the winds have stripped the trees of their leaves, roost shooting for crows can be very productive. This is exciting shooting and involves much less preparation and equipment than an ambush from a hide.

Considering that crows can be quite solitary birds, it is surprising how they often gather in great flocks to roost, particularly during the colder months. Their roosting sites are usually

A simple rattle made from an old camera film canister with airgun pellets inside will mimic the magpie's chattering call.

fairly easy to find in the woods because the ground beneath them will be splattered with watery white droppings. Alternatively, you can just wait in the woods until sundown and listen to hear where the noisy crows gather as darkness closes in. Crows are the last of the birds to turn in for the night so be prepared to wait a while.

Once you have located the roost, it's best to arrive about an hour before you expect the crows to turn up – for your first session at least – so you can get settled into the right place without drawing attention to yourself.

Find a spot that offers you clear shots at one or two of the tallest trees around the roost. Being the cagey creatures they are, crows will usually land first in a place that provides a good lookout before they decide it's safe enough to drop down to more sheltered branches, so make sure you'll be able to get an aim on them. The position you choose should also give you a reasonable amount of cover to keep you out of sight.

When I'm roost shooting for crows, I don't build a hide but try to make as much use of natural cover as I possibly can. Even something like a tree trunk can improve the effect of camouflage clothing. The important thing to do is cover up any pink patches of skin. Your hands and face will stand out like a beacon when the light of the rising moon catches them as you stare upwards from the gloom of the twilit woods. The crows will be away at the first sight of you, so a head net and gloves are essential to keep you concealed.

Once you're settled in, roost shooting for crows brings an indescribable feeling of excitement and anticipation. The woodland environment is a magical place to be as darkness falls, and the experience can be a little unsettling too if you let your nerves get the better of you. Many of the creatures of the woods become very active as night arrives and it's surprising what a noisy place a seemingly empty wood can be. Your senses will be heightened and the screech of an owl, the bloodcurdling shriek of a vixen or just the sound of a badger snuffling through the leaf litter can be enough to really put your nerves on edge. I once had a heart-stopping moment when a spooked deer came bolting through the darkness and almost piled straight into me. I had no idea what it was until it came to a skidding halt about five feet away from me, narrowly avoiding a head-on collision before it turned on its heels and bolted off. I don't know who was the more terrified but it certainly left my pulse pounding.

Once the crows start circling overhead, the job in hand should be enough to distract you from the spookiness of the night-time woodland. The usual form is for one or two crows to wheel high above the woods, letting out the occasional croak as they let the rest of the clan know that the coast appears to be clear. More birds eventually join the initial scouts, and it's not uncommon to have a dozen or so birds overhead before one lands, but once one drops in, it is usually quickly joined by its companions.

Raise your gun to your shoulder very, very slowly (better still, have it ready when the birds are circling) because the crows will be scouring all around for any sign of danger, and it doesn't take a lot of movement to catch their eye. Now, pick out the one that offers you the clearest shot of its head and, using a tree to steady your aim if you shoot a recoilless gun, allow the crosshair to settle on its mark. When the shot is on, touch off the trigger and prepare for all hell to break loose.

As I described, crows often hurl themselves into a very bizarre and noisy frenzy when one of their numbers gets bumped off. Their ritual is usually even more hysterical when the loss occurs at the roost, so brace yourself.

Within moments of the shot bird hitting the deck, the chances are that crows will be flinging themselves into a swooping, screeching fit of confusion. Black shadows with wings outstretched with fill the sky and the shrieks and rasps from the angry crows may be almost deafening. You can expect one or two agitated magpies to add their rattling, clacking calls to the howling congregation. If the screech of a distant tawny owl was enough to unsettle you, this could completely shred your nerves, but you'll need to keep cool in order to capitalise on the opportunity. As with the hide-shooting scenario, crows lose their natural caution when they enter this strange frenzy, so you can expect to shoot a few more when they glide in for a closer look. The light should be really going by now but you can extend your effective hunting time by winding down the magnification of your scope. On a lower mag, the scope will more efficiently transmit whatever available light remains and give you a brighter sight picture. The crows' noisy funeral gathering will eventually calm down and the birds will back-off when they wise-up to the fact that there's danger below, but the urge to roost should bring them back in ones and twos until it gets too dark to shoot.

What to do with them

Making use of what I kill is as important to me as having a good reason for killing it in the first place. While I don't have (and have never felt inclined to look for) a good recipe for corvids, there are profitable uses for shot birds.

Most members of the corvid family have feathers that are incorporated into lure patterns tied by fly-fishermen, and there are several companies willing to buy these materials to sell on to anglers. The list of saleable parts includes the wings of crows, jays and jackdaws, and the tails and wings of magpies. Admittedly, pairs of wings and individual tails are only worth pennies, but it's better than nothing.

What I do is keep wings and tails in a bag in the freezer and, every so often, when I've accumulated a few dozen, I post them to a buyer as a batch. This makes me enough cash to cover the cost of my ammunition. You should be able to find details for numerous fur and feather dealers on the internet. Alternatively, you might be able to strike up a deal with a fly-fishing friend. Perhaps he would be willing to buy you the occasional pint in exchange for fly-tying materials, as and when you acquire them.

Brown rat

The brown rat (*Rattus norvegicus*) is the most notorious vermin species in the world, and not without good reason.

Rats achieved infamy for being the carriers of bubonic plague – the Black Death – which ravaged Europe and Asia between the fourteenth and eighteenth centuries.

The plague was, in fact, spread by the black rat (*Rattus rattus*), which is now very scarce in the UK, but its larger, more aggressive cousin, the brown rat, carries all sorts of horrible diseases and has spread at a rapid rate since it first arrived in Britain in the early eighteenth century.

The brown rat is known to carry as many as 70 diseases, including Weil's disease and tuberculosis. Infection is spread through bites and contact with blood, urine and droppings, so never touch rats with your bare hands and be very careful anywhere you think they may be present.

Weil's disease (also know as Leptospirosis) can be very dangerous if not treated promptly. After being passed in a rat's urine the infective bacteria can survive outside of the body in a moist environment. So, great care must be taken around sources of water including ditches, ponds, animal troughs and even puddles, where infection can enter through cuts in the skin or through the membrane of the throat. Never touch dead rats with your bare hands and always clean your hands when you've been anywhere near rats.

Symptoms of Weil's Disease include fever, chills, aches and pains, loss of appetite and nausea. In its early stages it can easily be mistaken for 'flu or an inexplicable fever. The infection becomes more violent in its later stages, with symptoms such as bruising of the skin, sore eyes, anaemia, nose bleeds and jaundice. Symptoms usually appear within a few days of infection but can take several weeks to manifest. Most people recover completely after treatment with antibiotics but the illness can cause permanent damage to internal organs and can even result in death.

If you ever feel feverish after spending time in a place you know is frequented by rats, you should contact your GP immediately. Tell him or her that you suspect Weil's Disease because many doctors will not have encountered the condition and rapid diagnosis and treatment are vital.

Despite relentless efforts to control their numbers, the UK rat population is on the rise and is now estimated at over 60 million. This hike in numbers can be attributed to warmer winters and the increase in filth around towns and cities; urban rats quickly cotton on to food sources including litter bins and discarded takeaways. Consider the rat's ability to give birth to six or more young as many as five times a year from the age of three or four months, and the potential growth of their population is alarming, to say the least.

Rats will eat virtually anything – including soap and plaster when they're desperate – and often make a real nuisance of themselves around the farmyard, where they can contaminate food and water supplies. Rat infestations need to be dealt with quickly in areas used to store food for human consumption.

Apart from the threat of disease, rats cause problems by munching into farmers' narrow profit margins. They also like to supplement their protein levels by predating on the eggs and chicks of wild birds and game birds. Ground-nesting birds such as pheasant and partridge are particularly vulnerable. During the colder months, rats often raid grain put out for pheasants, so are not at all popular with gamekeepers.

Closer to home, brown rats are often

encountered in the garden. Rotting vegetables on the compost heap and bread and seed put out for wild birds will attract the attention of rats and they will also steal from the vegetable patch. If you keep poultry, rats are inevitable because they can't resist the urge to scrounge an easy meal from the chicken feeders – they are also likely to steal eggs from nesting boxes. I always have a trap set in a small wooden tunnel on the outer edge of my chicken run. The trap is my first line of defence and I check it every morning. Catching a rat in the trap is my signal to investigate after dark with my air rifle at the ready, just in case there are others around.

Unless you are a professional pest controller tackling urban rats, most air-gunners are likely to encounter this vermin on the farm and in the garden; although food sources such as grain hoppers in pheasant coverts can also attract large colonies in woodland and hedgerows.

Around the farm, rats will nest virtually anywhere from hedge banks and ditches to hay barns, wall cavities and animal pens. They are attracted by easy pickings in the shape of food and grain stores, spilt animal feed and rotting silage.

Rats raid the farmyard in massive numbers in the winter. They are fairly timid, nocturnal creatures and tend to turn up *en masse* as the sun starts to go down. You can expect to encounter rats around the farm throughout the year but many tend to disperse into the surrounding countryside in the summer when natural food is abundant.

Brown rats are heavily built, have a grey/brown coat, a white belly and long scaly tail. They are big, distinctive rodents and are unlikely to be mistaken for protected black rats, which are smaller and uncommon. They are occasionally confused with the water vole (*Arvicola terrestris*), which is protected. Water

Rats can carry some very unpleasant diseases so never use your bare hands to clear up after a cull.

voles have smaller ears than rats and a very blunt head, whereas rats have long snouts.

The best time to control rats with an air rifle is at night when they are most active, and you are likely to encounter them if you stroll around with a lamp or night-vision scope. They can be surprisingly wary creatures and have an acute sense of smell and excellent hearing, so it's important to keep quiet when targeting them. Although roving tactics will help to reduce their numbers, a static approach can be a more effective way of getting past their natural defences.

Rats are incredibly tough, so head shots are the only way to kill them cleanly, and these shouldn't be too difficult to make at the close ranges over which rats are usually encountered. Rats might seem disgusting, but they are still entitled to the same respect as other living creatures and that means we have a duty to ensure a clean, humane kill at all times.

The threat of disease posed by brown rats can not be over-emphasised, so make sure you take proper precautions when culling them. Don't eat when on a ratting foray, don't touch dead rats with your bare hands, and wash your hands as soon as you can when the session is over.

Shooting brown rats

Rats provide some of the most exciting, and sometimes most hectic, shooting available to the air rifle hunter. Apart from being good sport, rat shooting is also a very useful service and many local farmers will appreciate your assistance in the control of this despised pest. The quiet operation and relatively low power of the air rifle make it the perfect tool for tackling vermin in the confined places where rats are usually encountered. On holdings where it is not practical for farmers to use poison or traps because of livestock, shooting is about the only option. And, because the anti-coagulant effect

of most poisons causes a slow and lingering death by internal bleeding, shooting with an air rifle is certainly one of the most humane solutions.

Most farms harbour a population of rats but some are more prone to infestation than others. Pig and poultry farms generally host rats throughout the year, whereas rats tend to congregate around dairy farms through the winter months when livestock is moved inside. On vegetable farms, storage areas are often frequented by rats, and the filth and warmth around compost heaps is also an attraction. One of my rat shoots is on a large market garden where the owner, who is reluctant to waste anything, has established several massive compost heaps to convert surplus or damaged vegetables into nutritious feed for his crops. These steaming heaps of rotting food are like a magnet to rats in the winter. Interestingly, and quite disgustingly, rats shot on this holding are frequently dragged away and devoured by their companions – their unvaried diet of vegetables obviously leaves them craving protein.

The very fabric of a farm can influence the likelihood of rat infestation. They certainly like old, tumbledown farms with lots of small,

Dark, slug-shaped droppings are a sure sign of rats.

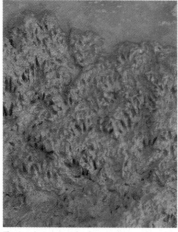

Footprints reveal a busy rat-run on the edge of a muddy puddle.

A well-used rat hole in the side of a festering compost heap.

Ambushing rabbits on the farm as the summer sun sinks beneath the hills.

A hunter's-eye view of a rabbit ambush.

The limited power of air
rifles is an asset when
controlling vermin
around farm buildings.

Rabbit *(Oryctolagus cuniculus)*

Grey squirrel *(Sciurus carolinensis)*

Brown rat *(Rattus norvegicus)*

Woodpigeon *(Columba palumbus)*

Collared dove *(Streptopelia decaocto)*

Carrion crow *(Corvus corone corone)*

Magpie *(Pica pica)*

Jay *(Garrulus glandarius)*

Rook *(Corvus frugilegus)*

Jackdaw *(Corvus monedula)*

The hunter weaves a hide into the hedgerow at the end of the day.

An understanding of the countryside will enable the hunter to predict the habits and whereabouts of quarry species in relation to their seasonal food sources.

There are few things more rewarding than turning the result of a successful day in the field into a tasty meal.

The hunters head for home
after an evening in the woods.

untidy buildings where nesting sites are abundant. Conversely, large modern farm buildings made from huge slabs of impenetrable concrete are less prone to intrusion by rats. Wherever you encounter rats, their numbers are likely to be highest from late autumn through to early spring. Many of these large rodents spend the warmer months in the countryside where natural food is abundant, and then swarm to the farmyard as pickings get lean towards the end of the year. It is during this time that big tallies of twenty or more rats can be made in a few hours. Rats don't like really cold weather, though, and are often reluctant to venture far from their nests on frosty nights.

Because they are nocturnal creatures, the best time to hunt rats is from dusk and into the night. However, farms are potentially dangerous places, packed with lethal hazards, so it's always wise to arrive during daylight so you can get your bearings and note important considerations such as livestock and machinery. As well as ensuring that your shooting doesn't pose any risk, it is also essential to ensure that you don't place yourself in any danger. Farmers are notoriously untidy folk, and leg-breaking hazards in the shape of discarded machinery, dumped feed sacks and goodness knows what else have a habit of cropping up where you least expect them – much better to locate objects like these in the day rather than stumbling across them in the dark.

I once had a very close call on a farm I had visited on many occasions. It was a wet night and my friend and I were having a walk around with our guns in the hope of spotting a rat or two. As I made my way towards one end of the yard, I slowly traipsed through what I thought was just a very large puddle. It was a puddle (at one end, anyway) but it disguised the edge of a submerged slurry pit, the first indication of it being the sensation of my feet disappearing from beneath me. Luckily, my mate was standing close by and managed to grab my shoulder and drag me away from what would have been a thoroughly unpleasant, and frighteningly dangerous, dunking in the 'fallout' from 200 dairy cows. That was a serious reminder of the importance of being familiar with your surroundings, and how easy it is to overlook hazards when your mind is on other things.

Arriving while the light is still good will also enable you to have a thorough look around for signs of rats. Unless you're dealing with a major infestation, it is unlikely that you will actually see any rats during daylight, but these animals leave several calling cards that will indicate places worth investigating after dark. Holes are an obvious sign of the presence of rats, and are often found around the edges of buildings, in silage heaps, amongst piles of bricks and rubble, beneath hay bales, storage crates and piles of pallets, and in the sides of earth banks close to farm buildings. Black, shiny, slug-shaped droppings between 2cm and 3cm in length also betray the presence of rats, as do signs of chewing around feed sacks, vegetables and even cables and woodwork. Rats prefer to travel along defined routes, and their runs between nesting sites and feeding zones are usually easy to spot. Look for smooth, compacted trails through the soil and flattened pathways through grass or animal bedding. After wet weather, rats' footprints can often be found in patches of soft mud and around the edges of puddles – areas of heavy footfall are certainly worth targeting.

Although it is possible to make good tallies of rats by walking around the farm and hunting them on the move, systematically and thoroughly targeting specific areas usually makes for more effective pest control – it's also a heck of a lot safer than wandering around. Some of

It might not smell too good in the kitchen but liquidised cat food is a terrific holding bait for rats.

The light from a scope-mounted lamp also comes in handy for reloading.

A scope-mounted lamp is a useful piece of kit for controlling rats after dark.

the best places to concentrate on are the runs you locate between nesting and feeding areas because these places are likely to guarantee a fair amount of ratty traffic throughout the evening. The problem is that rats are very fidgety creatures, and you'll be lucky to get reliable shots at them as they scuttle along their runs. Baiting is the solution.

A tempting bait laid along a rat run should hold your target still long enough for you to make a telling shot, but it has to be the right bait. Cat food is a real favourite; rats can't resist the appeal of this stinky, greasy meat – especially the really fishy flavours. However, it is no good just spooning chunks of cat food straight from the tin because greedy rats will just pick them up and run away. The way to make your bait stop rats in their tracks is to liquidise it. That way they have to stand still and lap it up – while you take your time to compose a nice, steady shot to the head.

Granted, using the family kitchen to prepare batches of cat-food slop for rat bait is not going to make you very popular with the rest of the household. I have a food processor dedicated to this task (because there was no way I was going to use it for food preparation once it had been filled with stinking cat food) and try to prepare my fishy soup in large batches when there's nobody else in the house. After blitzing a few cans into a pungent brown sludge, I separate it into sealed bags and freeze it, ready for action. Take a bag out to defrost a few hours before your ratting session and you'll have hassle-free bait at the ready.

If you aren't brave enough to prepare and use cat-food slop, there are alternatives, but I've yet to find one as good. Liquidised sweetcorn makes for a sweet, sugary meal that rats find hard to resist, and can be prepared and stored in exactly the same way as cat food – only without the stench. I've also had good results with chocolate spread, peanut butter and soft, smelly cheese; these baits just need to be smeared along the base of the wall or on hard ground along a rat run.

In terms of illumination and optics, there are several effective options for night-time ratting. Night-vision scopes are the high-tech, expensive choice and provide absolute stealth, allowing you to hide in total darkness and snipe unsuspecting rats as they emerge. Although I rarely use them, laser sights allow you to take a fast aim and are more suited to shooting rats on the move and at very close quarters. My favourite choice of optic and illumination for general rat shooting is a conventional telescopic sight mounted with a small lamp. As most rat shooting tends to take place at ranges of between ten and twenty metres, the average scope-mounted lamp will cast plenty of light for your needs. It will also provide useful illumination for tasks like reloading, but it's sensible to take a back-up light, too. Often, rats are encountered at such close ranges that the light cast from your lamp will be enough to unsettle them. Some lamps have a fader switch to adjust brightness, although most shooters clip a coloured filter to the lens to soften the light.

One great way to create an unobtrusive light source for rat shooting in a barn is to ask the farmer to leave the light on until a few hours after nightfall in the days leading up to your visit. If he's willing to assist, you can switch the light on for illumination – but remember the rats will be spooked if they aren't given a few days to become accustomed to the light.

Your typical ratting session will start with an observational mooch around the farm buildings. You decide on a spot that enables you to cover two busy runs in a large barn that contains numerous pig pens, then unfold your stool and place it in a shadowy corner that allows you to

Regular tallies like this will soon make an impression on a rat infestation.

cover the likely looking areas from about 15 metres. It's a rough night outside and your hiding place provides welcome shelter from the elements.

You slip on your gloves and take the bag of smelly slop and a spoon from your bag. Stroll over to the opposite wall, where you can see the holes the rats are using to creep in and out, and spoon a couple of good dollops of bait on the run. Keep your bait a little way from the holes so the rats have to crawl into full view and ensure that they're positioned right against the wall so shots strike harmlessly into the concrete backstop.

Back at your base, you tie up the bait bag and stow it safely away before slipping your airgun from its case. Clip on the lamp, plug in the wires and have a quick shine around to make sure everything is working as it should. Now, load up and make sure the safety catch is set.

All you can do now is sit back and hope the rats put in an appearance. The light is starting to fade and the wind is rattling the tin roof of the barn, but you're wrapped-up warm and it's surprisingly cosy inside with the sweet smell of straw filling your nostrils and the occasional contented grunt from the pigs at the other end of the building.

As the light starts to fade, you flick on the lamp, shoulder you gun and shine along the far wall to see if there's anything about. There isn't, so you switch off and sit tight. A moment later, you hear the squeal of bickering rats at the other end of the barn – they're on the move.

Because of the livestock, the far end of the building is out of bounds, but be patient because, judging by how well worn it is, not to mention the amount of droppings, the run in front of you is obviously a regular route. After a short wait, you switch your lamp back on and a big rat scurries away from one of the bait piles and disappears into a hole. Keep the light on and watch the hole through your scope because old ratty will probably be back now he's had a taste of the grub. Sure enough, you soon see the glow of his beady red eyes reflecting the filtered light back at you from just within the crevice. Don't shoot yet, though – wait until he's out in the open. Your patience pays off a few moments later when the scaly-tailed rat slips out of the hole and skulks along the edge of the wall towards the bait. It stops at the liquidised cat food and hunches down to stuff its face. Steady yourself, push off the safety catch and allow the crosshairs to settle just behind the greedy rat's eye. The pap from your air rifle is followed by the smack of the pellet walloping into the wall. You didn't miss; the shot passed right through the rat's skull and your quarry in now lying lifeless in a pool of red lamplight. Take your time and shoot carefully, and a good bag could be on the cards.

What to do with them

There's only one answer to the question of what to do with rats, and that's get rid of them as safely as possible.

Because of the disease threat, rats should never be touched with bare hands. I always take a tough pair of gloves and some pliers to pick them up by their tails as a last resort, but you can usually find a shovel on most farms. Ask the owner where you should dispose of the corpses – most farms have a fire site that serves the purpose well. It's also worth asking your host if there's anywhere you can clean yourself up at the end of the night. Some farms are filthy places and it's handy if you can use a hose and brush to get the worst of the muck off your wellies before you drive home. There may also be a sink where you can give your hands a scrub – I always carry a bottle of alcohol-based, antibacterial hand wash just to be on the safe side.

CHAPTER 8
More tips and tactics

Hide shooting

Successful air rifle hunting depends on the ability to get close to your quarry. Concealment is the key to going unnoticed, and hide building is a very effective means to achieve that end. The skilled hide builder will be able to create a discreet screen to keep himself out of sight wherever and whenever a hunting opportunity arises. Unlock the secrets of creating a really good hide and, apart from being able to get yourself a whole lot closer to your intended target, you'll probably witness some amazing spectacles of nature as wild creatures go about their daily business oblivious to your presence. A well-concealed hunter enjoys the privilege of seeing the natural world from a perspective very few people ever get to experience.

Types of hide

A hide can be literally anything that creates a screen to keep you hidden, from piles of branches and stacks of hay bales to tent-style shelters and scrim nets. Most have their uses, but some are far better than others.

Over recent years, the instant pop-up hide has established a popular following – more from clever marketing than from actual results in the field, I fear. These hides usually consist of a sheet of modern camouflage material stitched to an integral frame. They usually come packed neatly into a carrying bag, and pop up in seconds, courtesy of the sprung frame, as soon as you unpack them from their case. Such hides are very quickly assembled and usually provide a weather-proof shield as well as visual concealment. Be warned, though, some models can be absolute devils to pack away. Trying to compress the sprung frame back into the position it was packed in at the factory can be virtually impossible with some models. Packing away a test model I was once sent really was akin to wrestling a very large, and very stubborn, jack-

Shooting from a hide provides the hunter with ultimate concealment.

Pop-up hides are quick and convenient but they don't blend-in with the countryside like a net hide.

A pair of gloves and billhook are useful for clearing the hide site and cutting weeds to dress the net.

in-the-box. I couldn't fit it back in the car let alone back in the bag so it ended up on the farm's fire site with the rest of the rubbish.

Another problem with some tent-style hides is the fact that they have a very bold outline. Things in the natural world tend to have ragged outlines, so it can take a lot of natural cover to make such hides blend in. You're also stuck with whatever camouflage pattern they come printed with and, even if it's the best pattern in the world, it won't work if it's not in the right surroundings. To add to this gloomy list of gripes, the small windows that are usually cut into these hides also provide a very restricted field of view from which to observe and shoot your quarry.

In spite of my misgivings, I will concede that some pop-up hides are worth their price tag, as long as you are prepared to use one or two branches to help them blend in with the countryside. Better models are quite straightforward to assemble and pack away once you get the knack, and they can be useful for keeping out the wind and the rain when the weather is not ideal. Just remember to choose carefully before you part with your money.

My favourite type of hide is built from a camouflage net draped over either purpose-made hide poles or hung from a fence or bushes. Although net hides take a while to construct, you can adapt them to perfectly suit the job in hand. Hide netting is reasonably inexpensive and comes in numerous colours and sizes. My advice is to buy a fairly large sheet of netting. This will enable you to build a big hide if you need to, but it can also be folded in half and doubled up when you don't need so much.

Hide construction

One of the most important considerations when building a hide is its location. It needs to be situated in a discreet place within range of where you expect your quarry to present itself. There's nothing worse than a hide that stands out – in fact, you'd probably be better off with no hide at all. Wild creatures are as familiar with their territory as you or I are with our homes, and you'd soon notice if someone built a shelter in your lounge. The best way to create an unobtrusive hide that will escape the attention of wily wild creatures is to incorporate it into existing cover. I try to construct them against a tree or bush, or weave them into the hedgerow so the resulting screen is just a subtle extension of the existing countryside. What is behind your hide is also very important. I always ensure that I build mine in front of a backdrop that prevents light from shining through. Chinks of light passing through the hide will reveal your

silhouette whenever you move – even a slight movement like raising your gun to shoot – and this is likely to spook quarry. My favourite backdrop is a dense hedgerow, but if there isn't anything appropriate in the immediate vicinity then I'll drape a dark-coloured net behind my hide.

I keep a billhook and a pair of gloves with my hide-building kit. This enables me to clear the ground where I plan to sit without ripping my hands to pieces on brambles or stinging myself on nettles. The weeds that I cut back are kept to one side because they have a useful role to play later on.

With the site cleared, the next thing to do is position the poles to create a frame for the camouflage net. You can buy extendable hide poles from most good gun shops or you can make your own from straight hazel rods. If you use hazel sticks, all you need to do is push your knife into the top end and twist it to make a split in which the net can rest, then make a point on the end that goes in the ground – and please make sure you have permission from the landowner before you start hacking at hazel bushes. Sometimes it's possible to eliminate the need for poles by fixing your hide net to a fence or bush with a few twists of stiff wire.

Whatever means of support you opt for, the hide needs to be draped in a way that gives you enough space to sit and shoot comfortably. It can be quite miserable sitting in a cramped hide when there isn't much happening; ensure that you've got adequate headroom and space to stretch your legs and you'll last a lot longer before the fidgets set in. On the subject of comfort, a beanbag seat is about the best way to avoid the condition of 'numb bum', which is synonymous with hide shooting. It's also wise to take a drink and something to eat; sufficient provisions will keep your mind from drifting to the creature comforts of home when action is slow and there's a sneaky winter breeze cutting through the hide.

To keep you out of sight, the hide needs to create a screen around you and above you, and its important to remember to leave a 'door' where you can slip discreetly in and out. It is very annoying to go to all the trouble of building a hide only to realise that you can barely squirm into it. One extra touch that can really improve a hide is to use pegs (either tent pegs or sticks from nearby) to fix the net to the ground. Once tensioned with pegs, a hide net can't attract unwanted attention by flapping in the wind.

With the shell completed there's still one very

Set up in the right place, and thoroughly dressed with weeds, a hide like this provides a very discreet hiding place.

important job left to do – the hide needs to be dressed. Dressing a hide with vegetation is the best way to make it disappear into its surroundings. Secateurs make this job a lot easier, and remember not to cut anything apart from weed species; the landowner will be understandably disgruntled, or more likely, furious, if you hack at anything else. Typical weeds for hide dressing include nettles, brambles, docks, clematis, ivy, elder, burdock and thistles – anything apart from hardwood tree species, really. Gather a few armfuls and place them against the outside of the hide net until it just looks like another part of the countryside. Remember to place plants the right way up because wild things will shun your hide if anything looks amiss, and remember to leave one or two clear 'windows' to observe and shoot through. With the dressing finished, all that remains is to scatter the weeds you cleared from the ground at the outset around the base of the hide so it blends seamlessly with the surrounding environment.

Admittedly, building a hide from scratch sounds like a lot of hard work, but it isn't. It doesn't take long to get familiar enough with the procedure to throw one up in about 20 minutes. It doesn't take long to pack away either; whip off the weeds, unpeg the net, slip it off the poles and fold it away, and all that's left to do is pull up the poles. Spend another minute tidying after yourself and nobody will ever know you'd been there.

A variation of the standard net hide has saved my planned shooting trip on more than one wet weekend. By swapping the hide poles for a large fishing umbrella, you can create a waterproof support for your net. Such a brolly doesn't cost much and can come in very handy when the weather turns foul.

Of course, you don't need to spend money

Hides don't have to be bought from a shop – branches can be used to break up your outline.

A hide net draped over a cheap fishing umbrella will provide shelter and concealment on a rainy day.

on any equipment to build a good hide. Sometimes, when shooting in the woods, you need do little more than lean a few branches against a tree trunk, wigwam style, to create enough of a screen to break up your outline and enhance the effect of your camouflage clothing.

Branches can also be used to create a more substantial hide. On one or two of my woodland shoots, I have built screens from piles of fallen branches. These haphazard brash-wood dens help to keep me out of sight and have the added advantage of being taken for granted by local wildlife because they are always there. I usually add a few more windblown branches every time I visit them so they grow sturdier and more substantial as the seasons pass.

Hunting in company

The company of a friend brings an extra element of enjoyment to an outing in the field. A successful hunting trip brings with it a tremendous sense of achievement, and it's great to be able share the satisfaction with someone else.

Companionship can improve your shooting. Two brains are better than one and, with help from a friend, you should be able to think up even more ways to hone your technique and outwit your quarry. Best of all, if you're starting out in the world of shooting and are fortunate enough to be able to befriend an experienced hunter, you can expect your skills to improve rapidly as you learn from your mentor.

Nonetheless, it must be acknowledged that the presence of another shooter can also prove to be a disadvantage. Two people can't move with anything like the stealth of one, and few things strike more fear into the heart of a wild animal than the sound of human voices. Hand signals are one way to get around the problem of causing disturbance by talking. You don't

113

Companionship brings an extra element of enjoyment to days in the field.

need a sophisticated code, just a few simple gestures that you'll quickly learn to give and understand if you frequently shoot with the same companion. That said, there will be times when it's virtually impossible to keep quiet. A bit of quiet chatter can be very welcome when you're sharing a hide and there's nothing much happening, and it's very difficult to keep silent when somebody makes a particularly good shot, or misses an absolute sitter.

Of course, the presence of another person also brings an added safety concern. To mitigate this, you'll need to enforce a few simple guidelines, the same as when shooting in the garden.

The best way to shoot safe with a friend is to stay close so you both know each other's exact whereabouts at all times. A good approach when shooting in close proximity to a companion is to shoot back to back so you can cover a wide area while making shots in a safe direction. If, at any time, either of you intends to move – perhaps to collect shot quarry or to find a new hiding place – make your intentions clear to your companion before you leave your position.

Sometimes you might not be able to shoot close enough together to be able to see each other. In this situation, it's wise to make sure there is a considerable distance between you (a couple of hundred yards or more) to ensure that you stay safely out of each other's way. When shooting out of sight of your companion, it's a good precaution to make sure you both have mobile phones. This will enable you to keep in contact and notify each other of your exact whereabouts and proximity.

When hunting on the move with a companion, it's best to walk side by side. This is obviously going to make you rather more conspicuous if you're stalking but it's certainly preferable to having someone walking in front of a gun.

I do most of my hunting on my own. These solo trips are usually the most productive but the days spent in the company of a good friend are by far the most enjoyable.

Garden pest control

From time to time, some of the vermin species on the quarry list make a nuisance of themselves around the garden. The modest power and quiet operation of air rifles make them ideal for pest control in these circumstances.

The aspects of law, safety and consideration previously described in relation to shooting targets in the garden still apply. Ultimately, it is your responsibility to ensure that the dimensions of the garden you are shooting in, and the way you conduct yourself while doing so, are conducive to safe pest control.

Rats are a common garden pest, usually attracted by the rotting contents of compost bins, by the rich pickings to be found inside the poultry run or by spilt feed from guinea pig and rabbits hutches. Often it can be unsafe to deploy a trap or poison in the garden environment, so shooting is one of the few available options for controlling rats.

When culling rats around the garden, the first thing to establish is a safe backstop to catch your pellets. If you're lucky, the rats will be patrolling along a wall that will do the job;

otherwise, you can use the large paving slab you place behind your paper targets. A handful of chicken-feed or birdseed should have sufficient appeal to draw and hold intruding rats in front of the backstop while you take aim.

Few gardens escape visits from scavenging grey squirrels. These cunning little rodents are expert at emptying and devouring the contents of bird feeders – even most of the squirrel-proof ones. As well as stealing their food, grey squirrels also like to eat the eggs and young of garden birds and can soon make quite an impact on their numbers. A fistful of peanuts placed in front of a decent backstop is an effective way to bring troublesome squirrels to book.

Rabbits can make a real nuisance of themselves in the garden by nibbling down vegetables and scraping holes in the lawn. Their nocturnal habits mean that dusk and dawn vigils are likely to be most effective. Luring rabbits to exactly where you want to shoot them is virtually impossible, so the best option is to work out where they are likely to emerge and position yourself in a spot that ensures your shots are heading towards a safe backstop. Sloping banks can be utilised to catch stray pellets when shots are taken at a downward angle.

From time to time, avian pests cause problems in the garden. It might be crows or magpies stealing eggs, or pigeons hammering the vegetable patch. Whatever flying vermin you find yourself controlling in the garden, never be tempted to take shots up into trees because the chance of a shot straying beyond your boundary is just too great to risk.

I treat avian vermin in much the same way as rabbits; it's difficult to persuade them to land exactly where you want them to, so the best option is to get yourself in a position that ensures safe shots. Wait until avian pests land on the ground before you take a shot and, as with rabbits, make sure it's at a downward angle. In a large garden, baiting and decoying tactics can be employed to encourage pigeons, crows or magpies to land within range of the gun.

Many of the tactics described in the chapters dedicated to controlling specific quarry species can be applied in the garden. Refer to them for in-depth information.

Air rifles are excellent tools for garden pest control as long as you take proper precautions.

CHAPTER 9

FAC-rated air rifles

Air rifles described as FAC-rated produce power levels beyond the 12ft.lb unlicensed legal limit and can only be acquired by persons in possession of a firearms certificate, which is issued by your local police force.

At some point or other, many people who hunt with air rifles will consider a move to a high-powered firearms-rated air rifle, often because they become seduced by the notion of a gun with more power and increased hunting range. Admittedly, the effective range of a conventional air rifle is limited, and FAC power can increase hunting distances, but don't expect the extra grunt to enable you to cut corners in terms of field craft. Even high-powered air rifles are relatively feeble guns compared with live-ammunition weapons, so you need all the same skills to hunt effectively with them. I regard FAC-rated airguns as useful tools in the hands of highly experienced air rifle hunters but, without the skills acquired through years of

triumphs and tribulations with a legal-limit airgun, it's not going to be worth the hassle or expense of obtaining one.

On the subject of power, I would urge anyone starting out in the hobby of air-rifle hunting not to get too fixated on it. Some people get obsessed with trying to squeeze every last ounce of power out of their guns, and their efforts are almost always counter-productive. An air rifle producing something around 11ft.lb muzzle energy is all the gun most hunters will ever need. Airguns generally perform at their best around these power levels, and I know many experienced shooters who have actually tuned their guns down to around 10ft.lb to make them shoot smoother and more accurately. After all, accuracy is the key to success with any air rifle.

I had been hunting with airguns for more than 20 years before I decided to get my first FAC air rifle. One of the things I enjoy most about

117

FAC-rated air rifles are well suited to long-range hunting from a bipod.

hunting with airguns is the pure simplicity of the sport; ammo is cheap, propulsion is free (if you use a springer or stirrup pump) and their use is less restricted than that of high-powered firearms. What's more, I get a buzz from the challenge of getting close to my quarry, and find the thrill of using field craft to hunt at close range as satisfying as making a good long-range shot. For these reasons, I was reluctant to get caught up in the technical and bureaucratic complications of more powerful guns. Nonetheless, I acquired my firearms certificate several years ago and, in that time, have come to realise the advantages and disadvantages of high-powered airguns.

Applying for a firearms certificate

The application process can be a long-winded affair, and this alone is enough to discourage some people. My ticket was eventually granted more than three months after I sent off the completed paperwork.

An FAC application form can be obtained by telephoning the firearms licensing department of your local constabulary or downloading it from their website. It is a fairly involved piece of paperwork, but that is to be expected as it is used for the licensing of weapons far more powerful than FAC air rifles.

The form requires the usual details such as your name, address, occupation and contact information, but there's more to it than that. The police need to know whether you have any criminal convictions, and also require details of medical history, alcohol or drug-related conditions, and whether you have ever received treatment for depression or any other kind of mental or nervous disorder. Checks will be made with your GP.

The form then moves on to the nub of the application: which gun you want and why you want it. As well as explaining the sort of gun you intend to acquire, you must provide the police with a 'good reason' for needing it. You must also to tell the police where you have permission to use the gun and provide contact details for the landowner. Checks will be conducted to ensure that the ground is suitable for the use of a high-powered weapon. The form also asks how much ammunition you plan to purchase and store; this question really refers to live-round ammunition used in rim-fire and centre-fire rifles, and not to airgun pellets.

Gun storage is also a very important issue that needs to be detailed for police approval. The form states that firearms should be stored out of sight and under lock and key. Most police authorities prefer British Standard gun safes made of at least 2mm steel and with a minimum of two five-lever locks. The cabinet should be kept hidden from casual visitors – generally in an upstairs room – and bolted to the fabric of your home.

Gun safes are pretty hefty pieces of kit – I had a real job getting mine up the stairs on my own – and fitting them to the fabric (brickwork) or your home is quite an undertaking. They have to be fixed securely to a structural wall (a partition wall is not acceptable) and to the floor, with special bolts that have expanding metal collars to lock them to masonry.

Returning to the application form, you need to provide the names and addresses of two people who are prepared to act as referees. These must be people you have known for at least two years and 'of good character'. Your referees can not be members of your immediate family, registered firearms dealers, serving police officers or police employees.

Each of your referees will have to fill in a reference form stating how they know you and for how long. Although they are not expected to guarantee your future good behaviour, your referees have to give their opinion of your suitability to own a firearm. They also have to comment on your personal history, domestic circumstances and what they know of your experience of and attitude towards guns. Your referees each need to sign a passport photograph of you and send it and the form direct to your local firearms licensing department. They should expect to be contacted by the police when the form is received.

Your application form wraps up with the usual declaration. When completed, it should be sent to the firearms licensing department along with a further two signed passport photographs of yourself and (at the time of writing) a cheque for £50. Before a decision is made on your application, you will be visited at home by a firearms officer. During this visit, expect details of your application, including that 'good reason' to be further discussed. The officer will also want to see where the gun is to be stored. If you are successful in your application, the certificate has to be renewed after five years. I found my local police firearms team very helpful, and willing to answer all the queries I had throughout the application process, but I would warn any would-be applicants to expect a lengthy wait for your ticket.

When you receive your firearms certificate, you are authorised to purchase whatever type of gun it stipulates. Details of any FAC gun you acquire or sell (either to the holder of a certificate with appropriate provision or a registered firearms dealer) must be promptly sent to the Firearms Licensing Department.

The easiest way to acquire an FAC air rifle is to buy a factory-made gun that has been built to FAC specification. Alternatively, some 12ft.lb airguns can be upgraded to FAC power either by the manufacturer or a certified gunsmith.

Never be tempted to attempt a DIY power upgrade on your legal-limit air rifle – it's illegal and it's potentially very dangerous. Most airguns are fitted with anti-tamper devices to prevent inexperienced hands from messing with their internals. Tinkering will void the manufacturer's warranty and could damage your gun or make it dangerous to use. Furthermore, it is likely that the gun will need specialist components to cope with the extra power – so leave power upgrades to the experts.

FAC airgun performance

In terms of performance, I noticed quite a few changes when I first used an FAC-rated air rifle – some good, some bad.

High-powered air rifles can produce anything up to 80ft.lb muzzle energy and beyond. Most hunters opt for one in .22 calibre turning out around 30ft.lb. Even at the low end of the FAC air scale, the gun's components will have significantly more work to do and this can manifest itself as a loss of smoothness and refinement in the cocking and firing cycle.

As well as being a little harder to cock and having a slightly heavier trigger, there is also a more distinct muzzle flip compared with a non-FAC air rifle. The additional kick is the result of the extra air needed to thrust the pellet to higher velocities – all that puff has to go somewhere – and this can impede accurate shooting. The increased blast of air also results in a louder muzzle crack, and you'll need a decent silencer to hush it down. You will also find that an air firearm will guzzle air very quickly compared with its 12ft.lb counterpart. This means a lot more refilling, and I would strongly recommend buying a large diving bottle (yet more expense, I'm afraid) rather than struggling with a hand pump.

If your budget can stretch to it, air rifles with an electronic firing cycle completely overcome the issues with cocking and trigger mechanisms, as these remain silky smooth at any power level. The added efficiency of the electronic system also improves the number of shots per fill and reduces muzzle flip considerably.

One of the biggest problems I encountered when I first took an FAC-rated air rifle on the range was finding a pellet that could handle the extra power. Most air rifles perform better with a particular brand of ammunition, but high-powered airguns can be incredibly pellet-fussy.

A lot of hunters opt for the added knock-down power of a heavy .22 pellet of around 20 grains or more. I tried this route but found the loopy trajectory affected down-range accuracy to the point that the benefits of the extra power were more or less lost. I eventually settled on a 16-grain pellet but expect this would be too light for an air rifle producing anything over 30ft.lb.

In the field, the benefits of the additional power quickly became apparent. My 30ft.lb air rifle is still turning out more power at 70 metres than the 12ft.lb version is at the muzzle, so the increased hitting power is obvious. When hunting with legal-limit air rifles, I usually opt for .177 calibre because of its fast, flat trajectory but I've been very impressed with the performance of the FAC gun in the bigger, heavier, harder-hitting .22 calibre.

The extra clout results in a bigger kill area. When hunting at 12ft.lb, I almost always take live quarry with head shots. At 30ft.lb, this is still the case with rabbits, but a direct hit to the upper body will cleanly despatch crows and pigeons.

As a basic comparison, I regard around 40 metres as the maximum hunting range for a legal-limit air rifle in experienced hands and in the right conditions. At 30ft.lb, there is still plenty of stopping power at 70 metres if you and your combo have the accuracy to exploit this. Realistically, though, I don't take many shots beyond 50 metres with my high-powered airgun, so the increase in effective hunting range is not vast. Accuracy is paramount and, for this reason, one of my favourite assignments for FAC-rated air rifles is ambushing rabbits off a bipod.

Of course, there are additional safety considerations to be addressed when shooting FAC airguns. The increased power means the shot will carry further, so it is vital to ensure that there is a suitable backstop behind whatever you are shooting at before you pull the trigger. When using my FAC air rifle, I generally limit myself to downward shots, or shots where a rising slope will ensure that the pellet's flight path is brought to an abrupt halt when targeting ground game. When shooting into trees – around roosts, for example – I am very strict about sticking to shots that will travel safely upwards at a reasonably steep angle away from where anyone is likely to be rather than rattling through the woods. When a steep shot runs out of steam, the pellet will tumble back down to the ground with little more clout than a falling acorn. If your shooting involves pest control around farmyards, the increased risk of damage or injury to buildings, machinery, livestock and even people means an FAC-rated airgun is certainly not for you.

FAC-rated air rifles undoubtedly have their uses. They provide a useful bridge in the gap between conventional air rifles and rim-fire rifles, but I would undoubtedly opt for the versatility of legal-limit power if I could only have one airgun.

My advice to anyone considering the purchase of a high-powered air rifle would be to start at sub-12ft.lb and properly learn the skills of stealth and accurate shooting. This will stand you in good stead should you then decide to move on to higher power.

CHAPTER 10
From field to plate

Making the most of what I shoot means a great deal to me, and it's hard to think of a better way to utilise something than turning it into a tasty, nutritious meal.

I get as much satisfaction from harvesting my own meat as I do from growing my own vegetables. There is something very heart-warming about overseeing, and taking responsibility for, the way our food is produced – something that brings us close to nature and reinforces our connection with the countryside.

One of the most fulfilling things about hunting with an air rifle is knowing that the meat you eat comes from an animal that lived as nature intended, running wild, feeding on a natural chemical-free diet until its life was ended swiftly and humanely. People regard pheasant as being some of the wildest meat available, and it is, but rabbit and pigeon is wilder still. Pheasants tend to be bred for shooting (wild stocks would never meet the demand for driven shooting) and

this usually means a life that begins in the incubator before moving on to the sort of conditions usually associated with farmed chicken. When they are old enough and big enough, pheasants are then moved into the woods, firstly to live in the confinement of release pens, and then finally given full freedom to roam. Even when enjoying life in the woods, and a fine life it is too, most pheasants still rely on grain from feed hoppers for a large part of their diet.

Compared with the existence of many animals that are reared for food, nobody can claim that the pheasant doesn't enjoy a life of wonderful freedom, but I would argue that the air rifle hunter's quarry lives better still. Rabbits and pigeons breed and live with virtually no human intervention; they are not farmed, their existence is a completely wild one.

The fine quality of life enjoyed by rabbits and pigeons is apparent in the flavour of the meat.

The taste is often described as gamey – a product of their rich, natural diet.

Woodpigeon meat tastes, and looks, gamier than rabbit. These birds have a very mixed diet comprising not only grain but also things like acorns, beech mast, kale, clover and ivy berries, depending on the season. It should come as no surprise that a diet of such strongly flavoured food gives the dark meat of the pigeon quite a distinctively gamey taste – gamier than pheasant, I would argue.

Rabbit, on the other hand, is subtler in flavour – more like chicken, in fact. The rabbit's diet of mostly grass is far less varied than that of the pigeon, and features nothing anywhere near as bitter as ivy berries. Its meat, therefore, is nothing like as strong tasting as pigeon.

The wild lifestyle of rabbits and pigeons also influences the texture of their meat. Unlike the sedentary existence of cooped-up farm animals, our quarry species use up energy foraging for food and escaping from predators. Consequently, they use their muscles a lot more, so the meat is comparatively dense and has very little fat. This is particularly true of the pigeon's breast meat, which comes from the muscle that powers its wings during miles and miles of flight each day. Such meat can be more than a little tough if not cooked in the correct way. Similarly, older rabbits tend to get tough and stringy. They're perfectly good for the table as long as you cook them slowly, but the best bunnies for the pot – the tastiest and tenderest – are always the ones that are about three-quarters grown, the kind that are abundant from mid summer through to late autumn.

So, rabbits and pigeons, two of the air rifle hunter's main quarry species, are raised to the highest welfare standards. Furthermore, their meat is lean, tasty and easy to prepare for the table. And, just in case you needed anymore encouragement to go out and harvest some for the pot, don't forget that it is also free.

I'm no chef and I confess that my talents in the kitchen are limited. Compared with many, my butchery skills are a little ham-fisted and my approach to cooking is far from elegant. But that doesn't stop me from making some delicious meals with meat harvested on hunting trips with my air rifle, and if I can do it, anyone can. The following recipes are simple, wholesome, affordable, adaptable and, above all, tasty. They have been begged, stolen and borrowed from family, friends and cookbooks. I've adapted them over the years with input from my wife and children – I regard children as the most honest of food critics, because if they don't like something they spit it out.

Hanging

Odd as it may sound, game needn't taste as gamey as most people assume it will.

Although it can't be denied that the diet and lifestyle of wild animals contributes to the added flavour of their meat, much of the gaminess commonly associated with game is a result of people slavishly following the tradition of hanging meat.

Personally, I don't subscribe to the theory that hanging improves the flavour or texture of pigeon or rabbit meat at all. True, it does 'develop' the flavour to a degree, but I'm not convinced that it's for the better.

If I can, I prepare quarry for the table the same day that I shoot it. Admittedly, a busy life sometimes makes this impractical – sheer tiredness often does, too – so I do sometimes leave it until the following morning.

For those of you who wish to experiment with hanging meat, I would recommend about four days as an absolute maximum in cool weather and just one or two when it's warmer.

Rabbits should be paunched before hanging to prevent the stomach contents from tainting the meat; pigeons can be left as they are. Your shot quarry should be hung in a cool, dry, well-ventilated place – a stone outbuilding or cellar is ideal, although the porch or garage are just as suitable.

Game preparation and recipes

RABBITS

Paunching

The first job to do when you shoot a rabbit is to empty its bladder immediately so the urine doesn't have time to taint the meat. Holding the rabbit head-up with its body dangling, all you do is slide your other hand down the bunny's belly and apply gentle pressure in a downward stroke to squirt out its 'dirty water'.

Removing the guts from rabbits (a task known as paunching) is also far better done in the field, where the remnants will be polished-off by foxes, badgers and crows. It does away with some of the hassles of waste disposal and I personally find it preferable to stick my hand inside a warm rabbit than a cold one!

I usually paunch the entire session's tally at the end of the outing so I don't have to spend my time in the field with rabbity hands. To begin, I lay a rabbit on its back and pinch up the loose flesh where the belly starts, just below the ribcage, and make a small incision cross-ways. Keeping the skin raised, I then slide the blade of my knife inside the slit at a shallow angle, so as not to puncture the intestines, and make a cut down towards the vent to expose the guts.

Next, I lift the rabbit in my left hand so that it's dangling and give it a bit of a jolt to help the guts on their way out. Then I push two or three fingers of my right hand up into the slit, right up behind the ribcage, and draw all of the innards down and out. And that's it, the rabbit is paunched.

Some hunters have perfected the knack of swinging a rabbit to literally flick the innards out of the slit made down the belly. My first attempt at hands-free paunching was a partial success – some of the guts came out, but I also got something thoroughly unpleasant splattered across my face. I didn't try it again.

Skinning

Although a sharp knife (a small and manoeuvrable one, and preferably not the one you use to cut foliage for your hide) is all you really need to prepare meat for the table, a robust chopping board, a cleaver and a pair of kitchen scissors are very useful tools to have at hand.

Assuming the rabbit is already paunched, take a cleaver, chop off the hind and front legs around the knee joint (there's barely any meat beneath there) and remove the head. If you don't have a cleaver, snap the legs at the joints to break the bone, then slice them off with a sharp knife (figure 1) – you can leave the head for now.

Now, peel the skin away from the meat at the belly and push your fingers around towards the back (figure 2) until you can reach right through around the rabbit's waist – at this stage the skin will still be connected at the front and back, forming a sort of handle in the middle. Push the hind legs up through the skin while pulling back at the 'handle' to pare the flesh and coat apart. Keep going until the rear section of the skin is removed. Once you've popped the back half of the rabbit out of its fur coat, grip just in front of the hind legs with one hand and pull off the rest of the skin in one swift, forward stroke with your

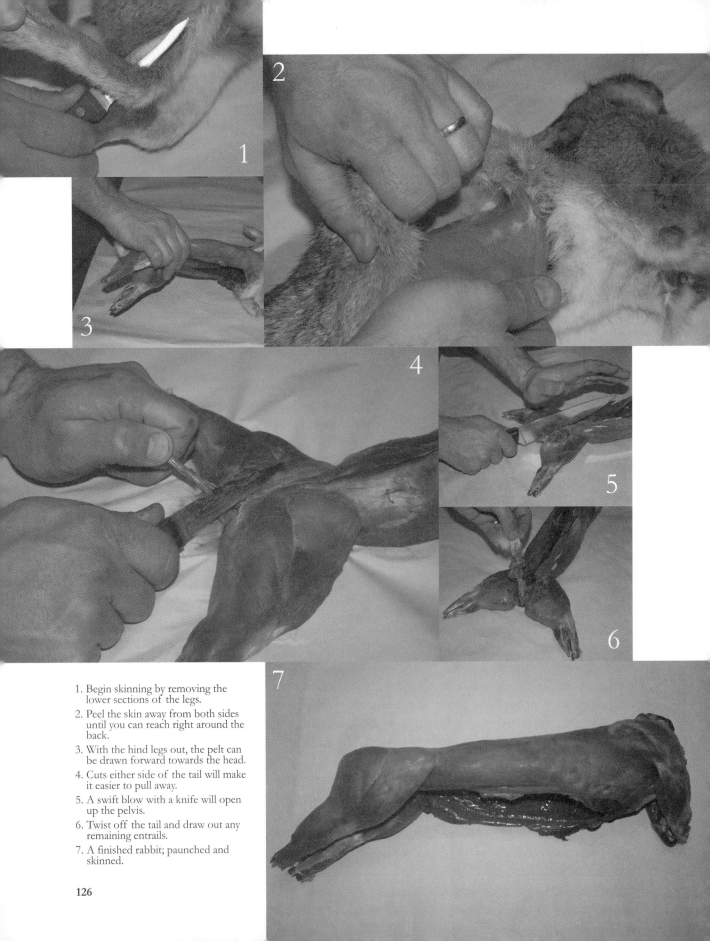

1. Begin skinning by removing the lower sections of the legs.
2. Peel the skin away from both sides until you can reach right around the back.
3. With the hind legs out, the pelt can be drawn forward towards the head.
4. Cuts either side of the tail will make it easier to pull away.
5. A swift blow with a knife will open up the pelvis.
6. Twist off the tail and draw out any remaining entrails.
7. A finished rabbit; paunched and skinned.

126

other hand (figure 3). If you removed the head with a cleaver, the whole skin will come right away. However, if you left the head on, pull the skin until it reaches the top of the neck, then lay the rabbit back on the board and cut off its head with your knife – it's much easier to slice through the neck with the fur out of the way. Next, make cuts either side of the tail (figure 4) – it will twist away along with the remnants of the intestine in a moment.

Place the skinned rabbit on its back with its feet towards you and extend the original belly slit right down to the end of the pelvis. Push the hind legs apart, then place the blade of your knife along the pelvis so the point is facing the front end of the rabbit. Now slam the base of your hand down onto the back of the knife (figure 5). The stiff blow will enable you to open the tract around the vent and remove any remains of the genitals, anus and intestines – often along with a few droppings – as you twist out the tail (figure 6). Rinse your rabbit under a cold tap and the job is done (figure 7).

Jointing and boning

Many rabbit recipes don't necessitate jointing; you just cook it whole and then flake off the meat, but it's useful to be able to butcher them down. For pan frying and casseroles, you don't need to do anything more than joint-up the legs and saddle, but I'll also explain how to remove the sinew to leave only the finest meat.

Begin by removing the hind legs. There's a distinct line around the joint between the hip and the thigh. Cut all the way around, then hold the rabbit chest-up with one hand and fold the leg right back with the other to break the joint. You will now be able to cut the rest of the way through to remove the thigh. To shallow fry, I would now chop the remaining saddle into two sections and leave it at that.

If you wish to remove the front legs, you'll be relieved to learn that they're not attached to the bone like the hind ones. You should be able to fold them back and cut straight through with a forward stroke from the ribs.

You are now left with the saddle. To remove the best of the meat, place the rabbit back-up and make a cut parallel to the spine from the shoulders to the hip joint. Make a downward cut at the end to release the flap of meat that can be easily pulled from the carcass.

The saddle you have prepared contains white sinew that can turn tough with cooking. Fortunately, it can easily be removed. Place the meat sinew-down on a board and run the knife along the underside to slice it away as if you were skinning a fillet of fish.

The hind legs (thighs) can be boned without much fuss. With the thick part of the thigh facing towards you, cut down into the meat either side of the thighbone – it is very easy to feel through the meat. Having exposed the bone,

Jointed rabbit meat ready for the table.

127

lift it away with your finger and thumb and slide the knife underneath to cut it clear. Pull the bone upwards and cut downwards to remove the meat. The remaining thigh meat has a seam of sinew that can be sliced away in the same manner as with the saddle.

When just using the best meat from the thighs and saddle, put the carcass and front legs to good use by boiling them down to make a wonderful stock.

Soaking

Whether using rabbit whole, jointed or boned, I like to soak it overnight in a homemade solution that I guess could be described as a brine. This soaking draws-off impurities, removing any bitterness the meat might have and also helping to make it tender. It doesn't do pigeon meat any harm, either.

All I do is place the meat in a large pan and cover it with cold water, then add a few good pinches of salt and a slosh of white wine vinegar. I'm not strict with the measurements for this, but I reckon a tablespoon of vinegar and a teaspoon of salt is about right for one litre of water.

After soaking, I rinse with cold water and the meat is ready for cooking or freezing.

Slow cooking

My favourite way to prepare rabbit meat for the table is in a slow cooker. This does away with all the fuss of jointing and boning, and results in wonderful, tender, flaky meat with minimal wastage. All you do is paunch, skin, soak and rinse your rabbit then slow-cook it whole – I can actually fit three in one of my slow cookers, which is very useful.

All I do is place the rabbit or rabbits into the slow cooker and add a pint or so of water and a pinch of salt. The flavour of the meat can be infused with subtle flavours by adding herbs, stock cubes, wine, cider or whatever you fancy.

When the rabbit is cooked through, all the meat literally falls off the bone so nothing goes to waste. This takes about three hours cooking time but I often put the slow cooker on a very low heat in the morning and leave the whole lot simmering away until I get home from work – the smell that greets me on my return is absolutely gorgeous. The meat can then be used in all sorts of recipes, or just served up with potatoes and vegetables. You can achieve the same result by placing your rabbit in a large pan, covering with water and simmering gently for two or three hours but you can't beat the convenience of a slow cooker.

RECIPES FOR RABBIT

Cidered rabbit parcels

To serve two

Ingredients

1 rabbit (skinned and ready
for the table)

3 thick rashers of smoky
bacon

6 sage leaves

A generous knob of butter

1 bottle of farmhouse cider
(just one glass for
the recipe)

Clarissa Dickson-Wright passed this recipe on to me a few years ago. I was interviewing her for a newspaper feature and couldn't help but ask for a suggestion for a simple recipe.

As the author of the shooter's kitchen bible, *The Game Cookbook*, Clarissa knows a thing or two about turning rabbits into a tasty meal. Here is what she suggested.

Cut the main fillets of meat away from the rabbit with a sharp knife – expect to get five or six pieces from a full-grown one, and don't worry about being too tidy. Wrap the chunks of meat in cling film, place on the worktop and use a rolling pin to beat them flat. Remove the cling film and spread the pummelled fillets flat on a large plate.

Place one sage leaf and half a rasher of bacon on each fillet, then fold in half and pin each one closed with a cocktail stick to make them into little parcels.

Next, melt a knob of butter in a frying pan, add the rabbit parcels and cook them gently until they are just starting to brown. Now pour in a good slosh of farmhouse cider – one large wineglass should be plenty. Allow to simmer for five minutes so the cider steams through the rabbit parcels, infusing them with flavour.

The freshness of the cider and sage makes this a great summer dish served with new potatoes and peas.

Don't waste the remainder of the rabbit carcass after removing the best chunks of meat. Cook it down in the slow cooker to make a rich stock.

Rabbit casserole

To serve four

Ingredients

2 rabbits (jointed but not
    boned)

1 onion (sliced)

2 leeks (sliced)

4 carrots (sliced)

1 stick of celery (chopped)

2 tablespoons wholegrain
    mustard

2 garlic cloves (crushed)

2 tablespoons of flour

2 chicken stock cubes

2 bay leaves

Olive oil

Half pint of farmhouse cider

3 tablespoons crème fraiche

Knob of butter

Salt and pepper

This is a really hearty rabbit dish that's great at any time of year.

Admittedly, this recipe needs more ingredients than most but it's still far from complicated. And you'll be glad that you went to the trouble when you catch a waft of the aroma when you lift the lid off the casserole.

This recipe will easily serve four, and can be stretched even further depending on what you serve it with.

Season half the flour with salt and pepper, then roll the rabbit joints until lightly coated. Heat the butter and oil in a wok or large pan and fry the joints until browned. Remove the rabbit, reduce the heat, add the onion and leek, and cook until they begin to turn soft. Add the crushed garlic gloves, the carrots, celery and remaining flour, and keep stirring while cooking for another couple of minutes.

Place the rabbit joints into a casserole dish and pour the contents of the wok over the top. Dissolve the stock cubes in half a pint of boiling water, add the cider and mustard and pour over the top of the casserole. Add the bay leaves, cover the casserole and cook in a preheated oven at 180°C for 90 minutes.

Remove and discard the bay leaves. Transfer the rabbit and vegetables to a serving dish. Add the crème fraiche to the cooking juices and warm through on the hob while stirring. Pour the sauce over the rabbit and veg, and it's ready to serve.

Serve with mashed potato for a really filling meal or just with a chunk of crusty bread to mop up the mouth-watering sauce.

Warrener's Pie

To serve four

Ingredients

For the filling:

2 rabbits (skinned and ready
 for the table)

4 rashers of bacon

Vegetable oil (one tablespoon)

1 large onion (finely chopped)

8oz mushrooms (chopped)

1 bottle of red wine (just one
 glass for the recipe)

2 Oxo cubes

Salt and Pepper

For the topping:

2lb potatoes (peeled and
 chopped)

¼ of a pint of milk

A generous knob of butter

This recipe is a rabbity twist on a traditional shepherd's pie. It makes for a wholesome meal that's ideal for a family dinner or a hearty supper after an evening's hunting.

Like burgers, it's a great dish to serve to newcomers to countryside fare because the minced meat is not obviously recognisable as game.

As an alternative dish for children, try swapping the red wine for a can of baked beans and add a dash of Worcester sauce for some tang. Whatever variation I opt for, I often double the ingredients and make an extra pie to put in the freezer for another day.

As with the rabbit parcels, the remainder of the rabbit can go in the slow cooker to create a flavoursome stock.

Cut the main fillets of meat away from the rabbits. Trim the rind from the bacon and pass through a mincer along with the pieces of rabbit.

Place the peeled and chopped potatoes in a pan of boiling water. Leave the potatoes to boil and heat the vegetable oil in a wok. When the oil is hot, add the chopped onion and fry for a few minutes until it begins to soften. Next, add the mushrooms and minced meat to the wok. Keep turning the ingredients in the wok until the meat begins to brown – this should take about five minutes. Pour in one glass of wine, crumble the Oxo cubes over the top and stir the mixture occasionally while letting it simmer for a further 15 minutes.

When the potatoes become fluffy (after about 25 minutes of boiling), drain off the water, add the milk and butter, then mash and season to taste.

The mince should now have reduced to a thick consistency. Season with salt and pepper and pour it into a baking dish. Spoon the mashed potato evenly and smoothly over the top, then cook in the oven at 200°C for 15 minutes or until the potato topping turns crisp and brown.

Serve with peas and carrots, or whatever seasonal veg you fancy.

Rabbit puff pastry pie

To serve four

Ingredients

2 rabbits (remove the best
    meat, as previously
    described)

1 packet of ready-to-roll puff
    pastry

1 large onion (chopped)

1 medium swede (diced)

2 large carrots (diced)

1 tin of peas

2 tablespoons of gravy
    granules

1 tablespoon of vegetable oil

Handful of flour

1 egg

1 knob of butter

Salt and pepper

This is a mouth-watering variation on a rabbit pie, and the texture of the crispy, fluffy pastry combines wonderfully with the rich, stodgy filling. This recipe works with frozen or even fresh peas, but there's something about the consistency of tinned peas that helps create the soft texture of a traditional pie.

Don't be tempted to trim off the excess pastry after pinching it closed. Just pinch the whole lot in and it will rise into a wonderful crusty shell – even if it does look a bit rustic.

Dice the carrots and swede and place in a pan of boiling water to simmer. Meanwhile, heat the oil in a wok or large frying pan and fry the onion until soft. Cut the rabbit into one-inch chunks, add to the pan and cook through – this takes approximately five minutes.

Drain the softened carrot and swede (which should have been cooking for about ten minutes) and keep back about a quarter of a pint of the water. Add the drained carrot and swede to the rabbit and onion in the wok, sprinkle the gravy granules over the top and gradually add the vegetable water while stirring until the mixture reaches a thick consistency. Drain the peas, stir them into the pie filling and remove from heat.

Dust the work surface with flour and roll-out the entire pack of puff pastry until it's about 5mm thick. Grease the inside of a baking tray with the butter and place the rolled pastry over the tray. Spoon the pie filling into the middle of the pastry, then draw -up the sides and pinch them together in the middle to form a large pasty. Brush with beaten egg and cook in a preheated oven at 200°C for twenty minutes, or until the pastry turns golden brown.

Serve with mashed potato or chips with shredded cabbage and brown sauce.

Rabbit stew

To serve four

Ingredients

Meat from 2 slow-cooked
    rabbits (flaked)

1 large onion (chopped)

1 swede (cut into chunks)

2 large carrots (diced)

2 celery sticks (diced)

1 large cooking apple (peeled,
    cored and cubed)

Frozen peas

1 pint of stock

Curry powder

Knob of butter

Salt and pepper

Most people regard stew as the classic rabbit recipe, but they also regard it as a meal that takes an absolute age to cook. By preparing the rabbit in a slow cooker before you get started, the cooking time is reduced and the meat is even more tender. Just put the rabbit in the cooker in the morning so it's ready to go when you return from work. I use the juices from the slow-cooked rabbit to make a stock, but you can use chicken stock cubes and water if you prefer.

Melt the butter in a large pan, add the onion and fry until soft. Add the stock, swede, carrots, celery, cooking apple and one heaped tablespoon of curry powder. Stir and bring to the boil. Reduce heat to a gentle simmer. Cover and cook for 45 minutes, stirring occasionally.

Add the flaked rabbit and four fistfuls of frozen peas to the softened vegetables. Season and add more curry powder according to taste. Cook for another five minutes, or until piping hot, stirring occasionally, then serve.

This spicy rabbit stew is great served with crispy roast potatoes, although my children love it with chips.

If you don't have a slow cooker, add chunks of rabbit to the frying onion at the start, extend the simmering time to 1½ hours and expect to need to add a little more water.

Bunny burgers

To serve four

Ingredients

Boned meat from 2 rabbits
(minced)

8oz belly pork (minced)

1 large onion (finely chopped)

1 handful of fresh herbs
(finely chopped)

1 tablespoon of wholegrain
mustard

1 handful of flour

Salt and pepper

Just like the pigeon burgers (p.138), these patties are a great way to serve game to first-timers. In fact, they're even better because the flavour is more subtle and nowhere near as gamey.

Regard the recipe below as a starting point and feel free to experiment with different flavourings of your own.

Pass the chunks of rabbit meat and belly pork through a mincer (remove the skin from the pork first). Place the minced meat in a large mixing bowl and add onion, herbs and mustard, then season. Roll up your sleeves and use your hands to thoroughly blend the mixture.

Dust the worktop with flour to create a non-stick worksurface. Scoop out the mixture by the handful and pat into nice, flat burgers. Then place on a large plate that has been dusted with flour to prevent them from sticking. Grill on the barbecue or shallow-fry for four or five minutes on each side.

Serve with chips or in a bap with fresh salad leaves and a good dollop of mayonnaise.

For a mouth-wateringly sweet version with a tang of orange, leave out the mustard and add three generous tablespoons of coarse-cut marmalade.

Freshly made burgers can be wrapped in cling film and stored in the fridge for a couple of days or in the freezer for several weeks.

Rabbit supreme

To serve four

Ingredients

Meat and strained stock from
2 slow-cooked rabbits

1 onion (chopped)

8oz mushrooms (sliced)

½ pint of single cream

Cider brandy

1 level tablespoon of
cornflour

Knob of butter

Salt and pepper

Although relatively simple to prepare and cook, this makes for a rich, creamy rabbit feast. If you want to serve rabbit at a dinner party, this is the recipe to go with.

Melt the butter in a hot pan, add the onion and fry until soft. Add the mushrooms to the pan and cook for two or three minutes until they start to turn golden brown.

Add large chunks of flaked rabbit, a cupful of stock and about two tablespoons of cider brandy to the pan. Blend the cornflour with the cream and pour over the top. Simmer gently until the rabbit is piping hot and the sauce is thick and creamy, then season to taste.

Serve with dauphinoise potatoes and seasonal vegetables. I'm often guilty of wanting to serve everything with potato but this dish is equally good on a bed of rice.

WOODPIGEON

Preparation

Preparing pigeon is very straightforward. I rarely go to the trouble of plucking and dressing the whole bird because the bulk of the meat is on the breast and there's really very little anywhere else. Therefore, all you need to do is remove the breast meat.

Begin by plucking the feathers from around the breast. This part of the bird is simple to locate; it's the plumpest part and you can easily feel the hard ridge of the breastbone (or breastplate) running along the centre. Above this is the crop where the pigeon's last meal is stored. There are two large pieces of meat either side of the ridge that need to be removed one at a time.

Plucking is easier soon after the bird is shot although it has to be said the pigeons are never particularly difficult to pluck – the feathers come away very easily. Just pluck a large enough area of feathers to clearly expose the breast to a little way under the wings. (figure 1) Woodpigeon feathers are fine and fluffy and seem to get everywhere. If plucking indoors, you can prevent feathers from floating all over the place by placing the bird inside a carrier bag, which should catch most of them. Giving the bird a thorough soaking before plucking is another way to stop fine feathers from wafting around.

With the breast clear of feathers, use a sharp knife to cut down into the top of the breast along the central ridge, paring the meat back away from the bone (figure 2) and towards the wing. Follow the line of the breast meat down to the base then cut back under the wing and up to where you started in the top centre of the breastbone. The trimmed-out breast meat should just pull away from the bone. (figure 3) Now do the other side and you have two pieces of pigeon breast ready to rinse and cook. If you wish to remove the skin it is easily peeled off.

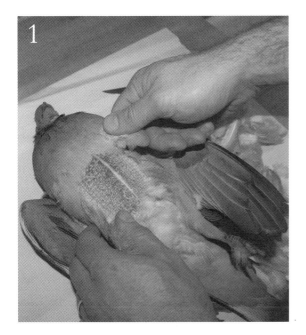

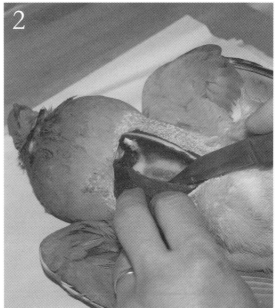

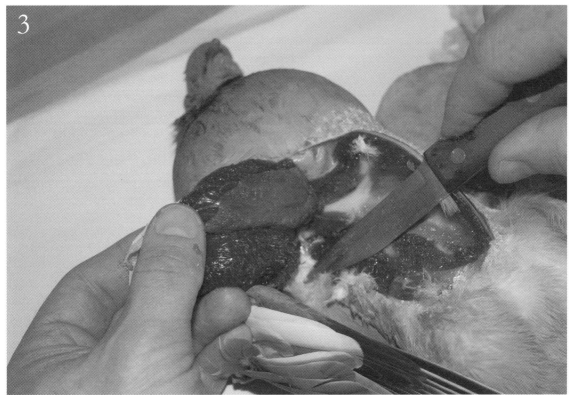

1. Pluck feathers from the breast and under the wings.
2. Cut down the central ridge of the breast bone and pare away the meat.
3. Cut back up beneath the wing to where you started and lift out the breast meat.

RECIPES FOR WOODPIGEON

Pigeon burgers

To serve four

Ingredients

Breast meat from 4 pigeons (minced)

3 thick slices of granary bread (blitzed)

1 apple (grated)

1 onion (finely chopped)

1 clove of garlic (crushed)

Mixed herbs

Salt and pepper

A handful of plain flour

These rustic burgers are a family favourite in our house, and they're incredibly versatile.

The robust flavour of the woodpigeon makes for a surprisingly 'beefy' burger. And, because the minced meat is disguised, they're a great way to tempt people who think they don't like game – especially children.

Mince the breast meat and place in a large bowl, then blitz the slices of bread in a food processor (it's best if they're slightly stale, but just place them in a toaster for a couple minutes to dry them out if they aren't) and add to the meat. Peel and grate one large apple and add to the mix along with the finely chopped onion and the crushed clove of garlic. Season with salt and pepper and add a pinch of mixed herbs.

Roll-up your sleeves and use your hands to make sure all the ingredients are thoroughly mixed – you'll be glad you used a large bowl. Next, take a handful of the mixture and roll into a ball. A dusting of flour on the worktop will give you a non-stick surface to work on as you pat the ball into a burger shape. Place the burgers on a plate that has also been dusted with flour to stop them from sticking. There should be enough mixture to make about eight good-sized burgers.

Shallow fry for about five minutes on each side (or a little longer under a medium grill) until brown and crispy.

Shallow-fried and served with chips, peas and brown sauce, pigeon burgers form the basis of a good, square meal. Alternatively grill or barbecue them and serve in baps with lettuce and whatever sauce you prefer.

Stir-fried woodpigeon

To serve two

Ingredients

Breast meat from 2 pigeons
(cut into thin slivers)

Olive oil (1 tablespoon)

1 large onion (coarsely
chopped)

1 red or green pepper
(coarsely chopped)

4oz mushrooms (sliced)

2 handfuls of frozen peas

Chow mein sauce (the ready-
made type in the plastic
packet)

Here's a fast way to turn pigeon breasts into a meal. And don't worry if you aren't particularly accomplished in the kitchen. This is a really simple recipe, based on the sort of meals I used to survive on when I was student. Anyone should be able to master this one, and it only takes ten minutes to cook.

The recipe I suggest is really just a guide, and you can use more or less whatever vegetables you like. If you experiment with different sauces, I'd recommend the stronger flavours because the more delicate ones get lost in the pigeon's depth of flavour.

Method

Heat the oil in a wok and add the onion and slices of pigeon breast. The oil should be sizzling hot so the pigeon starts to turn brown after two or three minutes; then it's time to add the pepper and mushrooms. Cook for another three minutes before adding the frozen peas and the sauce. Cook until the sauce is piping hot, and it's ready to serve.

This quick and easy pigeon feast is great served on rice or noodles.

Pan-fried pigeon breasts

To serve two

Ingredients

Breast meat from 2
    woodpigeons

Port

Hedgerow jelly or redcurrant
    jelly from the shop

Olive oil

Knob of butter

Salt and pepper

Pigeon breasts taste rather like sirloin steak and, similarly, need little more cooking than a quick browning in the frying pan. Although simple, this recipe has the added bonus of a delicious, dark sauce to pour over the finished meat.

Heat butter and a dash of olive oil in a frying pan. Season pigeon breasts with salt and pepper and add to the pan. Cook until the breast meat is nicely browned – about two or three minutes on each side in a hot pan.

Add two tablespoons of hedgerow jelly and a slosh of port to deglaze the pan. Remove from the heat and leave to stand for two minutes so the meat can relax.

Slice pigeon breasts in half lengthways to expose the tender, pink meat on the inside and serve on a bed of mashed potato. Pour juice from pan over the top and serve.

Cooked quickly in the pan, this pigeon dish can be enjoyed throughout the year. It's light enough to serve with salad in the summer but there's enough depth of flavour to hold its own alongside winter vegetables during the colder months. If you do want to give it a bit of an edge, try adding a crushed clove of garlic.

If you're rustling up this recipe after a hot day shooting pigeons over corn stubbles, you'll be too tired to mess about with mashed potato and vegetables. Serve with crusty bread and butter instead.

Don't be afraid to serve fried pigeon breasts pink in the middle. Overcooked woodpigeon tends to taste of liver.

Pigeon broth

To serve four

Ingredients

Breast meat from 4 pigeons

2 onions (chopped)

2 cloves of garlic

1lb potatoes (cubed)

1 parsnip (diced)

2 large carrots (diced)

6oz mushrooms (sliced)

1 tin of sweetcorn

Frozen peas

2 chicken stock cubes

Knob of butter

Salt and pepper

This is a great winter warmer that really sticks to the ribs. It's the perfect meal to enjoy in front of the fire while you wait for the feeling to return to your fingers after a bitterly cold evening spent in the woods waiting for pigeons to fly in to roost.

Melt the butter in a large saucepan, add the onions and fry gently until soft. Cut the pigeon breasts into one-inch chunks, add to the pan along with the mushrooms and crushed garlic, and fry for another few minutes until the meat begins to turn brown.

Pour in two pints of water and add the potatoes, parsnip and carrots. Bring to the boil and crumble in the stock cubes. Reduce the heat to a gentle simmer, cover the pan and leave to cook for one hour, stirring occasionally.

Finally, pour in the tin of sweetcorn and add four fistfuls of frozen peas. Bring back to the boil, simmer for a couple more minutes, season to taste and serve.

This is a wonderfully thick and chunky winter broth, and makes a great supper served with crusty bread and butter.

You might need to add the occasional extra drop of water during cooking if the broth starts to look a little stiff. The finished consistency should be that of a chunky soup, with the melting vegetables turning the water to a thick gravy. For a really meaty version, use the stock from the slow-cooked rabbit leftovers instead of water. This option means you won't need to use stock cubes.

Pigeon casserole

To serve four

Ingredients

Breast meat from 4 pigeons
(large chunks)

4 chunky rashers of bacon
(diced)

6 banana shallots (whole)

4 carrots (chopped)

1 bay leaf

1 fistful of fresh thyme (finely
chopped)

1oz flour

2 chicken stock cubes

Red wine

Knob of butter

Olive oil

Salt and pepper

This is a dish that really does transform the humble woodpigeon into a magnificent feast. It's not exactly a 'quick and easy' recipe, but it's simple enough for anyone to tackle, and you'll be glad you did when the time comes to serve it.

Fry the bacon with a dash of olive oil for two minutes. Add the butter and pigeon breast and fry until browned on both sides. Tip into a casserole dish, add the shallots, carrots, herbs and flour, then season and mix well. Dissolve the stock cubes in half a pint of water and pour over the top with the same amount of red wine. Cover and cook in a preheated oven at 180°C for two hours.

This is a very versatile dish that can be tailored to virtually any occasion, depending on what you serve it with. When you need more fuel in the colder months, it's great with roast or mashed potatoes and winter greens. For a lighter bite in the summer, serve with rice or even just crusty bread.

CHAPTER 11

The hedgerow harvest

One of the greatest things about the British countryside is that it yields such great pickings for anyone with the inclination to get out there and forage. And, although it's not directly linked to shooting with air rifles, I thought I'd include a chapter on hedgerow fruit because hunters have easy access to this bountiful harvest.

Because shooters tend to spend a lot of time out in the countryside, we can keep an eye on this natural crop and stuff our pockets when the fruits are ripe for picking. I try to keep one or two freezer bags in a pocket of my hunting jacket for just such occasions.

If there's public access to your shooting patch, or if you can arrange it with the landowner, leave your air rifle at home and take your family along to join in with the sweet, sticky harvest. Picking blackberries, sloes, elderberries and the like is great fun and thoroughly engaging for children. By getting little people interested in nature and foraging for food, you'll be setting them on the right path to a healthy, happy lifestyle. It's a great way to encourage them to think about where their food comes from, and to get them involved in preparing it. And, if you don't have kids, just get out there, enjoy the peace and quiet, and make the most of this wonderful free crop.

Just to be on the safe side, get yourself an illustrated pocket guide to native trees and shrubs and ensure that you know exactly what you're picking. Avoid bellyache by making sure you can tell your ash from your elder, so to speak.

Blackberry and apple crumble

To serve four

For the fruit filling

3 large cooking apples (peeled and cored)

1lb blackberries (rinsed)

2oz caster sugar

1oz butter

For the crumble

6oz plain flour

4oz butter (from the fridge)

4oz brown sugar

Pinch of salt

Pinch of cinnamon

This is a classic autumn pudding that can follow more or less any meal. It's an old-fashioned, no-frills dessert but it's still one of the best.

Luckily, blackberry season tends to coincide with a glut of cooking apples and it isn't hard to find them going cheap, or even free. Food tastes all the sweeter when you don't have to pay much for it.

Melt the butter in a saucepan over a low heat. Chop the apple roughly into one-inch chunks, add to the pan and cook for five minutes, stirring occasionally, until it softens. Add the blackberries and caster sugar, stir, remove from heat and pour into an oven-proof dish.

Sieve the flour into a large mixing bowl and add a small pinch of cinnamon. Chop the butter into small cubes and crumble it into the flour until it reaches the consistency of breadcrumbs (using cold butter helps to avoid getting into a sticky mess while rubbing between your fingers). Add the sugar (saving a good pinch of sugar to sprinkle over the top) and the salt, and mix thoroughly. Spread the mixture over the fruit and sprinkle with the remaining sugar.

Cook in a preheated oven at 190°C for 25 minutes or until the top turns brown and crisp.

The addition of a sprinkling of sugar over the top gives the crumble even more of a crunch, which contrasts wonderfully with the sweet, gooey fruit. It's best served with custard or cream, or both.

Hedgerow jelly

Ingredients

3lb crab apples

1lb sloes

1lb elderberries

1lb rowan berries

1lb rosehips

One lemon

Sugar

This tasty, sweet jelly can be spread on toast like jam or, if you enjoy meat with fruity sauces, served with rabbit and pigeon dishes.

The recipe is a very loose guideline that can be adapted to whatever you lay your hands on when plundering the hedgerow. Using three pounds of apples as the base – you can use cooking apples if you can't get crab apples – add haws (the red berries from hawthorn), blackberries and any of the fruit listed below to make up the quantities.

Rinse the hedgerow fruit and chop apples into chunks. Place all fruit, except the rowan berries, into a saucepan. Add the juice from the lemon – saving one good squeeze for the rowan berries – then pour in cold water until level with the top of the fruit. Put the rowan berries in a separate saucepan with the remaining lemon juice and cover with water as before. Bring both saucepans to the boil and simmer very gently until the fruit breaks down into a pulp – expect this to take 30 minutes or so, and a little longer for the rowan berries.

Strain the pulp through a scalded jelly bag for five hours – don't be tempted to squeeze it through as you'll make the jelly cloudy. Measure the strained juice and weigh out 1lb of sugar for each pint. Pour the juice back into a pan, heat very gently, add the sugar and stir until dissolved. Bring to the boil and cook rapidly until the jelly reaches the setting point. Pot into sterilised jars.

To sterilise glass jars, wash thoroughly, place in the oven, heat to 150°C then switch off and allow to cool. I prefer plastic-coated lids as the metal ones tend to rust. I place the lids in a pan of boiling water for five minutes to sterilise.

Elderflower cordial

Ingredients

30 elderflower heads

2 lemons (sliced)

1 orange (sliced)

1 tablespoon of citric acid
(from your local chemist
or winemaking shop)

3lb granulated sugar

3 pints of water

Elderflowers offer a free harvest at a time when the main hedgerow bounty of the autumn seems like a lifetime away.

Although elder is regarded by most landowners as a weed, its blossom can be turned into a refreshing cordial, so stuff your pockets when you see heavy bunches of this creamy white blossom in early summer.

Boil the water, pour into a plastic bucket, tip in the sugar and stir until completely dissolved. Leave to cool.

Next, give the flower heads a good shake to rid them of any lingering creepy-crawlies, then add them to the cooled sugar water along with the orange and lemon slices and citric acid. Give the solution a good stir, and don't expect it to look particularly appetising at this stage. Cover with a cloth and store in a cool, dark place. Stir the mixture twice a day for four days and use a fine sieve to remove any surface scum.

Strain through a fine sieve, doing your best to leave the sediment in the bottom. Leave for another two days, then strain through a muslin cloth and decant into sterile, screw-top bottles.

Dilute with about five parts water, or whatever ratio tastes best to you, to serve.

Stored in sterilised screw-top glass bottles, the cordial will keep for three or four weeks in the fridge. Alternatively, pour into plastic bottles – remembering to leave room for expansion – and put it the freezer where it will keep for months.

As well as making for a refreshing drink when diluted with water, elderflower cordial also makes a great mixer for spirits, especially gin.

The hedgerow provides a
free harvest, which is a
great way to get people of
all ages interested in
foraging for food.

Sloes

Of all the hedgerow harvest, sloes rate highest in my opinion – partly because it always amazes me how such a spiky and unwelcoming shrub as the blackthorn can produce such beautiful fruit.

Take a bite in their raw state, and the bitterness of sloes will leave you gurning with a dry mouth. However, this wonderful, deep purple fruit forms the basis of the countryman's favourite tipple: sloe gin.

Sloe gin is a wonderful festive drink that is very warming and literally tastes of the hedgerow. A tot of this crimson liqueur will warm your cockles when you slump into the sofa after a cold evening in the woods, and it's a great snifter to offer to dinner guests.

The recipe I have provided is a good starting point but you may wish to vary the ratios according to taste after your first batch. Of course, if you want to make more than one litre, just increase all the volumes, keeping the ratio roughly the same.

This is a fairly potent brew so, as with any other alcohol, it's not for drinking before venturing out with the gun. But nothing concludes a winter day's hunting better than a glass of sloe gin in front of a crackling fire – preferably accompanied by a big slab of Cheddar cheese or a plate of mince pies.

You'll find sloes in any overgrown stretch of hedgerow that contains blackthorn. The fruit is round, waxy-skinned, and dark purple to black in colour. You're unlikely to confuse sloes with anything else, apart from damsons, which are bigger, but make an equally nice brew.

Sloes tend to ripen between mid and late September, depending on the weather and whereabouts you are in the country. Sloes are hard and very bitter before they reach full ripeness, so leave them until they become plump and juicy for the best results.

You'll need a decent crop of sloes to make sloe gin, so you may need to gather your harvest over several shooting trips. Here's how I make mine when I've got enough for a brew.

Sloe gin

You will need

1lb sloes

1 litre of gin

6oz of sugar

Freezer bags

Screw-top bottle/s

Colander

Funnel

This time you will need

Your sloe gin

Measuring jug

Funnel

Screw-top bottle/s or a
  decanter

Fine sieve or tea strainer

Tea towel or muslin cloth

Method

Begin by rinsing the sloes in a colander under a running tap. The berries then need to be split to let the juice run out. This was traditionally done with a long thorn from a blackthorn bush, but pricking them in this way, or even with a knife, is a total waste of time. The single best way to split sloes is to put them in a plastic bag and leave them in the freezer overnight. Expansion caused by the freezing process bursts the skin of the sloes and leaves them oozing juice when defrosted.

Transfer frozen sloes from the freezer bag into a screw-top bottle and tip the sugar on top – this is easiest with a funnel. Pour in the gin (using the funnel again) and seal the cap. Some people like to add a drop or two of vanilla essence at this stage, but I think it overpowers the natural flavour of the sloes.

Next, give the brew a good shake to mix all the ingredients and store it away in a cool, dark place. Give the mixture a quick shake every day for the first week to help the sugar dissolve, and then give it a weekly slosh thereafter to help it blend. The sugary solution will draw the juice, colour and flavour from the sloes, producing a delicious, warming, syrupy liqueur. Ideally you should repeat the weekly sloshing ritual for three months or more. In our house, we decant the brew on Christmas Eve.

Decanting

The months of sloshing the burst sloes have most likely resulted in a fair amount of sediment. Don't worry, it's just dust, skin and pulp from the sloes, but you'll need to get rid of it.

Place a fine sieve or tea strainer over a measuring jug and then pour your sloe gin through very slowly. It is likely that the sieve will get plugged with sediment, so you'll need to give it a rinse from time to time.

When the measuring jug is about three-quarters full (you don't want it to be too much of a handful) you are ready to transfer the sloe gin into its final bottle or decanter, but I would recommend a further refining stage. To get the clearest, cleanest sloe gin that literally sparkles, line a funnel with muslin cloth or a tea towel. This will act as a very fine filter, straining out any remaining

149

impurities as you pour your brew from the measuring jug to the bottle. You can't do this without straining the solution first because the cloth would get completely clogged.

Repeat this process until you have decanted your whole supply of sloe gin. The resulting brew could be any colour from bright pink to a lovely festive purple. That's the great thing about making your own sloe gin – there is usually a slight variation from year to year depending on the weather, when and where you pick your sloes, and how many you put in.

I must confess that I'm always at a loss as to what to do with the leftover sloes. Infused with gin and sugar, they smell delicious and I'm sure they would be very tasty in a cake if only the stones weren't such a nightmare to remove.

Thanks

Luke Manning, Jeffrey Olstead, Ian Barnett, Fanny Charles, Tony Belas, Roe Norman, Edward Thring, the House family at Yarlington, Bob Down, Tony Gibson, Peter Martineau, Wes Stanton, Peter Carr, Terry Doe, Matt Clarke, Jed Woodhouse, Andrew Peden Smith, Blackmore Vale Media, Blaze Publishing, *Airgun Shooter* magazine, *Sporting Rifle* magazine, *Shooting and Conservation* magazine, *Air Gunner* magazine, the British Association for Shooting and Conservation, Daystate, Deben, BSA Guns, Hawke Optics, Weihrauch, Tower Guns and Mendip Shooting Ground.

Very special thanks

Kev Hawker, Nigel Allen and Tim Dunning – for your invaluable help, encouragement and entertainment over the years.

Convair
B-58 Hustler

Bill Holder

Schiffer Military/Aviation History
Atglen, PA

Acknolwedgments

1. John Marsh, Grissom AFB History Office
2. TSgt Devin Drisker/MSgt Scott Marin, Little Rock AFB
3. Carol Keck, Media Relations, Edwards AFB
4. Sonny/Betty Williamson, Lone Star Flight Museum
5. Stephanie Mitchell, Pima Air & Space Museum
6. Warren Domke, Kelly AFB Public Relations
7. Terry Vanden Heuvel, Davis Monthan AFB
8. Clifford Gaston, B-58 historical expert
9. Paul Reinman, former KC-97/KC-135 crew member
10. Roger Boan, former B-58 DSO
11. Bob Norton, B-58 Hustler Association
12. Joseph Baugher, B-58 Web Site
13. Karen Hager/Mike Moore, Lockheed Company
14. Jeanie August, AMC History Office
15. Octane Chanute Aerospace Museum, Chanute AFB
16. Jackie Sheffer, Former B-58 DSO
17. Wes Henry, Air Force Museum
18. Grissom Air Museum, Grissom AFB
19. Pat Smotherman, former B-58 Pilot
20. Larry Boggess, former B-58 Navigator

Book Design by Ian Robertson.

Copyright © 2001 by Bill Holder.
Library of Congress Control Number: 2001094411

Printed in China.
SBN: 0-7643-1468-8

We are interested in hearing from authors with book ideas on related topics.

Published by Schiffer Publishing Ltd.
4880 Lower Valley Road
Atglen, PA 19310
Phone: (610) 593-1777
FAX: (610) 593-2002
E-mail: Schifferbk@aol.com.
Visit our web site at: www.schifferbooks.com
Please write for a free catalog.
This book may be purchased from the publisher.
Please include $3.95 postage.
Try your bookstore first.

In Europe, Schiffer books are distributed by:
Bushwood Books
6 Marksbury Avenue
Kew Gardens
Surrey TW9 4JF
England
Phone: 44 (0) 20 8392-8585
FAX: 44 (0) 20 8392-9876
E-mail: Bushwd@aol.com.
Free postage in the UK. Europe: air mail at cost.
Try your bookstore first.

Contents

Foreword

I was contacted by the author of this book and asked a number of questions about my B-58 experiences. As we got further into the discussion, many fond memories of piloting the world's first supersonic bomber came to mind. The opportunity to be a member of that exclusive flying group was one of the most memorable periods of my 35-year career in the United States Air Force. It all began the very first time I saw the B-58 in person. I was flying the B-47 at the time at Eglin AFB, Florida. This is the location for much of the Air Force's follow-on flight testing, including the "Cold Weather Hangar," in which aircraft are "Frozen to test all systems in extremely cold temperatures." When I got a tour of the facility, I saw the most stunning shape of the delta wing, covered with frost and icicles hanging from the four large engine pods. At that moment I decided that I would do whatever was necessary to be assigned to fly that magnificent machine! After begging and pleading with the folks at SAC Headquarters, I was assigned to the 43rd Bomb Wing at Carswell AFB for B-58 Aircraft Commander training. Upon arriving, I was informed that the wing was under time constraints to be declared "combat ready." Time did not allow me to go through the F-102 lead-in training, and I directly entered into the TB-58 for two training sorties. On the fourth sortie, I was solo in the B-58 with my assigned crew. After completing seven training sories, a simulator check, and another in the TB, my crew and the 43rd Bomb Wing were declared "combat ready." A few of my memories of flying the B-58 include the first time to go Mach 2, the first outboard engine failure at Mach 2, fuel stacking at night over Dallas bomb plot at Mach 2, extreme low level flight on the Tonopah Test Range, and the first attempt at landing a TB-58 from the back seat. Of course, there are others, but the best memory of all is of the close friendship and association with a very unique group of professional officers and enlisted men who all had one common virtue—they loved this airplane!

Pat Smothermon
Major General, USAF, Retired
Former B-58 Pilot

Foreword

My first flight in the B-58 Hustler happened on Octber 9, 1962. It had only been 15 years earlier than the sound barrier had been broken, and there I was, navigating the world's first supersonic bomber. I felt a great sense of importance in being a B-58 crew member. This was an airplane very different from others. The sleek delta wing design sported four underslung engines with afterburners, giving it a unique appearance that was a sight to behold. Many things were added to improve the B-58 before it made its way to the bone yard...It seemed that the SA-2 Soviet missile worked very well against a Mach 2 target at 50,000 feet, at least well enough to change our war plan tactic to low level. Had technology given us the smart bombs then, perhaps B-58s could have been effective in the Vietnam war with iron bombs, when four bomb pylons were added. The B-58 was doomed to the bone yard. It is a sad note that while the B-58 was first in many design and performance capabilities, it seemed to be the forgotten bomber.

Larry Boggess
Col, USAF, Retired
Former B-58 Navigator

Foreword

I was part of the B-58 Program from 1961 until 1968, except for a short tour in Viet Nam. I came from an aircraft where ECM meant Extra Crew Member rather than Electronic Counter Measures. Coming to the B-58 was a significant step up in responsibility and capability. To come from an environment where the crew counted on me more for the correct flight lunches to an environment where the crew depended upon me for real mission accomplishment allowed me to keep my sanity and self respect. The performance of the aircraft was such that you had to learn to think ahead of the aircraft—to anticipate. As a Defensive Systems Operator, my roles included radio (HF and UHF) communications, fuel management, Center of Gravity control, 20 mm gun, defensive ECM, low level navigation, pilot's checklist, and assorted other tasks. Missions ranged from 50,000 feet at Mach 2 over Texas to 300 feet at 550 knots over Missouri, and a lot in between. The crews made fun of the aircraft, but did not allow anyone else the privilege. We maintained that the flight controls were created when three bikers collided at the bottom of the high, then the wreckage was welded together and placed in the aircraft. When everything worked, it worked well. When it went bad, it went bad in a hurry. Without the pod, the B-58 looks fast in the air and more like an ungainly stork while on the ground.

Roger Boan
Major, USAF, Retired
Former B-58 DSO

1
System Roots

It was an era of changing aviation times. First, World War II was just over, and the military was saddled with a huge fleet of out-of-date aircraft. Technology was pushing hard toward the jet age, and the B-58 was typical of a number of advanced programs that began in the late 1940s.

The requirements laid on the new bomber were many times more complex than anything before, and as such, resulted in higher design and development costs that really raised eyebrows in budget meetings.

A pair of Air Force studies in the late 1940s, called GEBO I and II, formalized the requirement for a medium bomber, and looked at many possibilities for such a system.

There were schools of thought that felt that the technology push was proceeding too quickly, and that a more reliable and economical system could be acquired. The B-52 heavy bomber was certainly a step in that direction, and it proved to be a correct choice, with a number of the final H models still flying in the 21st century.

Production money was also a heavy consideration, as during that period both the B-47 and early versions of the B-52 were being built in considerable numbers. There were also a number of fighters that were in development or early production. Many asked, what was the need for such a craft as the high-flying, super-fast Hustler?

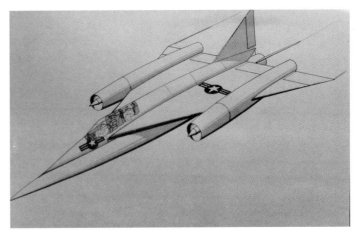

An early concept drawing of the B-58. Notice that this design integrated the engines into the delta wing. (Convair Drawing)

When B-58 design and development started just five years after the end of the war, the plan was for the model to replace the B-47, which was just starting to enter service. Obviously, that never happened, as the -47 was one of the finest light bombers in USAF history.

Also during this period, though, there were still many advocates of piston power, as was exemplified by the piston

The highly effective B-47 was the medium bomber that the B-58 was designed to replace. The B-58 numbers, though, would fall far short of making the replacement. (USAF Photo)

This Convair model shows how the concept on the previous page would have looked had it reached fruition. (Convair Photo)

Nope, this is not the early concept that had the B-58 serving as a parasite aircraft carried underneath a B-36 mother ship. This photo shows a B-58 being transferred to Wright Patterson AFB early in the program for structural testing. (USAF Photo)

engines of the giant B-36. And also, the early versions of the longstanding B-52 considered using prop power before turning to eight turbojet engines.

A little-known offshoot of the early program was a consideration to integrate the basic B-58 vehicle with the B-36 as a carried-along parasite aircraft. The B-58 would be carried aloft underneath the B-36, launched on a mission, and then re-attach for the return mission.

It was determined, though, that such a configuration would not be cost effective, so the concept was dropped in late 1951. It was assessed that a refueling capability on the future B-58 design would be a less complicated method for range increases.

At this time, the B-58 returned to its original concept, but some changes were made for addtional performance. Afterburners were incorporated on the model's four engines, and the crew was increased from its original two to three.

All well and good, but there was a contract to win before even considering production, and the competition was fierce for the winning award. The Air Force had requested proposals on the system from Douglas, North American, Lockheed, and Martin, in addition to the major Boeing and Convair players. The following is what is known about three of the design efforts:

Convair Designs

The eventual B-58 prime contractor Convair had some serious arguments in justifying its sleek, undersized bomber design. With comparisons to World War II bombers, it was pointed out that the B-58 could fly four times faster than the B-29, and could carry in one nuclear-capable bomb, the equivalent of the total tonnage dropped by the 8th Air Force during the great war.

Convair also considered a number of diverse configurations prior to settling on its well-known final design, which

This Convair concept drawing shows a B-58 four-engine delta wing concept design. The engine location was the interesting aspect of this design, with the inner engines carried on standard pylons, while the outer engines were mounted on the top of the wing. (Convair Photo)

Still another Convair concept, this time accomplished under the MX-1626 program, had twin engine pods flushed up under each wing. (Convair Photo)

Much of the B-58 design heritage can be traced back to the early XF-92, the company's first delta-wing design. (Convair Photo)

was developed within the MX-1626 program nomenclature. One design weighed in at a gross weight of some hundred thousand pounds, with a jettisonable pod for weapons and fuel.

In fact, a technique was considered where even a number of the plane's powerplants would be jettisoned, with the plane coming back on only one engine! Guess it isn't surprising that complex concept did not stick around for very long.

The company felt confident with its pure-jet, delta-wing configuration that was evolving, as it had considerable experience using such a wing design. The company had built three delta-wing fighters—the XF-92, followed by the operational F-102 and F-106 fighter systems—which proved the concept.

In fact, the XF-92 would provide important data for the company's B-58 design when the delta wing fighter was flight tested in the late 1940s. Needless to say, the delta wing application to a bomber aircraft was something quite foreign to the industry at the time.

With its vast bomber design and development experience, Boeing had to be considered the early favorite for the B-58 concept. This Boeing wind tunnel model shows the B-47 influence with the podded engines and swept wing design. (Boeing Photo)

This photo shows the delta wing Convair family tree, with the B-58 leading the F-102 and F-106 fighters. (Convair Photo)

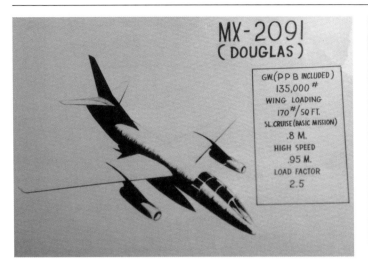

MX-2091
(DOUGLAS)

G.W.(P P B INCLUDED)
135,000 #
WING LOADING
170 #/SQ FT.
SL.CRUISE (BASIC MISSION)
.8 M.
HIGH SPEED
.95 M.
LOAD FACTOR
2.5

Douglas also got into the frey with its MX-2091 design. The high-wing design featured a pair of pylon-mounted engines mounted on swept wings. (Douglas Drawing)

This was an early B-58 mock-up that featured the not-to-be-adopted podded engine design. (Convair Photo)

Boeing Designs

Early Boeing designs showed their B-47/B-52-style configurations, which were so familiar. The needle-nose design sported a large high-mounted delta wing carrying four two-engine pods mounted on underwing pylons. It was coined the Model 484, and with the success the company had enjoyed in bomber development during the recent decades, Boeing had to be rated as a favorite. But the 200,000 pound design had one major strike against it; its top speed was only Mach 1.3, where the Air Force was looking for Mach 2! The Boeing work was accomplished under Air Force Program MX-1712.

Boeing also had another configuration considered, which was defined as the Model 474. The model, which was given the XB-55 designation, featured four turboprop engines driving three-bladed, countra-rotating propellers. The program never reached beyond the paper stage, although it was re-

ported that serial number 49-1946 had been reserved for one of the model.

Douglas Design

The Douglas proposal featured a jet-powered bomber configuration, but it would be an early casualty in the selection process.

Other Design Implications

Strenuous requirements were placed on the still-to-be-born Hustler, with "the capability to cover almost 5,000 miles in both directions, and possess high subsonic speeds when flying at low levels." It had to be "easy to fly, highly reliable, and requre few personnel for operation and maintenance."

The basic design for the model remained unchanged throughout the process, but there were a number of changes made.

Notice the forward cannards that were installed on this MX 1964 mock-up. Of course, there would be other changes, but the model was starting to acquire its final B-58 look. (Convair Photo)

This MX 1964 drawing shows an early powered pod design being launched from a B-58 mother ship. (Convair Drawing)

Notice the tip fuel-tanks integrated with the wing-tips in this concept drawing. (Convair Drawing)

This 1953 concept drawing shows the B-58 looking much like its final configuration, with the exception of the podded engines. (Convair Drawing)

Changes were made in the propulsion system configuration, with four pylon-mounted engines mounted separately instead of the original pair of two-engine pods. There were many engine locations and groupings considered during the design process. The fuselage would also be modified by the coke-bottle-shaped area ruling, which would allow the bomber to more easily pass through Mach 1. In addition, there were many changes made to the pod configuration. Of course, when changes were made to the basic airframe, changes were also required to make the pod compatible. Once Convair came up with its final proposal, the Air Force carried out a vigorous evaluation program, including wind tunnel testing, scale models, and other techniques. There were also considerations at the time to make the bomber capable of carrying a parasite fighter, but that concept would be dropped from consideration early.

After a year and a half of deliberations, Convair's design (which carried the MX 1964 company designation) was judged to be the best, and the award was made in late 1952. The Air Force would initially identify the program as MX-1626 before the XB-58 designation would emerge. It should also be noted that the new bomber model would be based around the new General Electric J79 turbojet engine.

The final B-58 configuration was finally almost attained with this company drawing, which was identified as showing the XB-58. Note that the engines are now hanging on four separate pylons. (Convair Drawing)

2

Design, Development, Test, & Production

Compared to other bomber development programs of the period, the B-58 took the longest time. From its development start (the issuance of the contract in February 1953) to the first operational delivery in November 1959, a long 81 months passed.

That figure can be compared to the B-47 with 62 months, and the B-52 was just ninety days short at 78 months. Another aircraft time period included 48 months for the C-5 transport.

Major Milestones

A number of key milestones highlighted the B-58 design, development, test, and production program. Following the Full-Scale Development (FSD) decision, a contract for the first 13 aircraft was issued in October 1954. The J79 powerplant was first tested aboard a test aircraft in November 1956.

The first supersonic flight of the B-58 occurred in December 1956, followed by the second prototype's first flight three months later. An additional 17 aircraft were ordered in the spring of 1957. Then, the first production B-58A took to the air in September 1959, with the first production aircraft (number 31) accepted two months later. SAC received the first B-58A with J79-GE-5A engines.

Design and Development

If you surmised that the development of the B-58 was a smooth operation, you would be wrong. The program was littered with many mountains and valleys, along with some changes in direction.

The so-called Configuration III was a new configuration for the fuel/weapon pod, having been shortened by some 50 feet and joining the under fuselage by a pylon. Crew positions number two and three were also reversed, pushing the DSO to the most rearward position. There were also modifications to facilitate these and other changes, all of which caused the mockup inspection of this version to be pushed back to September 1954.

The B-58 program was greatly reoriented in April 1953 when the decision was made that the first 30 vehicles would be classified as "Test Vehicles."

Then came the fourth configuration after the previous version had resulted in a near-fiasco. Initially, there was a consideration here for the front two crew members to be seated side-by-side, a set-up that would be quickly discarded.

This configuration was then officially referred to as the B/RB-58 configuration, and a number of other changes were introduced. External fuel tanks were eliminated, the tail area

There was no mistaking the early B-58 prototypes with their flashy red and white paint schemes. (Convair Photo)

There was a strenuous flight test program for the Hustler. Here, one of the test pilots consults with a maintenance crewman following a flight. (Convair Photo)

One of the early YB-52s awaits another test flight. (Convair Photo)

Major Joe Thornton, Chief of the Air Force Flight and Accessory Division, was heavily involved with the B-58 test program. (USAF Photo)

was increased to 160 square feet, and each of the four engines was suspended off the wing by an individual pylon.

All this activity occurred under a blanket of discontent from SAC, much of it coming from SAC Commander General Curtis LeMay. In fact, during 1955 a board was convened by SAC discussing whether the Hustler should be continued,

modified, or canceled completely. Considering the amount of money already spent, and the technology introduced by the design, it was decided that the program would continue.

The initial B/RB-58 made its first flight in November 1956 from the Convair Fort Worth facilities at Carlswell AFB, Texas. Early flights were all subsonic, but by December, supersonic

The sixth prototype (55-0665) shown from a front view and illustrating the size of the underslung pod. (Convair Photo)

With the completion of yet another B-58 flight test, a crewman descends the ladder. (Convair Photo)

The initial B-58 (55-0660) made its first flight in November 1955. In this photo, the nose is showing an increasing angle-of-attack while the main gear is still on mother earth. (USAF Photo)

The second prototype (55-0661) slows to a stop during a landing aided by its single drogue parachute. (USAF Photo)

The B-58 took on an entirely different, more sleek look without its pod. Pilots indicated, though, that the performance was not that much different with or without the pod. (Convair Photo)

A number of Convair test pilots pose in front of one of the early Hustlers. (Convair Photo)

Structural testing was a part of the overall development program for the B-58. Here, a Hustler is lifted into position for the testing, which took place at Wright Patterson Air Force Base. (USAF Photo)

speeds up to Mach 1.6 had been attained. This first plane was referred to as a prototype (the YB-58). No B-58 would ever officially receive the XB-58 designation, usually reserved for the first test aircraft.

Flight testing from the first three YB-58s brought forth some spectacular accomplishments and some severe deficiencies. The performance, of course, was outstanding, far surpassing any previous or future bombers.

Certain fuel system malfunctions were noted, with sloshing occurring when acceleration or deceleration took place. There were also minor cracking problems observed due to vibration, along with continuing brake problems causing tire failure in a number of different situations.

In 1958, the B-58 faced another crisis with a near-cancellation. The increasing costs and numerous problems with the advanced plane were again coming into play. There was

considerable concern with the disappointing range (only about 3,800 miles with refueling, and more than 40 percent less on internal fuel). But again, with what had been expended already, it was decided to go forth with the program, albeit at highly reduced numbers from what had originally been planned. Things certainly were not that much different from today, with the same type of thinking going on.

Testing

Due to the complexity of the B-58 system, the test program was altered from the norm. The Category I tests were initiated by Convair in November 1956. During the next six years, almost 3,000 hours of flight testing were completed. During the testing in 1959, the fifth YB-58 (55-664) was lost in an accident.

Some normal Category I tests were moved to the Category II test program, which was officially started in March

Test craft 55-0663 pours on the coal in a test flight. (Convair Photo)

As is easy to note, just the main structural components are in place for the structural tests. (USAF Photo)

An under view of the structural test Hustler as it is maneuvered into position for testing. (USAF Photo)

1959.

Actually, though, the Cat II testing began 13 months earlier. The reason given was the assuming of the test program by the weapon system office, although it was stated that SAC, as the primary user, would also be heavily involved in the program. A significant number of Convair representatives were also a part of the test force. After 256 sorties, representing 1,216 hours, Cat II testing was completed on 30 June 1960.

Although the testing was deemed successful, its results could well have spelled the plane's demise, as seven Hustlers were lost in the period between December 1958 and November 1959.

The crashes again brought on line the arguments to cancel the program. The B-52's stock went up again, along with

another interesting proposal to re-engine the B-47, increasing its speed and payload capabilities. Another argument that seemed to have a lot of validity was the fact that, with the stretched-out design program, the aircraft was getting obsolete before it was deployed. And at SAC Headquarters, there wasn't anyone that had a good word to say about the Mach 2 bomber.

But the program continued, with Category III testing beginning in August 1960 and lasting until July 1961. Certain structural modifications were accomplished to the test aircraft before this final test phase began.

An interesting aspect of the testing was that it contained combat training hours for B-58 crews. The crew training started out using TF-102As before the arrival of the first TB-58A trainer aircraft.

This model of the Hustler is tested in AEDC's 16-foot Transonic Wind Tunnel in 1957. (AEDC Photo)

Testing is a part of the design program of any new aircraft. Here, a B-58 enters the Climatic Laboratory at Eglin AFB. (USAF Photo)

During flight testing, it was necessary to assure that the B-58 design was compatible with inflight refueling operations. Here, a prototype is hooked up with a KC-135 tanker. (USAF Photo)

Production

The final phase for any military product is, of course, the actual production of the system for operational use. For the then-advocates of the system, they must have thought that it was never going to happen.

The Hustler had initially been planned for production to commence in December 1952. In fact, a year later, it still had not happened. By April 1954, the system still faced a situation of uncertainty about its future. In early 1955, the program was almost canceled. By mid-1955, it was given a two-steps-back order to a research and development status. On August 22, 1955, an amazing change in thinking took place, with the order to a production status and the first wing to be operational in mid-1960.

As it finally worked out, a total of 116 Hustlers were produced, a miniscule number compared to the numbers of other bombers and fighters of the era. The production involved the building of a pair of initial prototypes, 11 YB-52 production

A slight black exhaust smear can be seen being emitted by this test B-58 during a high-speed test. (Convair Photo)

Later versions of the B-58 carried the escape capsules for emergency crew exit. The system is shown here being tested with an actual B-58. (USAF Photo)

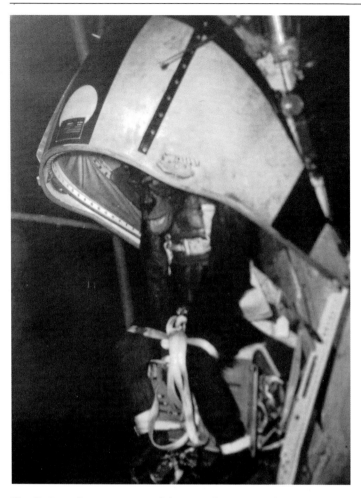

The first non-human testers of the capsule were monkeys. This rider appears to be very calm about his upcoming high-acceleration ride. (USAF Photo)

High speed ground testing of the B-58 Escape Capsule. (USAF Photo)

A close-in view of the capsule test sled, actually the front section of a Hustler. (USAF Photo)

No matter how well you became accustomed to the B-58, the size of that carry-along pod still gave the model a different look. (USAF Photo)

The B-58 test program, along with later operational service, was certainly not without disaster, as the remains of this Hustler vividly illustrate. (USAF Photo)

Production of the B-58 presented challenges never addressed in any other aircraft of the time. Here, a Hustler is in the production process, being secured in a production jig. (Convair Photo)

This test at Edwards Air Force Base in 1961, with an RB-58, failed during take-off. It was caused by landing gear problems, but the pilot was able to get it stopped before running out of runway. (USAF Photo)

This B-58 experiences the production build-up process at the Convair Fort Worth production facility. (Convair Photo)

B-58 59-2439 is shown in the final production process. (Convair Photo)

The Convair B-58 production facility was massive, and has continued to support other military aircraft programs following the Hustler. (Convair Photo)

prototypes, and 86 B-58As-produced in three lots of 36, 20, and 30 planes.

B-58 production presented problems never before faced by any previous bomber aircraft, nor with many that would follow it. It seemed that every aspect of the advanced bomber presented unique fabrication/production problems.

The internal structure of the delta wing used aluminum spars that reached the width of the complete wing and passed directly through the fuselage. The spars were placed very close together for strength reasons.

The longitudinal members were used strictly for attachment purposes, including the engine pylons, doors, landing gear struts, and elevons.

The wing covering presented a unique fabrication challenge, ie the honeycomb sandwich material. Between the layers of honeycomb were aluminum sheets with honeycomb bonded between them, making for a material capable of enduring the heats generated by the Hustler's high speeds.

The biggest aspect of the aircraft construction involved the building of the jig for the delta wing. It took Convair a year and a half for the device to reach the required tolerances of .003 inches.

The Convair B-58 nameplate which was riveted to every Hustler. (Convair Photo)

3
Parts and Pieces

For its time period, there was really nothing like the B-58, both from its dazzling (still looks good in the 21st century) looks and its Mach 2 performance capabilities. The craft pushed the state-of-the-art in many technologies, a fact that might have hastened its early demise.

On just about every aspect, the B-58 garnered a first. Obviously, the Mach 2 speeds it demonstrated were totally without compare. Its stainless-steel honeycomb construction was far beyond the current state-of-the-art. But it was the total configuration, with the fuel/payload-carrying pod being an integral part of the total aircraft system.

Quite frankly, the B-58 was a hugely-complex system. Every aspect of the bomber introduced new concepts, requiring new maintenance procedures and increased training requirements.

It was certainly a challenge to keep the Hustlers in the air, and any B-58 pilot would tell you that it was also a handful to keep up with from the pilot's seat.

The model empty, without the pod, only weighed 55,560 pounds, with a maximum take-off weight of 163,000 pounds.

After an in-flight refueling top-off, the weight could exceed 177,000 pounds.

The performance was 701 miles per hour at sea level and 1,322 miles per hour at altitude. Its range was about 5,125 miles without refueling.

The B-58 had a maximum drop weight of about 19,450 pounds, which could have included any of a number of different types of nuclear bombs, including the B43 and B61 weapon systems. The rear of the aircraft was protected by a single 20 mm T-171 tail gun.

Really, if this machine were to evolve as a concept bomber design in the first decade of this new century, it just would not look that much out of date. No stealth characteristics, of course, but otherwise very modern-looking.

Looking at the design, there was no doubt that it was built for speed from the beginning. That sleek fuselage with its needle nose, area-ruled mid-section and rearward-canted vertical tail all spoke of high-velocity intentions. The mid-fuselage-mounted sharply-swept delta wing recalled the company's earlier F-92 and F-102 fighter designs. Unlike

Without the pod, the B-58 was as sleek as an arrowhead. (USAF Photo)

Even with the weapons pod in place, the B-58 could still demonstrate an amazing rate-of-climb. (USAF Photo)

The Plane

The B-58 was not a big plane, and when compared with the monster B-52, it seemed almost tiny. That fighter size comparison when sitting next to the B-52 made one wonder how it ever got a "B" designation.

The wing span was almost 57 feet, with a length of 97 feet. It had a tail height of 31 feet, five inches.

This hot bomber had a maximum speed of 700 miles per hour at sea level, with a 1,322 mph capability at altitude. Its maximum range performance (5,125 miles) was initially provided by a quartet of J58 engines. Later models, though, would incorporate more powerful J79 engines with afterburners.

For its time period, the Hustler was extremely maneuverable. It was reported that in 1958, at a speed of about 600 miles per hour, a Hustler accomplished a complete roll. It also demonstrated 1 1/2 hours of supersonic flight on the deck. It was really something!

The Weapons Pod

If the design ended right there, the B-58 design would not have been that different, but there was one other aspect of the bomber that set it far apart from any other bomber design of the period or the future. In effect, the payload and a portion of its fuel load was carried in an attached pod joined to the lower fuselage. At first look, the pod looked like an afterthought on the design.

those designs, though, the B-58 wing was also asked to mount a quartet of pylons to carry the craft's four powerplants.

With the introduction of new fabrication technologies, the B-58 demonstrated an unheard-of characteristic of having its empty weight a miniscule 14 percent of its gross weight.

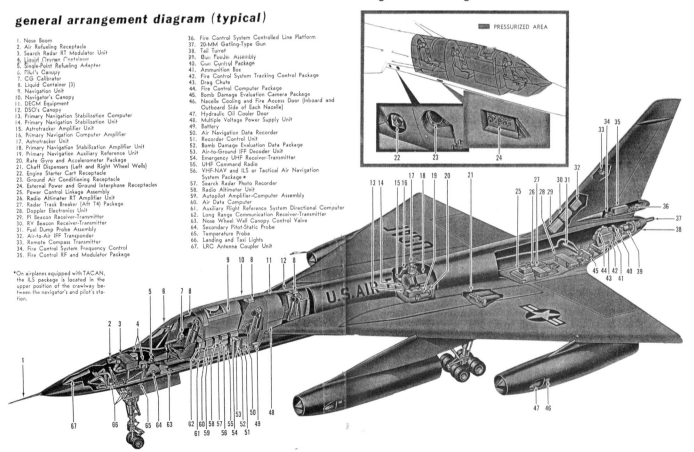

general arrangement diagram (typical)

1. Nose Boom
2. Air Refueling Receptacle
3. Search Radar RT Modulator Unit
4. Liquid Oxygen Containers
5. Single-Point Refueling Adapter
6. Pilot's Canopy
7. CG Calibrator
8. Liquid Container (3)
9. Navigation Unit
10. Navigator's Canopy
11. DECM Equipment
12. DSO's Canopy
13. Primary Navigation Stabilization Computer
14. Primary Navigation Stabilization Unit
15. Astrotracker Amplifier Unit
16. Primary Navigation Computer Amplifier
17. Astrotracker Unit
18. Primary Navigation Stabilization Amplifier Unit
19. Primary Navigation Auxiliary Reference Unit
20. Rate Gyro and Accelerometer Package
21. Chaff Dispensers (Left and Right Wheel Wells)
22. Engine Starter Cart Receptacle
23. Ground Air Conditioning Receptacle
24. External Power and Ground Interphone Receptacles
25. Power Control Linkage Assembly
26. Radio Altimeter RT Amplifier Unit
27. Radar Track Breaker (Aft T4) Package
28. Doppler Electronics Unit
29. PI Beacon Receiver-Transmitter
30. RV Beacon Receiver-Transmitter
31. Fuel Dump Probe Assembly
32. Air-to-Air IFF Transponder
33. Remote Compass Transmitter
34. Fire Control System Frequency Control
35. Fire Control RF and Modulator Package

36. Fire Control System Controlled Line Platform
37. 20-MM Gatling-Type Gun
38. Tail Turret
39. Gun Feeder Assembly
40. Gun Control Package
41. Ammunition Box
42. Fire Control System Tracking Control Package
43. Drag Chute
44. Fire Control Computer Package
45. Bomb Damage Evaluation Camera Package
46. Nacelle Cooling and Fire Access Door (Inboard and Outboard Side of Each Nacelle)
47. Hydraulic Oil Cooler Door
48. Multiple Voltage Power Supply Unit
49. Battery
50. Air Navigation Data Recorder
51. Recorder Control Unit
52. Bomb Damage Evaluation Data Package
53. Air-to-Ground IFF Decoder Unit
54. Emergency UHF Receiver-Transmitter
55. UHF Command Radio
56. VHF-NAV and ILS or Tactical Air Navigation System Package *
57. Search Radar Photo Recorder
58. Radio Altimeter Unit
59. Autopilot Amplifier-Computer Assembly
60. Air Data Computer
61. Auxiliary Flight Reference System Directional Computer
62. Long Range Communication Receiver-Transmitter
63. Nose Wheel Well Canopy Control Valve
64. Secondary Pitot-Static Probe
65. Temperature Probe
66. Landing and Taxi Lights
67. LRC Antenna Coupler Unit

*On airplanes equipped with TACAN, the ILS package is located in the upper position of the crawlway between the navigator's and pilot's station.

PRESSURIZED AREA

The B-58 was a complicated piece of military equipment. This chart shows the locations of its many systems and components. (USAF Drawing)

The B-58's ordnance is laid out in front of it, showing pods and nuclear bombs. (USAF Photo)

A B-58 Hustler resting next to a B-52, and looking very tiny in comparison. (USAF Photo)

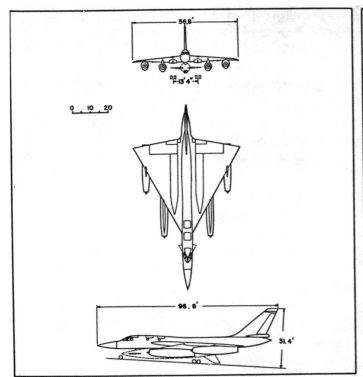

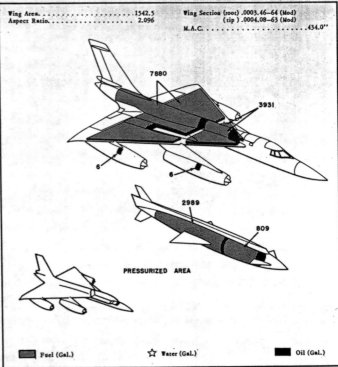

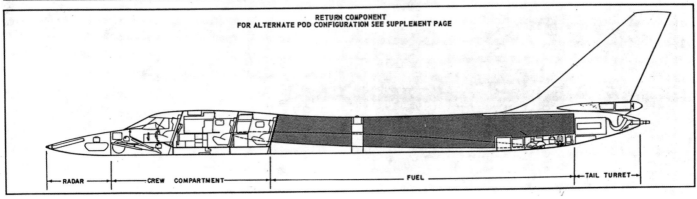

This official USAF drawing provides the aircraft dimensions, along with the internal layout. Note the particularly large percentage of the fuselage volume devoted to fuel storage. (USAF Drawing)

The initial-design MC-1C pod carried an equipment bay, a foward fuel tank and weapons bay, and an aft fuel tank. Reportedly, the pod could carry four nuclear weapons. The MC-IC weighed about 2,300 pounds empty and 18 tons fully fueled and carrying a nuclear warhead. It featured four 90 degree-spaced tail fins.

The later design TCP (Two Component Pod) could actually discard its top and bottom fuel cells in flight following fuel use, and while retaining the weapons section. The upper weapon and fuel component of the TCP weighed in at about six tons, with the bottom fuel pod coming in at an additional 26,000 pounds. A single control surface at the 12 o'clock position identified the TCP configuration. The fuel capacities of both the MC-1C and TCP pods were very similar. For example, the front sections were 12,496 and 11,988 pounds, while the after tank had capacities of 14,625 and 13,266 pounds, respectively.

Frankly, the weapons pod was a distinct entity and could be launched or dropped separately. Separation from the B-58 itself was a touchy affair, with care being taken not to effect the plane's critical center of gravity, along with not affecting the programmed trajectory of the weapon.

The Fuselage

The B-58 got its most attention during its short lifetime with the many speed records it set during its career. In addition to its vaunted velocity capabilities, the B-58 also could fly intercontenental ranges, as it possessed an in-flight refueling capability. The refueling probe was located in the forward fuselage, directly in front of the aircraft commander's crew compartment.

The fuselage sizewise was fighter-like for its three-man crew. Certainly, with its dimunitive size, there was no walking around like in the monster B-52, or even to some extent in the smaller B-47. Once in the seat, the crew member was there for the duration of the mission.

The "pinched fuselage" design of the B-58 is clearly visible in this overhead photo. The pinch allowed the Hustler to pass easily through the speed of sound. (USAF Photo)

Compared to the monster B-52, the B-58 was a tiny bomber. The size of the B-52 can be seen in this shot, making even the large KC-135 tanker appear small. (USAF Photo)

A view of the front probe on the nose cone of the B-58. This particular B-58 is on display at the Air Force Museum at Wright Patterson Air Force Base, Ohio. (Bill Holder Photo)

There were three completely separate compartments, one behind the other, for the trio of crew members. The positions, front to rear, were for the pilot, bombardier/navigator, and the Defense system operator (DSO). Each location featured its own rocket-powered escape module, which were pretty dependable in the cases when they were required to operate.

The pilot had the best view, looking out over the needle nose of the craft. A large six-piece windshield also provided for a 180-degree view to the sides. It must have seemed like entering a fighter for the crew, getting into their separate compartments. "Separate" was definitely the correct descriptor, as each crew member entered the Hustler through separate openings in the upper forward fuselage.

If you had claustrophobia, the rear two crew positions were certainly not for you. First of all, there was practically no visibility to the outside, with just a pair of small windows to indicate that there was still an outside. The locations were

The forward pod-mounting mechanism is shown here. (Bill Holder Photo)

A head-on view of the weapons pod attached to the lower B-58 fuselage. (Bill Holder Photo)

two component pod (blu-2b)

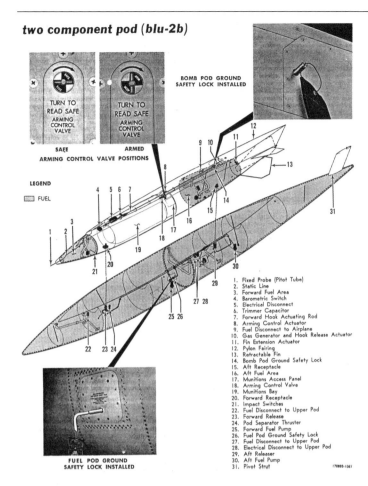

ARMING CONTROL VALVE POSITIONS

SAFE / ARMED

BOMB POD GROUND SAFETY LOCK INSTALLED

LEGEND
☐ FUEL

1. Fixed Probe (Pitot Tube)
2. Static Line
3. Forward Fuel Area
4. Barometric Switch
5. Electrical Disconnect
6. Trimmer Capacitor
7. Forward Hook Actuating Rod
8. Arming Control Actuator
9. Fuel Disconnect to Airplane
10. Gas Generator and Hook Release Actuator
11. Fin Extension Actuator
12. Pylon Fairing
13. Retractable Fin
14. Bomb Pod Ground Safety Lock
15. Aft Receptacle
16. Aft Fuel Area
17. Munitions Access Panel
18. Arming Control Valve
19. Munitions Bay
20. Forward Receptacle
21. Impact Switches
22. Fuel Disconnect to Upper Pod
23. Forward Release
24. Pod Separator Thruster
25. Forward Fuel Pump
26. Fuel Pod Ground Safety Lock
27. Fuel Disconnect to Upper Pod
28. Electrical Disconnect to Upper Pod
29. Aft Releaser
30. Aft Fuel Pump
31. Pivot Strut

FUEL POD GROUND SAFETY LOCK INSTALLED

Internals of the Two-Component Pod. (USAF Drawing)

pilot's main instrument panel (typical)

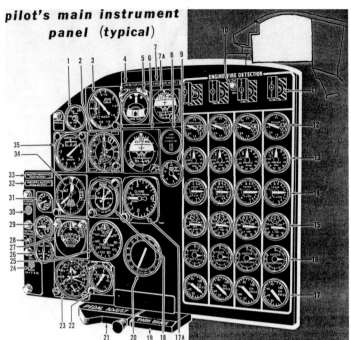

A view of the maze of instruments that constituted the pilot's main instrument panel. (USAF Illustration)

like a cocoon. Once seated, a crew member was in that location from engine start to engine shutdown.

Aircraft control was accomplished via a maneuver stick, instead of the conventional control stick. There was also an autopilot that could overrule pilot commands that might place the aircraft in danger.

A unique indicator was also available to the pilot in the form of an elevon position indicator. This enabled the pilot to be aware of the positions of the combination of ailerons and elevators. The gross weight computer provided roll and pitch corrections during flight.

A rare view of a weapons pod on its ground handling equipment. (USAF Photo)

No other bomber has ever had a trio of seating compartments like the Hustler. Each was completely separate. (USAF Photo)

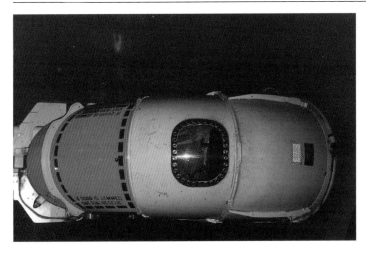

A view of the B-58 escape capsule in the closed position. (Bill Holder Photo)

A view of the B-58 forward fuselage showing cockpit details. (Bill Holder Photo)

The vertical stabilizer of the Hustler featured a highly-sweptback leading edge. (Bill Holder Photo)

Looking into the front wheel well of the Hustler. (Bill Holder Photo)

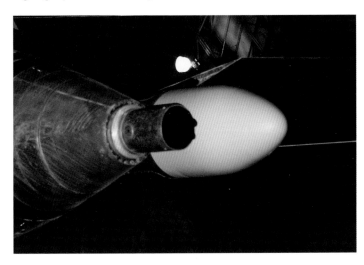

This will get your attention! The potent Gatling Gun was the only defensive weapon on the B-58. (Bill Holder Photo)

From the front view, the B-58 had a bit of a spindly look, standing relatively high on its tricycle landing gear. (USAF Photo)

A landing gear door for the front gear is shown in the open position. (Bill Holder Photo)

Each of the B-58's fuselage-mounted landing gears featured eight tires, in groups of two. (Bill Holder Photo)

By the name of his position, the bombardier/navigator had a multitude of responsibilities in the middle crew position. His basic job was to interface with the 1,200 pound navigation and bombing system. Recall that this was the vacuum tube era, thus causing the massive weight. Although there were problems, when operating correctly the system was able to direct the Hustler to the correct location, and then accomplish the launching and guiding of the particular weapon to the target.

Then came the final rear position, where the DSO had a close relationship with the pilot in aiding with checklists, overseeing fuel use, and monitoring the ever-important aircraft center-of-gravity. There were also ECM responsibilities, along with the operation of the six-barrel rear gatling gun. Potential targets were viewed on a scope, and the 20 mm cannon could be directed onto the targets.

Beneath the crew canopies were packed a number of systems, including the Long Range Communications Receiver-Transmitter, Directional Computer, Air Data Computer, Radio Altimeter Unit, Search Radar Photo Recorder, Navigation System, UHF Command Radio, Air-to-Ground IFF Unit, Bomb Damage Evaluation Data Package, Recorder Control Unit Batteries, and Multiple Voltage Power Supply Unit.

There was also considerable electronic equipment in the rear portion of the fuselage beneath the vertical stabilizer. The equipment included the Power Control Linkage Assembly, Radio Antenna, Radio Altimieter Amplifier Unit, Radar Track Breaker Package, and Doppler Electronics Unit.

In the lower leading edge of the vertical stabilizer were the PI/RV Beacon Receiver-Transmitters and Air-to-Air IFF Transponder, along with the remote compass transmitter.

A major portion of the fuselage, though, was dominated by internal fuel stores, two in the main fuselage (20,000

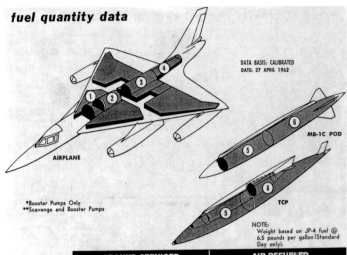

fuel quantity data

DATA BASIS: CALIBRATED
DATE: 27 APRIL 1962

AIRPLANE

MB-1C POD

TCP

*Booster Pumps Only
**Scavenge and Booster Pumps

NOTE:
Weight based on JP-4 fuel @ 6.5 pounds per gallon (Standard Day only).

		GROUND-SERVICED				AIR-REFUELED			
TANKS		FULLY SERVICED IN GROUND ATTITUDE (2.3° Nose Down)		USABLE FUEL IN NORMAL FLIGHT ATTITUDE (2.5° Nose Up)		FULLY SERVICED AIR REFUELING ATTITUDE (6.5° Nose Up)		USABLE FUEL IN NORMAL FLIGHT ATTITUDE (2.5° Nose Up)	
		U.S. GALLONS	POUNDS	U.S. GALLONS	POUNDS	U.S. GALLONS	POUNDS	U.S. GALLONS	POUNDS
AIRPLANE	FUEL LINES	103	672	32	211	120	781	32	211
	1 FWD	3,202	20,811	*3,172 **3,195	20,619 20,770	3,177	20,648	*3,147 **3,170	20,456 20,607
	2 RES	610	3,963	607	3,945	640	4,163	638	4,145
	3 AFT	5,893	38,306	*5,816 **5,884	38,000 38,245	6,122	39,794	*6,075 **6,113	39,488 39,733
	4 BAL	1,219	7,925	1,206	7,839	1,261	8,195	1,248	8,109
MB-1C POD	5 FWD	1,922	12,496	1,912	12,426	2,008	13,055	1,998	12,985
	6 AFT	2,250	14,625	2,244	14,585	2,306	14,991	2,300	14,951
TCP	5 FWD	1,844	11,988	1,837	11,941	1,870	12,154	1,863	12,107
	6 AFT	2,041	13,266	2,031	13,204	2,092	13,601	2,083	13,539

The huge fuel volumes of the B-58 are clearly shown here. (USAF Drawing)

pounds in the forward tank and 4,200 in the rear location). There was also another fuel storage location in the tail—8,200 pounds to be exact—with that aft-most location also used to help maintain the Hustler's center of gravity, a critical situation in the flight of the Hustler.

Located at the mid-fuselage point, far aft of the crew compartments, were the systems which constituted the Hustler's navigation system. The system was highlighted by its large stabilization unit.

View of the joining of the wing root to the mid-fuselage position. (Bill Holder Photo)

Cooling was a big requirement for this aircraft, and to accomplish that need there were a pair of 18-ton capacity refrigeration units. The heat was generated by the friction generated at the plane's high speeds, causing the temperatures to rise within the aircraft. Not only did the living inhabitants of the beast need to be cooled, but also the large electronic presence.

Like fighters of the era, the B-58 fuselage featured the pinched area rule design that eased transition from subsonic-to-supersonic speeds. Seventy percent of the fuselage was covered by the light, and extremely strong, honeycomb skin. With the Mach 2 capabilities of the Hustler, aerodynamic heating had to be considered in the plane's design. Beneath the honeycomb structure was an inner skin bonded to an aluminum shell, greatly aiding heat dissapation.

The Raytheon Search Radar was located in the forward section of the fuselage, directly behind the long, protruding pitot tube.

In addition to providing lift for the craft, the wings were also the mounting position for the four J79 engines. (USAF Photo)

A view of the rear look of the Hustler. (USAF Photo)

A single landing gear was located under the forward fuselage, and consisted of a dual-tire arrangement. The fuselage was completed by the expected rear horizontal stabilizer, which carried an approximate 45 degree sweepback.

View from underneath the rear of a Hustler. (Bill Holder Photo)

Mounting details of a J79 engine to the underside of the wing. (Bill Holder Photo)

The rear cannon protruded out beyond where the rear of the stabilizer joined the upper fuselage.

The Wing

Describing the wing as "wet" would be putting it mildly, as a massive amount of fuel was carried within its confines. The foward wing tanks (one on each side) carried a total of 20,811 pounds, with 38,306 pounds in the rear wing tanks. Of course, as the fuel was being burned off, it was necessary to keep trimming out the ship to maintain the center of gravity location. Besides providing lift and storing JP-4 fuel, there were a number of other functions performed by the 1,543 square foot delta wing. First, the main gear was attached underneath with a pair of four-wheel landing gears, two behind two on each gear. The 22-inch diameter tires had an amazing air pressure of 240psi! Located internally in left and right wheel wells were chaff dispensers, which served to confuse enemy radars.

Then, there was the final job, that of carrying the four J79 turbojet powerplants. The engines were attached to four py-

Location of the attachment points for externally-carried weapons. (Bill Holder Photo)

The J79 engine system, four of which powered the Hustler. (Bill Holder Photo)

Inlet cone of a B-58 J79 engine. (Bill Holder Photo)

Ions on the bottom side of the wing. All the gears were built with heavy-duty specifications, such that they could continue to support the weight of the aircraft should tires blow, which they did on numerous occasions.

Also beneath the wing were four hard points which could be used to carry different types of bombs, or the ADM-20A Quail diversionary missile. The trailing edge of the 60-degree delta wing carried an additional ten-degree sweep back to tail cone. The wing tips were also cambered and rolled downward. In addition, there were also large elevons located on the wing's upper surfaces.

The Engines

The J79 powerplant was an excellant match for the performance goal of the B-58, with its 15,600 pound thrust capability during maximum afterburner operation. One of the most highly-used military powerplants, the J79's most famous use would have to have been with the F-4 Phantom fighter.

The B-58A used the J79-5B augmented version, which was rated at 15,600 pounds of thrust at maximum afterburner. The engines were equipped with a variable position center inlet spike. Depending on engine conditions, the spike would select the most optimum position. The unique device aided in preventing compressor stall.

The engine also had the capability to provide optimum thrust and fuel consumption in a number of different engine conditions. Additionally, the engine had the capability to operate at 104 percent of rated thrust for short periods of time. Also, for bursts of up to five seconds, the thrust could be kicked up to as high as 107 percent.

Another function of the engines (actually engines 1, 2, and 3) was to drive a number of generators to provide the variable voltage to power the instruments, fuel pumps, and aircraft controls.

With a fully loaded Hustler at take-off, the quartet of engines was capable of pushing the craft to a climb rate of 17,000 feet per minute. When the plane was empty, and with the engines at full afterburner, the climb rate could reach an amazing 46,000 feet per minute!

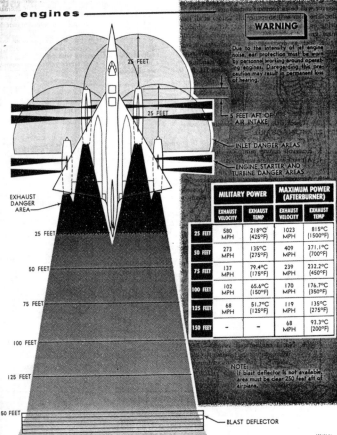

This Air Force chart shows the danger areas that existed behind the Hustler when the engines were in operation. (USAF Drawing)

4
Models and Mods

Although all Hustlers produced carried the basic B-58 in their nomenclature, there were many add-on letters and numbers that set many of these models apart.

Through the years, many Hustlers served different research, training, and other functions. Produced models were all the B-58As, with many deviations being added after the production run. Like many other operational aircraft, future versions of the model were proposed, with a number of performance improvements and additional missions. None, however, reached operational status.

Production Models

The initial two prototypes were first unofficially identified as XB-58-CFs (numbers 55-660/661), but the "X" was not continued. They were initially flown without the weapons pod and used J79-CE-1 engines. Later, the production prototypes (YB-58A-CFs), of which 11 were produced and Identified as numbers 55-662-through -672, were powered by the more powerful CE 5 version of the J79 engine. Next came the actual production model, the B-58A-CF, of which 86 were constructed. Built in three lots, the first 36 Hustlers were identified as B-58A-10-CFs, the next 20 carried the B-58A-15-CF designation, while the final lot of 30 were called the B-58A-20-CF. The aircraft numbers were 59-2428 through -2463, 60-1110 through -1129, amd 61-2051 through -2080.

55-0664 was the fifth YB-58, posed here with a number of crews. (Convair Photo)

Later, 17 of the B-58A-10-CFs were converted to RB-58A-CFs, each of which carried a ventral reconnaissance pod. The program was carried out in the late 1950s, with the first pod delivered in June 1958. The first RB-58 that carried the pod was lost in a crash in June 1960. During its lifetime, the program was reinstated once and canceled twice.

Then, with the Cuban Missile Crisis in 1962, the program was brought back to life again with Project Mainline, which

55-0660 was the first B-58 and carried the model designation of YB-58A. (USAF Photo)

This B-58A (60-1118) was built in the second production lot of 20 aircraft. (Convair Photo)

B-58A(61-2054) was built in the final production lot. (Convair Photo)

The enlarged window area of a TB-58 is quite evident in this photo of number 56-0670. (Convair Photo)

View of the instructor pilot's position within a TB-58. (Convair Photo)

involved modifying 44 B-58As and ten MB-1 pods. The modification involved the incorporation of a KA-56 panoramic camera into the nose fairing of the weapons pod. The modification was successfully flight tested in 1963.

Also, eight YB-58A-CFs were converted to operational trainer aircraft, the TB-58A, with dual controls for student and instructor in tandem. The first TB-58A, 55-670, was delivered to the Air Force in August 1960. It had been constructed from the remains of thirty test planes.

The flight characteristics of the TB version and its Mach 2 speed capabilities required such an aircraft for training new pilots. The TB-58A was a ton and one-half lighter than the standard B-58A configuration. The reduction in weight was achieved by removing all the offensive and defensive aspects of the craft. For pilot training, the bombardier/navigator location was replaced with a complete pilot's station.

Projected Future B-58 Models
With more powerful versions of the J79 engine and a longer fuselage, Convair proposed the B-58B version. The extra length was to be accomplished by insertion of a plug in the

fuselage. The wing also benefitted in the proposed upgrade, with extensions being added to the inboard leading edges. Research showed that the modifications should add greatly to the high angle-of-attack capabilities of the Hustler.

The B-58B would, of course, have a significantly greater payload capability over the A model. It also offered a conventional weapon capability, which was not available on the B-58A. Standard iron bombs were visualized as being carried in a larger weapons pod. Then, there was an amazing proposal to carry and air-launch small ballistic missiles from wing mounts.

An additional proposal, the B-58C configuration, made use of the more modern J58 non-afterburning turbojets, which had sizable thrust improvements over the existing J79s. The time period for the early phases of the B-58C were at the same time as the North American B-70 Valkyrie program, with the Convair considering that system as a possible competitor to that program.

Like the B-58B, this model was also enlarged from the basic system with a significant five-foot fuselage extension, a new wing leading edge, and more tail area. One big strike

55-0663 was one of the first YB-58s, later to be converted to a TB-58. It is shown here on display at Grissom Air Force Base. (Grissom Air Museum Photo)

The Kingfish was a proposed variant of the B-58, a system which lost in a competition with the Lockheed A-12, shown here in construction. (Lockheed Photo)

55-0661 served as a testbed for several functions, including proving refueling techniques and certification of the crew capsule. (USAF Photo)

the proposal had against it, when comparing it with the B-70, was the fact that the B-58C was based on an older design, plus it lacked the growth potential of the much larger B-70 design. Also, the Air Force doubted the 5,200 mile range capability quoted by the Convair contractor. Finally, the extensive use of aluminum caused concern because of the long exposure to sustained high-speed flight.

With the cancellation of the B-70 project after only three models were built, interest in the B-58C program also faded, with cancellation occurring in early 1961. There was also concern that continued use of older technology could cause future problems for the model.

The existence of later proposed Hustler versions gets more on the hazy side, but it has long been reported that there were also D and E versions; however, no available USAF documents verify that the programs officially existed. Little is known about the progress on these programs, or what the configurations actually resembled.

Nope, that isn't a weapons pod under this B-58A, but a J93 engine, which was being tested for the XB-70 Mach 3 bomber. (USAF Photo)

In the mid-1950s, yet another version of the B-58 was proposed which called for the development of a reconnaissance version carrying an AN/APQ-69 side-looking radar system. The radar was extremely large, with a 50-foot-long antenna—one of the largest to ever be attempted to be carried by an aircraft.

The XB-70 was designed to either replace, or supplement, the B-58. It did neither, being canceled after several prototypes were built. (USAF Photo)

This tenth B-58 produced was used to test the navigation/bomb system. (USAF Photo)

The radar system was to be contained within a special pod, which was flight tested in late 1959. The seriousness of the concept was verified from the fact that over two-dozen flight tests were carried out with the pod. The size and shape of the new pod, though, presented problems with the performance of the combination, religating it back to subsonic top speeds.

A later program, with the code name of Quick Check, which was based on the Goodyear AN/APS-73 radar system, was also carried out. In order to carry the system, it was necessary not only to modify the MB-1 pod, but the actual aircraft structure, as well. A little-known fact is that the Quick Check aircraft actually overflew Cuba during the Cuban missile crisis. But like so many other B-58 follow-on programs, the Quick Check program was canceled with completion of the flight test program.

Although there was no export version of the B-58 ever built, there was at least one attempt to accomplish such a sale. Convair, in the late 1950s, proposed a stripped-down version of the Hustler to the Australian Air Force. The modification envisioned the use of wing pylons to carry conventional bombs. However, interest from the Ausies was not forthcoming, and the concept was dropped shortly thereafter.

In 1957, the contractor proposed what would have become the largest modification of the B-58, a program which was given the name Super Hustler.

The concept envisioned a basically standard B-58 carrying a new-design parasite aircraft in the normal pod position. There were two components of the payload; one was the

powered manned vehicle carrying a crew of two, while the second carried either fuel or the payload.

It was likely that aerial reconnaissance was the most probable mission of the combination. Power for the parasite aircraft was to be by an airbreathing ramjet, with the craft returning to base under its own power. Prior to landing, the expendable component of the craft would have been dropped off.

A high-altitude capability of up to 90,000 feet, plus a Mach 2 speed capability, would have made the parasite craft a tough target to intercept. However, the Air Force never showed any interest in the project, and it was canceled while still in the paper stage. Certainly, it was an ambitious project for the state of-the-art during the time period.

A final footnote on the program, though, was that a variant of the system—codenamed the Kingfish—was entered in the competition to fulfill a CIA reconnaissance requirement. But again, the proposal would not be adopted, the agency instead opting for the Lockheed A-12 system, the earlier version of the famous SR-71 Mach 3 Blackbird.

The final reported Hustler modification program was called the Snap Shot program, and it had the mission of mounting ballistic missiles for air-launch from beneath the B-58 fuselage.

The missiles were to be launched from a centerline pylon on the fuselage underside, while Lockheed was contracted to build a missile based on a number of existing missile systems.

Four of the solid-rocket-powered, 30-foot-long missiles were ordered with all flight tested. After the first missile test failed with control problems, the second test was a complete success, achieving a range of 185 miles. The final two launches were also successful, with the final missile carrying a camera to photograph the Explorer IV satellite in orbit.

As was the usual situation, though, there was little interest in the demonstrated capability, and the program did not move forward from that point.

As strange as it might seem, the B-58 was even considered in a company program for use in a supersonic airliner application.

55-0671 was an early B-58 that was used in test missions at Kirkland Air Force Base. (USAF Photo)

The 22nd B-58 produced (58-1015) was a heavy contributor in gross weight testing. (USAF Photo)

With its military configuration, it is hard to imagine that such a model could evolve, but Convair derived its Model 58-7, which had the appearance of a greatly-stretched B-58. Reportedly, the fuselage was stretched to the point that it could accommodate over fifty passengers. The long-forgotten transport was to be powered by the same J58 non-afterburning powerplants that had been planned for the never-built B-58B configuration.

One of the strangest modifications considered for the B-58 was a proposed configuration to investigate the effects of supersonic flight on passengers in a supersonic transport. The concept consisted of a modified weapons pod, which would be used to carry up to five personnel for test purposes. It never happened. There was also a proposal that such a modification could be used to carry high-ranking government or military officials in a special pod during possible national emergencies. This too was never carried beyond the paper stage.

Testbed Models

With its unique altitude and performance capabilities, it is not surprising that the B-58 would find itself in demand for use as a testbed aircraft. As such, a number of Hustlers received one-of-a-kind modifications supporting research efforts.

The second B-58A (55-0661) was a real test workhorse, proving the Hustler's capability to be aerial refueled. It accomplished the first hook-up to a KC-135. The plane was later extensively used in proving the crew ejection seat. Following its testbed duties, the craft was converted to the TB-58A configuration.

One of the YB models, the third B-58 built, would later be modified to a NB-58A-CF, a testbed model that was modified to carry a giant J93 jet engine in the location normally assumed by the weapons pod. The test engine was designated for Mach 3 B-70 and the projected F-108 Rapier. The testing, with speeds up to Mach 2, was for the development of a plane with even greater performance capabilities than the Hustler. Unlike the B-58, the B-70 would never enter series production.

After this testing was completed, the Hustler was reverted back to a TB-58A configuration and actually flew B-70 chase missions at Edwards Air Force Base.

The tenth Hustler built (55-0668) served as the test vehicle for the navigation/bomb system, along with being used as an engine test vehicle for advanced engines.

B-58 55-0671 would be converted to a testbed aircraft, performing a number of missions at Kirkland Air Force Base before being modified into the second TB-58 trainer. The 22nd B-58 built (58-1015) was modified for gross weight testing, and later was converted to an RB-58 configuration.

Also, the Hustler played an important role in development of the first control system for the YF-12A Mach 3 fighter. This particular system had originally been developed for the canceled F-108 Rapier fighter, which had been designed to be an escort fighter for the B-70.

Since this testing was to take place in the late 1950s, and the YF-12A was not yet ready, it was decided to use a modified version of the B-58 to accomplish the testing. 55-0665 was the particular B-58A selected for the job, but as far as is known, it never received any special designation for the testing.

The modifications were substantial, as it was necessary to add substantial length (about seven feet) to the fuselage in order to accomdate the large AN/ASG-18 fire control system. In addition, sensor domes were mounted to the forward fuselage on both sides. Changes were made to the middle crew position to enable that crew member to monitor the testing.

The GAR-9 air-to-air missile system was the recipient of the AN/ASG-18 data, and it too would be tested in this particular Hustler. To that end, a single ventral pod was developed to carry one GAR-9 missile. The radar testing took place in 1960, with the first GAR-9 launch occurring in 1962.

This B-58A would never see any follow-on operational service, continuing to be used in a test role and being placed in a photo test range at Edwards Air Force Base. Its ultimate disposition is unknown.

B-58A number four (55-0663) was another active test participant, performing the first pod drop and also the first pod drop at supersonic speeds. This Hustler was also the first to flight test at above 60,000 feet.

This is a YF-12A Mach 3 fighter. A B-58 testbed aircraft was important in the development of its control system. (USAF Photo)

55-0663, the fourth YB built, performed a testbed function performing the first pod release. (Convair Photo)

5
Operational Service

Amazingly, with the fanfare the B-58 had received, the numbers finally produced would result in only a pair of operational units being fielded, the 43rd and the 305th Bomb Wings. Their locations were Carswell AFB (later Little Rock Air Force Base) for the 43rd, and Bunker Hill Air Force Base (later Grissom AFB) for the 305th.

The minimal deployment was surprising since the B-58 was the first, and still the only, true Mach 2 bomber. But even as the plane was being deployed, there were still a number of reservations and worries about its reliability and safety.

An interesting note is that earlier, a 40-45 plane contingent would normally have been called a group. But with the increasing costs of the B-58 and the feeling that there would be fewer than hoped for built, the designation was instead changed to Wing for the two units.

Operational Bases

After production had begun five years earlier, operational capability was initally achieved for the Hustler when the first lot of 12 started arriving at the 43rd Bomb Wing at Carswell, Texas, in August 1960. The base was located in close proximity to the Convair production facility. The 43rd consisted of the 63rd, 64th, and 65th Bomb Squadrons. It would be well into the following year before the unit would achieve full operational capability with 36 of the model.

Later, that number would be slightly increased, a number that would include four of the TB-58 models.

It had been hoped that the 43rd would have been operational much earlier, but a number of problems, including ground support equipment shortages, continuing maintenance problems, the unreliable bombing and navigation system, and involvement with the Category III testing set it back.

The cover of the B-58A Flight Manual. A look at this document quickly showed what a complex bird the Hustler really was. (USAF Document)

A pair of B-58 crewmen dash for their Hustler on a SAC Alert. (USAF Photo)

Nothing slow during an alert, as this trio sprints to their B-58A, and hopefully into the air within four minutes. (USAF Photo)

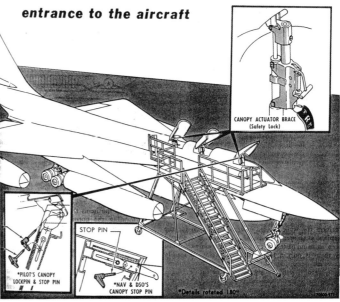

The B-58 could only be boarded from the right side by means of this special unit. (USAF Photo)

Later, a physical relocation was made in 1964 when the 43rd was moved in total to Little Rock (Arkansas) Air Force Base. It would remain there until the call-down of the Hustlers late in the decade.

The second SAC B-58 wing, the 305th, started receiving its first B-58s in May 1961 at Bunker Hill Air Force Base as it started phasing out the B-47s it formerly had. Twenty KC-135 tankers were already in place at Bunker Hill when the transition began. The 305th consisted of the 364th, 365th, and 366th Bomb Squadrons.

Each wing would have six RB-58s among its number. One of those planes photographed the destruction caused by an Alaskan earthquake during the 1960s, providing amazing pictures.

Hustler Operational Flight Incidents

All did not go well, however, with a number of accidents occurring at the bases. Included were Carswell accidents, with the destruction of 58-1017 on an aborted takeoff and the loss of 59-2459 due to mechanical failure of the flight control sys-

55-0668 was the ninth B-58 constructed and spent its career with the 43rd Bomb Wing. During its career, it had the nickname "Wild Child II," and later "Peeping Tom." (USAF Photo)

This B-58A (59-2451) is shown during a take-off. It too was a member of the 43rd Bomb Wing. (USAF Photo)

This 43rd Bomb Wing B-58A (59-2442) rolls along the ramp toward a take-off. Note the high stance of the plane. (USAF Photo)

tem. At Little Rock, 58-1016 and 59-2437 were destroyed during hard landings. At Bunker Hill, 59-2462 was destroyed due to a control system failure during takeoff, 60-1116 was written off due to collapse of the landing gear during taxiing, 60-1128 was lost when it left the runway during a landing, 61-2061 crashed due to mechanical failure after takeoff, 61-2063 was destroyed during a hard landing, and 61-2065 was lost due to loss of control during initial climb after takeoff. In addition, there were also a number of inflight failures from the operational bases.

The 64th Bomb Squadron of the 43rd Bomb Wing was identified by this flashy patch. (Bill Holder Photo)

The 43rd Bomb Wing patch, of blue and gold, had roots stretching back to World War II. (Bill Holder Photo)

The Mach Crow patch was worn only by DSOs after both a Mach 2 flight and ECM run were accomplished. (Bill Holder Photo)

The 43rd Bomb Wing trophy patch was highlighted by the number of the performance trophies won by aircraft of the organization. All 43rd personnel were eligible to wear it. (Bill Holder Photo)

Where the Hustler did its best job, high and fast. This 43rd BW Hustler is outlined by a high cloud formation. (Larry Boggess Photo)

One of many B-58 crews during the 1960s. This particular 43rd Bomb Wing Crew consists of (L-R) then-Captains Pat Smotherman, Larry Boggess, and Jackie Sheffer. (Larry Boggess Photo)

Flying the Hustler

The 43rd and 305th frequently flew missions of 12-to-20 hour durations, accomplished with multiple refuelings. There were also flights that included considerable supersonic flight time.

One would have thought that with the huge discrepancy in speed capabilities of the B-58 and the KC-135 tanker, aerial refueling might have been a problem. But most tanker pilots indicated it was no big deal.

Former KC-135 tanker pilot Eban Parker recalled hooking up with the Hustlers for a drink:

Granted, refueling a B-58 was a lot different from a B-52. The B-58 did require a higher formatting speed from us. The Hustlers liked the operation to take place at about 330 knots to start with, and more speed as they got heavier. This was not far from our red line. The rendezvous was no problem, and the higher speeds during refueling were actually more

This 43rd BW Hustler is shown rolling on a taxi-way, minus its weapon pod. (Larry Boggess Photo)

comfortable for us. The tanker seemed to be more stable the faster you went.

We had little trouble making the refueling altitudes in the upper 20,000s. The B-58 pilots were very good on the end of the boom. Pilots seldom had unplanned disconnects, and I attribute this to them being the best of SAC at the time.... The B-58 felt more like a fighter behind us than the bigger RC-135 and B-52 with their bow waves.

Turns and turbulence did not appear to be a problem with a B-58 on the boom, and there were no pumping problems during the fuel transfer operations.

The most interesting aspect of a B-58 refueling operation, though, was the break-off, when the Hustlers would drop down out of the observation position and move out ahead of us, sometimes with afterburners lit. They would leave us like we were parked on the ramp!

Retired USAF General Pat Smothermon was a B-58 pilot during those operational days, and as a Lieutenant and Captain, served at Carswell from 1961-1964 and Little Rock from 1964-1966. He came out of the B-47 program to the Hustler:

"Believe me, the B-58 was a handful to fly, but there were similarities to the B-47, both being sporty, but complex aircraft. The landing was tough to accomplish because of the plane's visibility problems.... For me, the refueling operation was a piece of cake. I have fond memories of the B-58; it was one of the finest planes that I ever flew.

There was a smooth transition as you passed through Mach 1. You didn't know that you had done it, with changes on your instruments giving you the only indication that it had been accomplished."

With characteristics of a fighter of the time, the B-58 was stressed for a negative two and a positive three Gs. A similar-

The "Can Do" patch of the 305th Bomb Wing. (Bill Holder Photo)

This TB-58A (55-0663) was attached to the 305th at Bunker Hill Air Force Base. (Grissom Air Museum Photo)

ity to the B-47 was the fact that the Hustler had to be flown exactly as explained in the manual. During take-off, strict attention had to be paid to angle-of-attack. Too much, and velocity was killed off, and the pilot was faced with a possible serious situation.

The plane was built to lift from the runway at just less than the 8,000 foot location. At which time, the Hustler accelerated like a fighter that it so closely resembled. With a full load, the B-58 was capable of climbing at over 45,000 feet per minute.

An interesting phenomena occurred when the B-58 exceeded the speed of sound, and then again at Mach 2. At those speeds, it was necessary to adjust the plane's center of gravity by transferring fuel to different locations in the aircraft. The four-ton ballast tank in the tail was the reference point about which these changes were made.

Of course, one of the Hustler's strongest flying attributes was its capabilities to fly at high speeds at low altitudes. One

former Hustler pilot recalled an operational mission from Carswell when a mission was flown at 500 feet altitude or less all the way to Edwards Air Force Base. The delta wing design was such that it allowed stability at Mach .9 for the low altitude missions.

Landings were made with a 15-degree nose-high angle of attack—enough that the pilot could not see the runway. The pilot would look for equal amounts of concrete on each side of the nose and ease off on the power. If the nose was too high, as had happened, the aircraft would touch down first on the engine nacelles and then roll over onto the wheels.

Larry Boggess was a Navigator with the 43rd Bomb Wing from 1962-1966 at Carswell and Little Rock:

"I recall the job being easier in the B-58 than in the B-47 I had flown in earlier.

I flew in aircraft with both the initial ejection seat and later the escape capsule. Like any former B-58 crew member will tell you, the capsule was like sitting in a cocoon. There was

At altitude, this 305th Bomb Wing B-58A (60-0118) shows its supersonic lines. (USAF Photo)

This operational B-58A (59-2435) looks like a dart flashing through the sky. Note that one external bomb is visible mounted under the wing. (USAF Photo)

58-1012 was destroyed in 1959 at Carlswell Air Force Base by a fuel leak and accidental ignition. (USAF Photo)

Depot maintenance on the B-58 Hustler was accomplished at Kelly Air Force Base, Texas. (USAF Photo)

A SAC maintenance man checks out the weapons pod. (USAF Photo)

With the pilot's compartment open, maintenance is performed on this particular Hustler. (USAF Photo)

The B-58A was an excellent bomber in accomplishing the refueling maneuver. KC-135 pilots indicated that there were no unique problems in refueling the supersonic machine. Boom Operator's view of a Hustler receiving a drink of JP-4. (USAF Photo)

Moving in for a hook-up, this 43rd Bomb Wing Hustler moves in for a fill-up. (Larry Boggess Photo)

enough room to move a little, but if you happened to drop a pencil, there was no way you could pick it up. The capsule presented problems to the bigger guys, some losing toes when it was closed, both on the aircraft and also in simulators."

air refueling boom envelope limits

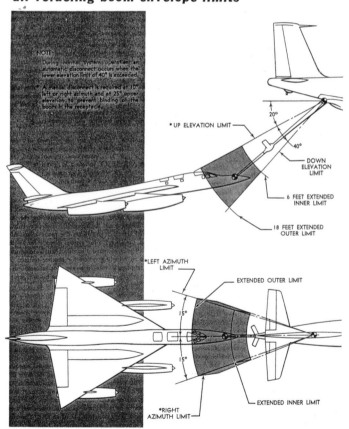

This page from the Flight Manual shows the positive angle-of-attack of the B-58 when it is hooked to a KC-135 tanker. The refueling receptacle is located near the apex of the nose cone. (USAF Drawing)

In describing the navigation system, Boggess explained:

"When it was working, it was great; however, in the early days there were quite often problems—some that could be worked around and some not. The system was highly integrated, and problems could pop up quickly. The main system was an inertial platform assisted by a doppler and a star tracker. I believe that most of the doppler-related problems were caused by bolting the antennas to the frame rather than a stabilized platform."

Then-Captain Roger Boan was a DSO with the 43rd. He explained the many duties of the position:

"The job included acquiring clearance for take-off, certain pilot-type duties, aircraft weight and balance and aircraft performance calculations, fuel consumption, deception equipment, and control of the rear gatling gun. It was like I was the co-pilot, along with a lot of other duties.

By the way, the rear gun could not be fired at supersonic speeds. Actually, the rounds, which were being fired in the other direction, could run out of energy before reaching the target."

Boan also remembered a low-tech message center within the Hustler:

"I think it was a local retrofit, where a clothes line ran through all three compartments. That way, written messages could be passed between the crew members."

This former DSO also remembers what it was like to exit a Hustler after a 12-hour mission:

"While you were in there in the capsule, there was no way to stretch, and I sometimes needed help getting out, being so stiff. There were a lot of guys that were openly afraid to use the capsule to eject."

Boan explained that there were two types of missions during operational service:

"One type was flown when the aircraft was taken off alert, and a second was for an aircraft that had been off Alert for a

A pair of sleek machines joined together as one, with one plane getting lighter and one picking up weight. (Larry Boggess Photo)

while. The difference being that an aircraft coming off alert had ammunition on board, and therefore on part of the mission would be on the Gunnery Range off the coast of Fort Walton Beach, Florida.

"B-58 Mission planning began the day before, and there were slight variations between crews who accomplished each task.

Basically, each crew had a list of objectives to accoomplish each quarter, and it was our task to accomplish them as quickly as possible. Runs against a Radar Bomb Scoring (RBS) site, refueling, and fighter intercepts were scheduled at the Wing level. The rest was mainly up to each crew.

Gunnery missions were interesting. We would fly out to the range, the Navigator would scan the area to be sure that the range was clear, and then the DSO would begin to fire the gun. As the gun fired, the excess brass was discharged from below and allowed to fall into the Gulf. After the first burst, it was a fairly general practice to lock onto the expended brass and use that as a target. Fighter intercepts and gunnery practice were never accomplished on the same mission.

We were limited to two-second bursts because of the heat generated by such a rapid rate of fire, and because we only had 12 seconds worth of ammo. There were occasions where someone fired for more than what was recommended, the barrels warped, and a round got stuck in the barrel."

Another former DSO, Jackie Sheffer, recalled a special "Poker Deck" reconaissance pod, which provided excellent

An Air Force Maintenance Technician works in a B-58 cockpit. Maintenance was definitely one of the big problems faced by the Hustler fleet through its lifetime. (USAF Photo)

Ground support equipment used to support the movement and attachment of the pod to the B-58. (USAF Photo)

This B-58A is shown minus its pod, with all three canopies in the open position. (USAF Photo)

photo capabilities. "I recall being able to see the puffs off running cattle's hoofs as we photographed using the system."

A dozen crews at both Wings were selected to participate in low-level photo reconnaissance missions. Some weapon pods were modified to carry cameras in the nose. Low level runs were made on Army routes over Missouri, Arkansas, and Louisiana at 550 knots at 300 feet.

In the 1966 time period, the crews involved with the low level photo missions were tasked to participate in a test of a "Pathfinder" capability. The question was whether the B-58 could be used as a pathfinder for F-105 and F-4 fighters in Viet Nam. The tasking was split into two roles, navigation and bombing. The navigation role went to Bunker Hill, and

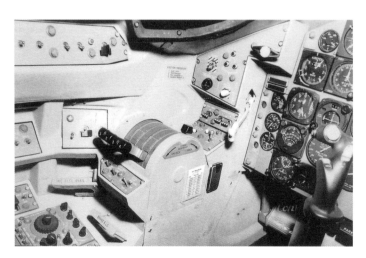

View of the Pilot's station, looking at the left-hand console. (USAF Photo)

No time to close the doors on this alert drill. (USAF Photo)

View of the Bomb/Nav station. (USAF Photo)

The DSO station is accentuated by a mass of buttons and switches. (USAF Photo)

Little Rock received the bombing role. The capability was tested, but it would never be developed further.

Boan recalled that the humidity was always very low in the aircraft:

"If you took an inflight meal that included a sandwich, you encountered an interesting effect while eating it. The air was so dry that the top surface of the bread would dry out as you were eating, and the bread would begin to curl up. It always bothered me that you got a quart of coffee and a quart of cold water for each flight, but the urinal was only capable of holding only a pint.

The aircraft skin presented some unusual handling techniques, such as having to wear booties while walking on the wings. They prevented scratches on the surface. Boan commented, "People had the habit of writing on the skin with a pencil to note loose rivets or some other minor problem until they found out that the chemical reaction etched their notes into the aircraft skin."

Aircraft Changes During Operational Service

The initial B-58As reached operational bases without the Tactical Air Navigation (TACON) systems. They would later be retrofitted. And, as has been mentioned earlier, the escape capsules would replace the ejection seats during the early 1960s.

Another retrofit was the re-equipping with sturdier wheels and new tires. It fixed a longstanding problem. Also, there would be changes during operational service that would allow the plane to carry a wider variety of weapons, four of which could be carried externally.

A number of the different nuclear weapons that were carried by the B-58A fleet. In the foreground is the B61 Nuclear Bomb. (Bill Holder Photo)

The B-63 Nuclear Bomb was another B-58A weapon. (Bill Holder Photo)

6

The Demise

The announcement came down with no emotion, but it left no doubt as to the future of the Hustler.

It happened in December 1965 when Secretary of Defense Robert McNamara directed the phaseout of the complete B-58 fleet by the end of June 1970. The same announcement contained the information that the FB-111 would enter production, effectively replacing the Hustler.

How could this happen to this advanced bird? It was one of the sleekest, most beautiful bombers ever built. It had a Mach 2 speed capability, twice that of other operational bombers of the time. But it wasn't enough. There were just too many problems facing the Hustler that eventually caused its end.

The termination announcement, not surprisingly, was met with a huge objection from the Strategic Air Command, which pointed out that even though there were problems in early production, many of the weaknesses had been addressed and solved. SAC pushed to have the fleet stay around at least until 1974, but its objections went ignored and the termination decision would end up being carried out on schedule.

Even still, the Air Force initiated several improvement programs in the penetration and countermeasures area in hopes of changing some minds. But when 1969 arrived and there was no waivering in the demise decision, all those follow-on programs were canceled.

When all was said and done, though, the major shortcoming of the model was that its bombing and navigation system was far less reliable than those of the B-47 and B-52. And, as it worked out, there was not an easy solution for the deficiency. There was also high-level concern with the Hustler because of its vulnerability from surface-to-air missiles. There was also the fact that the system was based on vacuum tube technology. Modern transisters could possibly have rescued the Hustler from this problem.

Quite simply, that AN/ASQ-42 system was a very complex unit, with the wiring considered a nightmare by repair technicians. As time went by, problems with the aging equipment became harder to locate and repair. A number of proposals for remedying the problem were submitted by industry, but the cost was deemed highly impracticable.

SAC kept trying, though, to improve the major weakness. In a last-ditch attempt in 1966, with Modification 1180, a new techique was attempted to improve control deficiences. The system, however, did not function as planned.

The beginning of the end. One of 84 B-58s that arrived at Davis Monthan AFB for its final disposition. (USAF Photo)

The less-expensive, slower, and more payload-capable B-52 would replace the Hustler. It still remains on station in the 21st century. (Boeing Photo)

Interlocked like cordwood, these Hustlers were not waiting for their next mission, but instead waiting to be turned into aluminum ingots. (USAF Photo)

The engines of these waiting Hustlers were covered should they ever need to be reused. (USAF Photo)

Several former B-58 crew members also recalled an unplanned maneuver which sometimes occurred while the plane was under autopilot control. For a totally-unknown reason, the plane would accomplish a snap-roll, which certainly must have been disconcerting to the crew.

From a maintenance point-of-view, there was also another major hang-up. The entire aircraft had to be placed in a jig should it be necessary to remove a single body panel. Reportedly, the plane could not be moved until the panel was secured back in position! This caused the particular aircraft a serious amount of downtime and spiraling maintenance costs.

Many Air Force personnel associated with the Hustler in various aspects also pointed out other deficiencies. It was a "Hangar Queen," one former B-58 DSO recalled. "There was a tale going around that some 35 manhours of maintenance

was required for every hour of flight...Also, the maintenance crews just hated to have to work on the flight control system. There were many pulleys oriented in different directions."

Also, a larger-than-normal attrition rate plagued the sleek bomber through its short lifetime. There did not seem to be a pattern in the causes of the crashes, but one of the most common problems was "A loss of control," many times occurring in normal flight. There were also aircraft losses due to landing gear problems and hard landings. One plane was even lost due to a landing gear failure which occurred during taxiiing! You just never knew what to expect from the Hustler.

Then there was that matter of aircraft cost. In 1960 dollars, the Hustler cost was a massive $34M per copy, which would be something like the B-2 cost 35 years later. For sure, it was many times more expensive than the B-52. So when it

Even though the end was near, these B-58s were still aligned perfectly on the Arizona desert floor. (USAF Photo)

Hard to believe that such an advanced weapon system could meet its fate after such a short service period. That fate was usually reserved for aircraft with decades-long careers. Such was not the case with the Hustler. (USAF Photo)

A rear view of a pair of rows of doomed B-58s with their rear Gatling Guns seemingly pointing at each other. (USAF Photo)

Looking like they are awaiting the command for a mass take-off, though that is far from the truth, as the only mission left for these sleek machines is a trip to meet with cutting torches. (USAF Photo)

came down to it, you could have a great deal more B-52s than B-58s for the same dollars. Looking at the situation from that point-of-view, it's not hard to understand why the decision was made the way it was.

The B-58 officially left Air Force service in November 1969 after the first Hustlers had been operational for only some nine years. Once the retirement started, it moved quickly, and actually finished six months ahead of schedule. The completion occurred in January 1970, when the 305th's final pair of

Hustlers were transferred to the Davis-Monthan AFB boneyard.

By 1970, the remaining fleet of 84 B-58s were all sitting in the arid heat of the Arizona desert awaiting their fate. But not all of them were to meet their fate, instead becoming fixtures as gate guards or quietly resting in museums across the country.

Then, one by one, the beautiful Hustlers were cut up and turned into very non-airworthy aluminum ingots that were sold to industry. The process was completed by 1978.

The B-58 was gone!

A B-58A being processed at Davis-Monthan AFB. (USAF Photo)

The FB-111, shown here being refueled, was the replacement for the canceled Hustler. (USAF Photo)

7
Remaining Hustlers

Sure, the order came down for the Hustler to cease to exist as an operational weapon system. And when the order came down the fleet, over a period of time, was sent to the expected final location before the eventual meltdown occurred.

That was what happened to the Hustler fleet; a small number of the majestic machine, however, escaped to aviation museums across the country, and they remain there today. A view of one of these planes up close and personal, and realizing that the roots of the design stretch back into the 1940s, provides an idea on how advanced it was for its time period.

The best records show that there are ten of the planes still in existence. Here is a listing of their locations, and any data that is available on each of them:

TB-58A, 55-00663. This former 43rd Bomb Group Hustler was received at the Grissom Air Museum in November 1995. It is on display for the public.

B-58A, 55-00665 ("Snoopy"). This Hustler is located on the Edwards Air Force Base photo test range.

B-58A, 55-00666 ("Greased Lightning"). This early Hustler was acquired in November 1995 and is on display at the Octave Chanute Aerospace Museum at Chanute Air Force Base, Illinois.

TB-58A, 55-0668. This Hustler has had quite a history in its retired state. Initially, it was put on display at the South-

west Aerospace Museum in Fort Worth, Texas. Following the closing of that museum, the Hustler was transferred to Meacham Airport for a proposed museum that was later canceled. It was then briefly displayed at the 50th anniversary of AF Plant No. 4. In October 1966, the plane was moved to its present location, the Lone Star Flight Museum in Galveston, Texas.

B-58A, 59-02437. This B-58 has been at Kelly Air Force Base, Texas, serving as a gate guardian. With the closing of the base, its ultimate disposition is unknown. The plane has been at Kelly since June 1996.

B-58A, 59-02458. One of the most famous Hustlers ever, this particular B-58 was the recipient of both the Bendix and Bleiot Trophies. It has been on display at the Air Force Museum at Wright Patterson Air Force Base since June 1995.

B-58A, 61-02059. Received in June 1995, this Hustler has since been a part of the Strategic Aerospace Museum at Offutt Air Force Base, Nebraska.

B-58A, 61-02079. During the 1990s, this Hustler was brought up to flight status at Davis-Monthan Air Force Base and flown to the Air Force Academy near Colorado Springs, Colorado, where it was placed on display.

B-58A, 61-02080. The Pima County Museum has had this Hustler on display at the Pima County Aerospace Museum in Tucson, Arizona, since January 1970.

This TB-58 (55-0663) served with the 43rd Bomb Group and has been at the Grissom Air Museum since 1995. (Grissom Air Museum Photo)

"Greased Lightning" was the nickname given to 55-0666, a B-58A on display at the Octave Chanute Aerospace Museum at Chanute Air Force Base. (USAF Photo)

A view of the B-58 which was on display at Kelly Air Force Base. (USAF Photo)

55-0665, although not on public display is still showing its lines on the Edwards AFB Photo Test Range. Here, it is in flight earlier in its career. (USAF Photo)

B-58 Escape Capsule. One of the escape capsules is located at the Smithsonian's Silver Hill, Maryland, facility.

Granted, the B-58 is now gone from all but the aforementioned museum locations, but many of the former crew members have not wanted to forget those Hustler experiences and are members of the B-58 Hustler Association. President Bob Norton explained the hows and whys of the Fort Worth, Texas, based organization:

The last B-58 flew in January 1970, when it was delivered to the Military Aircraft Storage and Distribution Center at Davis Monthan AFB. The air crews were assigned to many different assignments, from F-4s to O-1s to helicopters, along with B-52s and FB-111s. Additionally, some crew and staff members retired from the Air Force.

The Bendix Trophy-winning B-58A (59-02458) is on display at the Air Force Museum. (USAF Photo)

View of the Air Force Museum's Bendix Trophy B-58 being restored before public display. (Air Force Museum Photo)

More restoration activity on the Air Force Museum's B-58. (Air Force Museum Photo)

At Davis Monthan AFB, this Hustler was brought up to flight status and flown to the Air Force Academy for display. (USAF Photo)

The honor is complete at the Air Force Museum, with the Bendix Trophy also displayed. (Bill Holder Photo)

A large model of the Hustler at a B-58 Hustler Association gathering. (Bob Norton Photo)

B-58A 61-2012 is proudly displayed at the Pima Air & Space Museum in Tucson, Arizona. (PASM Photo)

There are many that remain that still have a love and passion for that magnificent supersonic bomber. Many of them gather every other year with the Hustler Association to recall the Hustler. (Bob Norton Photo)

The emblem for the B-58 Hustler Association flaunts all the trophies the model garnered. (Bill Holder Photo)

One of those who retired was a Grissom AFB pilot named Collins Welsh, who had settled in the Fort Worth area. In 1973, it was Collins who became a driving force to form a B-58 Hustler Association. Through his efforts and those of many others who lived in Fort Worth, the first reunion was held at the Green Oaks Inn in Fort Worth in the spring of 1974. It was attended by over 200 people and became an immediate success. Reunions were held annually until about 1976, when it was decided to have them every even-numbered year. The reunions have been attended by as many as 350 people.

The Association, headed by Bob Norton, is headquartered in Fort Worth, and all the reunions have been at the Green Oaks Inn. The Association is composed of those who built, flew, maintained, and supported the world's first supersonic bomber—settter of 19 world records and the winner of six top aviation trophies. Aficionados are welcome as associate members with full privileges.

Information about joining the Association can be received via U.S. Mail at PO Box 126158, Fort Worth, Texas, 76126.

8
Hustler Records

The B-58 Hustler did not stay around for that long, but during its lifetime, it was a public relations dream. The model was a tiger in the sky and set a multitude of records, many that seemed unbelievable for the time period. Expensive (certainly) and controversial (without a doubt), but the B-58 could fly like a rocket, and many of its records stayed around for many years.

During its design and development program and early operational service, the new high-tech bomber also demonstrated some significant firsts that need to be recognized.

International Speed and Payload Records
The first historical achievement took place on January 12, 1961, when a Hustler from the 43rd Bomb Wing set six international payload and speed records in a single flight. The accomplishment was significant in that five of the records broken were previously held by the Soviet Union.

The flight was made on a 620-mile (1,000 kilometer) closed course with 4,400 pound and 2,200 pound payloads, and then with no payload at all. The top speed attained was 1,284.73 miles per hour. For that accomplishment, the honor of the prestigious Thompson Trophy was awarded. It was the first time in over a decade that a medium bomber was awarded the trophy.

Next, with an average speed of 1,302.07 miles per hour, a B-58 on May 10, 1961, flew 669.4 miles in thirty minutes and 45 seconds. As a reward, the pilot, Major Elmer Murphy, was awarded the French Bleriot Cup.

That same B-58, 16 days later, flew 4,612 miles from New York to Paris in three hours, 19 minutes, and 51 seconds. The B-58 traced the same route as Charles Lindbergh's famous 1927 effort, but it was accomplished in about one-tenth the time. That epic high-speed trip earned its crew the MacKay Trophy.

This crew of Captain H.S. Blaias, Major H.E. Confer, and Major R.E. Weir of the 43rd Bomb Group set closed course speed records carrying payload weights of 1,000 and 2,000 kg, respectively. (USAF Photo)

Left: The famous Firefly B-58A set a New York-to-Paris speed run in May 1961. Needless to say, it was accomplished in considerably less time than the Lindbergh flight. (USAF Photo)

No doubt about this Hustler's accomplishments, as the Bendix Trophy is lettered on its forward fuselage. (Bill Holder Photo)

The Fort Worth, Texas, paper headlines the Japan-to-Britain speed record set in 1963. (Fort Worth Star-Telegram Photo)

This speed merchant B-58A set a record for an Anchorage-to-London run. (USAF Photo)

The following year, another B-58 slashed three speed records on March 5, 1962, made during a New York-to-Los Angeles run. The 43rd Bomb Wing aircraft, with three inflight refuelings, made the trip in four hours, 41 minutes, and 15 seconds, with an average speed of 1,044 miles per hour. For its efforts, the Mackay Trophy also came this Hustler's way.

A portion of that particular flight was also worthy of note, as during the return trip back to New York (which took only two hours and 59 seconds) it showed an average speed of 1,214.65 miles per hour. That effort got the crew the Bendix Trophy, with that particular B-58 still carrying the Bendix Trophy lettering as it currently rests in the Air Force Museum.

On September 18, 1962, another Hustler was awarded the Harmon Trophy for payload and altitude records. Additional performance records—five of them to be exact—were set on October 16, 1963. A non-stop trip from Tokyo was made to London by a 305th Bomb Wing Hustler. The time for the 8,028 mile trip was eight hours, 35 minutes, and 20 seconds, which equated to a speed of 938 miles per hour.

Finally, another B-58 in a trip from Tokyo to Anchorage, Alaska, and then on to London, set a number of speed records. The 305th Bomb Wing Hustler accomplished this record run on October 16, 1963.

Hustler 59-2431 set a number of speed records, one being a 70-minute flight completely at Mach 2 speeds. (USAF Photo)

55-0664 was the first to release its pod at Mach 2, along with also establishing the record of being the first Hustler to reach 60,000 feet. (USAF Photo)

This B-58A won the 1960 SAC Bombing Competition over all other B-58s and other model bombers. (USAF Photo)

59-2431, the 34th B-58 built, demonstrated a number of speed and endurance records. (USAF Photo)

Test Program Accomplishments

The number two B-58 (58-1015) was a significant performer during the design and development program when it was used in gross weight testing. In September 1959, the craft was pushed to its limit with a 1,200 mile trip, flown completely at 500 feet altitude, where it averaged an amazing 610 knots. Shortly thereafter, 58-2431 made a one hour-ten minute flight completely at Mach 2!

The fourth B-58 built, and shown here in its colorful test configuration, also had its claim to fame, being the first B-58 to release its pod at Mach 2, along with also being the first to fly above 60,000 feet.

The third YB-58, number 55-0662, was the first to complete the Hustler test program. The ultimate in reliability, the model demonstrated 256 flights without a missed, or late, take-off.

Early Operational Accomplishments

The 34th B-58 constructed was one of the most famous in the record-breaking business. This plane held the Mach 2 speed for an amazing 78 minutes in a 1960 flight. During this same time period, another operational B-58 stayed aloft for over 18 hours, covering over 11,000 miles at a speed of over 620 miles per hour. After being operational for only a month and one-half, one B-58, 59-2433, won the 1960 SAC Bombing Competition. The Hustler was first in both high altitude navigation and radar bombing.

The crew platform was an elaborate structure that allowed the three-man crew to enter and leave the Hustler. (Roger Boan Photo)

Ammunition loading for test range operations is shown in this photo. As can be seen, this operation was certainly more than a one-man job. (Roger Boan Photo)

A pair of 43rd Hustlers maneuver for a KC-135 refueling, as seen from this considerable distance away. (Roger Boan Photo)

That smoke you see in this photo is a result of rounds emitting from a B-58 tail stinger on the gun range at Schilling AFB. (Larry Boggess Photo)

s the Air Force for you?

Find out

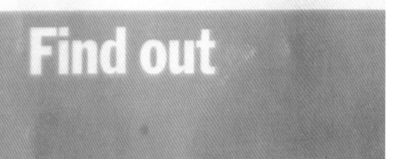

Although the B-58 had a relatively short operational lifetime, it was extremely popular with its dart-like appearance and stunning performance. It was also used on recruiting posters. (USAF Poster)